No Going Back

Letters to Pope Benedict XVI
on the Holocaust,
Jewish-Christian Relations
& Israel

Pope Benedict XVI. In May 2009, Benedict XVI makes an historic pilgrimage to the Holy Land, which includes visits to Jordan, Israel and the Palestinian Authority. This book of essays addresses some of the issues he is likely to face in the region during his visit. Courtesy of Sergey Kozhukhov.

No Going Back

Letters to Pope Benedict XVI
on the Holocaust,
Jewish-Christian Relations
& Israel

Edited by

Carol Rittner Stephen D. Smith

Managing Editor
Wendy Whitworth

Quill

in association with

THE
HOLOCAUST
CENTRE

No Going Back

Letters to Pope Benedict XVI on the Holocaust,
Jewish-Christian Relations & Israel

Edited by Carol Rittner & Stephen D. Smith

Published in Great Britain by
Quill Press in association with The Holocaust Centre
The Hub,
Haskell House,
152 West End Lane
London.
NW6 1SD

British Library Catalogue in Publication Data
A catalogue record for this book is available from the British Library.

ISBN 978-0-9555009-2-3
0-9555009-2-3

Design and artwork, The Holocaust Centre
Printed and bound by Cromwell Press Group, Trowbridge

For all those Christians, Jews and Muslims over the years
who despite misunderstandings, discouragement and setbacks
continue to try to understand and to show respect
for each other's religious traditions and beliefs –
and who teach their families, friends, neighbours and students
to do the same.

Table of Contents

Introduction

Pope Benedict XVI is not the first pope to visit Israel and the Holy Land. His predecessors, Popes Paul VI and John Paul II, both paid visits previously. Pope Paul VI went to Jordan and Israel in January 1964, and in March 2000, Pope John Paul II visited Jordan, Israel and the Palestinian Authority. Today, Pope Paul VI's visit to Israel is a distant memory, but many people across the world still remember Pope John Paul II's visit there. Thanks to television, millions saw the aged and increasingly frail Pope engage Israelis and Arabs from all walks of life and from across the political, religious and social spectrum. Wherever he went, crowds of people were on hand to greet him – he met Israeli Jews and non-Jews, Palestinian Christians and Muslims, politicians, religious leaders and, at Yad Vashem, Holocaust survivors. Much good will was built up as a result of Pope John Paul II's statements and gestures of respect, honesty and understanding.

Nine years on, another pope is going to the Holy Land – Jordan, Israel and the Palestinian Authority – as a pilgrim. Much has changed in the intervening nine years; much has happened to undermine the confidence of Catholics and Jews about their ongoing institutional relationships. The emergence of radical Islamic fundamentalism as a threat to world security and peace, the bombing of the twin towers in New York City, the war in Lebanon and the invasion of Gaza, the ongoing wars in Iraq and Afghanistan, the breakdown of relations between Israel and Hamas, are but a few of the incidents that have clouded international relations. In addition, the affair involving the lifting of the excommunication of the four bishops illicitly ordained by Archbishop Marcel Lefebvre, the Holocaust denial of Bishop Richard Williamson, one of the traditionalist bishops, and the re-wording of the Good Friday prayer by Pope Benedict XVI have aroused consternation. Now that the Vatican archive is open, there has been better news about the positive actions of Pius XII during the Holocaust, although there still remains uncertainty among scholars, and some concern about his possible beatification. All of these issues have served to undermine confidence in Catholic-Jewish relations among both Catholics and Jews, officially and unofficially.

The visit of Pope Benedict XVI is going to be of great significance, politically, religiously, theologically, institutionally and socially. It will focus minds and hearts, for many will see it as an opportunity to clarify some delicate issues that are troubling people of good will in Israel,

Palestine and beyond. The question is, will Pope Benedict's visit help to move things forwards – or backwards?

We invited a number of people, men and women, well-known and not so well-known, scholars and others – Catholics, Protestants, Jews and Muslims – from various places around the world to write to the Pope on the occasion of his visit to the Middle East. What would you say to Pope Benedict XVI if you had five minutes with him? Most of those we invited to participate in this project accepted our invitation, but a few did not. Of course, we were disappointed, particularly because we found it almost impossible to entice Muslims to participate, but we did try. *No Going Back: Letters to Pope Benedict XVI on the Holocaust, Jewish-Christian Relations & Israel* is a collection of responses to our invitation. We have organized these "letters" into themes to make their reading more coherent.

As the editors of *No Going Back*, we want to stress that we do not necessarily agree with the content of all the letters. Sometimes they are contrary to or disagree with our own religious, theological or political views. However, in an effort to represent a cross section of opinion, we have chosen to print them for your benefit, unexpurgated and unabridged. We have done so on the grounds that a full range of views and opinions needs to be heard if a way forward toward respect, understanding and peace is to be found.

We asked each writer to include questions for discussion and readings that might help to expand and enrich the reader's views and insights about the complexity of some of the issues addressed in the book.

One might argue that the Roman Catholic Church has more to offer than any other institution toward strengthening Jewish-Christian relations and engaging people of faith to forge new paths to peace in the Middle East. If that is so, there is no one better positioned to influence Roman Catholics, indeed, people of good will, on these matters than Pope Benedict XVI. We hope he will find the time to read what many different people have to say. We think he may find that what they have to say is challenging, indeed, even inspiring.

Carol Rittner
Stephen D. Smith
May 2009

Acknowledgements

We would be remiss if we did not thank every one of our contributors for their contributions. They generously responded, meeting an impossibly short deadline, but doing so graciously and with care. We thank them. We have made every attempt to contact copyright owners of photographs and thank those who have generously allowed us to use their images. We also thank Dr Wendy Whitworth, our Managing Editor, who worked with her usual diligence, accuracy, good humour and speed. And we thank the staff of our publisher, Quill Press, especially Glen Powell, who with creativity and patience has produced an attractive and easy-to-read volume.

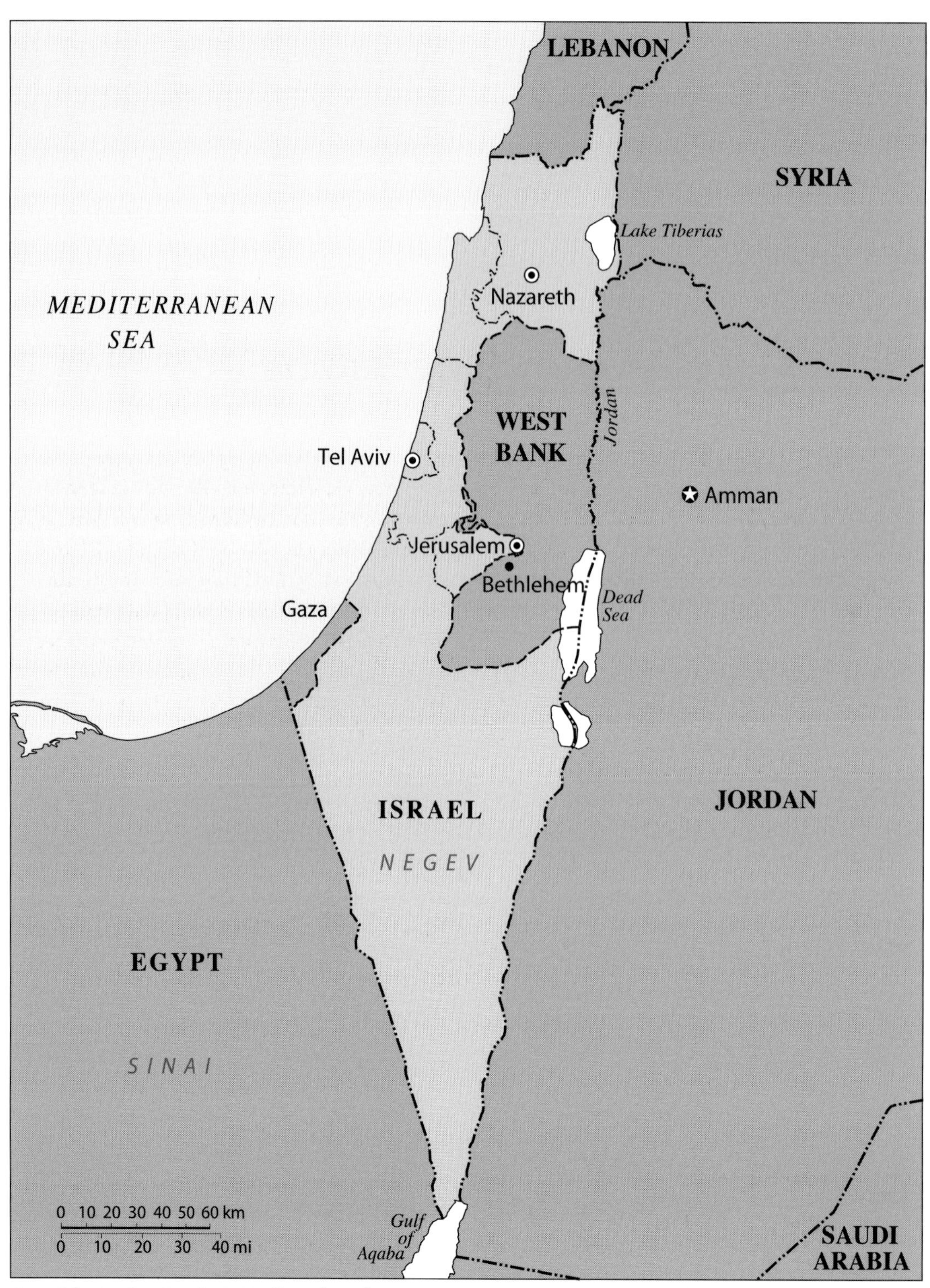

Some of the cities Pope Benedict XVI will visit during his May 2009 trip to the Middle East.

Dates & Documents

What follows is a sampling of dates and documents that have had a significant impact on interfaith relations, particularly Catholic-Jewish relations. While our selection of documents does not pretend to be complete, anyone interested in discovering how Christian-Jewish relations have developed in the Roman Catholic Church since the end of World War II and the Holocaust, particularly since the death of Pope Pius XII in 1958, the time of Vatican Council II (1962-1965) and the years following Vatican II up to the present, should consult these documents. Because this is primarily a list of significant documents and dates for the development of Catholic-Jewish relations, no attempt has been made to list documents or statements issued by other Christian traditions. Helpful websites where one can find many of the documents highlighted here are provided at the end of this chronological list.

1958

9 October	Pope Pius XII (Eugenio Pacelli) dies.
28 October	Cardinal Angelo Roncalli is elected Supreme Pontiff of the Roman Catholic Church. He takes the name Pope John XXIII.

1959

25 January	Pope John XXIII announces plans for an Ecumenical Council, which becomes known as Vatican Council II.

1962

11 October	Pope John XXIII opens Vatican Council II. He makes it clear that he did not call the Council to refute errors or to clarify points of doctrine. The Church today, he said, must "make use of the medium of mercy rather than of severity".

1963

3 June	Pope John XXIII dies.
21 June	Cardinal Giovanni Battista Montini is elected Supreme Pontiff of the Roman Catholic Church. He takes the name Pope Paul VI.

1965

28 October	The bishops at Vatican II approve *Nostra Aetate* ("In Our Time"), which contains a key statement on Catholic-Jewish relations. The document revolutionizes Catholic thinking and theology about Jews and Judaism and has a significant impact on Christian thinking and theology.
7 December	The bishops at Vatican II approve *Gaudium et Spes* ("Joy and Hope"), the Pastoral Constitution on the Church in the Modern World), which also impacts interfaith relations.

1974

1 December	The Vatican issues *Guidelines and Suggestions for Implementing the Conciliar Declaration, "Nostra Aetate".*

1978

6 August	Pope Paul VI dies.
26 August	Cardinal Albino Luciani is elected Supreme Pontiff of the Roman Catholic Church. He takes the name Pope John Paul I.
28 September	Pope John Paul I dies suddenly.
16 October	Cardinal Karol Wojtyla is elected Supreme Pontiff of the Roman Catholic Church, taking the name Pope John Paul II. He is the first Polish pope.

1979

7 June	Pope John Paul II is the first pope ever to visit Auschwitz. While there, he pays homage to Holocaust victims.

1984

	Roman Catholic nuns establish a Carmelite Convent in one of the buildings in the grounds of Auschwitz. Jews object because the nuns' activities will celebrate Christian martyrs on a site where more than one million Jews perished.

1985

24 June	The Vatican issues *Notes on the Correct Way to Present Jews and Judaism in Preaching and Catechesis of the Roman Catholic Church.*

1986

13 April	Pope John Paul II is the first pope to visit the main synagogue in Rome, where he delivers an allocution affirming all that Vatican II taught about the Jews and Judaism. In his talk, Pope John Paul II declares that "it could be said that you are our elder brothers."
26 November	Pope John Paul II gives an "Address to Jewish Community Leaders" in Sydney, during his pilgrimage to the Roman Catholic community in Australia.

1988

The Bishops' Committee for Ecumenical and Interreligious Affairs of the National Conference of Catholic Bishops (USA), issues "Criteria for the Evaluation of Dramatizations of the Passion".

September — The Bishops' Committee on the Liturgy, National Conference of Catholic Bishops (USA), issues "God's Mercy Endures Forever: Guidelines on the Presentation of Jews and Judaism in Catholic Preaching".

1989

February — The Pontifical Commission "Justitia et Pax" promulgates a document, *The Church and Racism: Towards A More Fraternal Society*, written at the request of Pope John Paul II "to help enlighten and awaken consciences about the reciprocal respect between ethnic and racial groups as well as their fraternal coexistence".

1992

2 November — The Catholic Bishops' Conference of Australia issues "Guidelines for Catholic-Jewish Relations".

1993

30 December — With the signing of the "Fundamental Agreement Between the Holy See and the State of Israel", the Vatican and Israel establish full diplomatic relations.

1995

23 January — The German Catholic Bishops issue a "Statement on the 50th Anniversary of the Auschwitz Liberation". The Catholic Bishops of Poland issue a similar statement on the same date.

The Catholic Bishops in the Netherlands publish their statement, "Supported by One Root".

1997

30 September — The Catholic Bishops of France issue a "Declaration of Repentance" concerning the silence and passivity of the Church in the face of the Holocaust.

1998

16 March — The Pontifical Commission for Religious Relations with the Jews issues *We Remember: A Reflection on the Shoah*. In March, the Catholic Bishops of Italy write a "Letter to the Jewish Community of Italy", and the Bishops' Conference of England and Wales responds to the *We Remember* document.

1999

October	The Vatican appoints a Commission of six Catholic and Jewish historians to review published Vatican documentation on the role of the Holy See and Pope Pius XII during the Holocaust.
December	The study of the topic "The Church and the Faults of the Past" is proposed to the International Theological Commission by its President, Joseph Cardinal Ratzinger, in view of the celebration of the Jubilee Year 2000. A sub-commission is established to prepare this study, which is promulgated in March 2000 as "Memory and Reconciliation: The Church and the Faults of the Past".

2000

12 March	Just before leaving for his pilgrimage to Israel and the Holy Land, Pope John Paul II, in an elaborate and moving ceremony in St Peter's Basilica, asks forgiveness for the past sins of the Church, including its treatment of Jews.
21-26 March	Pope John Paul II arrives in Israel on 21 March 2000 for a historic five-day visit, during which he visits the holy sites of the three major religions and meets with Israel's political leaders and Chief Rabbis. Though ostensibly a religious pilgrimage, the Pope also touches on political issues, blessing Israel, expressing support for a Palestinian homeland and apologizing for sins committed by Christians against Jews.
6 August	The Congregation for the Doctrine of the Faith, headed by Cardinal Joseph Ratzinger, issues *Dominus Jesus* ("Declaration on the Unicity and Salvific Universality of Jesus Christ and the Church").
September	*Dabru Emet*, a Jewish Statement on Christians and Christianity, is published in *The New York Times*. It is signed by more than 220 rabbis and intellectuals from all branches of Judaism, although few of the signers are from the Orthodox branch.
13 October	The Canadian Catholic Bishops issue a statement, "Jubilee: Renewing Common Bonds with the Jewish Community".

2001

July	The Vatican-appointed Jewish-Catholic Scholars' Commission formed to review published documentation on the role of the Holy See and Pope Pius XII during the Holocaust suspends its work because it contends that it cannot get full and free access to the needed Vatican documents to do its work.

	August	The Vatican's Pontifical Biblical Commission issues "The Jewish People and Their Sacred Scriptures in the Christian Bible".
2002		
	12 August	"Reflections on Covenant and Mission" is issued by the Consultation of the National Council of Synagogues and the Delegates of the American Catholic Bishops Committee for Ecumenical and Interreligious Affairs.
	September	The Christian Scholars Group on Christian-Jewish Relations, comprised of 21 prominent Catholic and Protestant scholars, releases the document "A Sacred Obligation: Rethinking Christian Faith in Relation to Judaism and the Jewish People."
2004		
	September	After Mel Gibson's film, *The Passion of the Christ*, is released and causes much concern and controversy among Jews and Christians, a group of "concerned Christians" in the USA publish a statement, prepared by Dr Peter A. Pettit and Dr John C. Merkle, entitled, "'The Passion of the Christ,' Jewish Pain and Christian Responsibility."
2005		
	2 April	After 26 years as Supreme Pontiff, Pope John Paul II dies. He is buried from St Peter's Basilica on 8 April 2005, after a funeral mass concelebrated by Cardinal Joseph Ratzinger and several hundred priests, bishops, archbishops and cardinals. Millions around the world view his funeral via television broadcast.
	19 April	Cardinal Joseph Ratzinger, a German, is elected on the second day of the papal conclave to succeed Pope John Paul II as Supreme Pontiff of the Roman Catholic Church. He takes the name Benedict XVI.
	18-21 August	Pope Benedict XVI makes his first official visit to his native Germany, where he participates in World Youth Day activities. While there, the Pope meets with members of the Jewish community in the Roonstrasse Synagogue in Cologne on 19 August, where he delivers an address which is very favourably received.
	September	Remarks by Pope Benedict XVI in a speech in Germany at the University of Regensburg, entitled "Faith, Reason and the University: Memories and Reflections", provoke outrage in the Muslim world and lead to demands that the pontiff apologize for "insulting" Islam. Following this controversy, Pope Benedict XVI makes efforts to repair relationships with Muslims.

2006

26 May — As part of his official visit to Poland, Pope Benedict XVI visits Auschwitz as "a son of the German people", where he denounces the "unprecedented mass crimes" of the Holocaust and underlines the reality of Hitler's campaign to wipe out European Jews.

2008

February — Pope Benedict XVI makes the decision to reformulate the Catholic Church's traditional Good Friday prayers. It proves to be a controversial decision for both Catholics and Jews.

15-20 April — Pope Benedict XVI visits the United States, where he meets with President George Bush as well as Catholic educators and interreligious leaders in Washington, DC. He moves on to New York City, where he delivers a speech at the United Nations, visits a synagogue and extends Passover greetings to the Jewish community, meets with survivors and family members of 9/11 victims and celebrates Mass in Yankee Stadium before thousands of Catholics.

2009

24 January — In a decree dated 21 January and released to the public on 24 January, Cardinal Giovanni Battista Re, prefect of the Congregation for Bishops, announces that Pope Benedict XVI has lifted the excommunications of the bishops who lead the traditionalist Society of St Pius X (SSPX), excommunications imposed on 1 July 1988 after the bishops were ordained by the late Archbishop Marcel Lefebvre in defiance of Vatican orders. Richard Williamson, one of the men illicitly ordained by Archbishop Lefebvre, is known for his antisemitic views and for denying the Holocaust. Jews and Catholics, including the bishops of Germany and Austria, are outraged. Pope Benedict XVI does his utmost to assure everyone of his continuing commitment to furthering good relations with the Jewish community, his respect for Judaism and his efforts to denounce antisemitic and anti-Jewish views.

12 March — In an effort to stem the tide of outrage and criticism, and to clarify his commitment to ongoing Catholic-Jewish relations and condemnation of the Holocaust and its crimes against the Jewish people, Pope Benedict XVI writes a Papal Letter on the Society of St Pius X concerning the remission of the excommunication of the four bishops of the Society of St Pius X that were ordained by Archbishop Marcel Lefebvre in 1988.

8-15 May	Pope Benedict XVI visits the people of Jordan, Israel and Palestine. While in the Holy Land, he expresses his solidarity and closeness to the people of Israel, Palestine and, through them, all the peoples of the Middle East.

For further information about "Dates and Documents", see:

Boston College, Center for Christian-Jewish Learning
http://www.bc.edu/research/cjl/

Council of Centers on Jewish-Christian Relations
http://www.ccjr.us/

Institute for Christian & Jewish Studies, Baltimore, Maryland (USA)
http://www.icjs.org/

International Council of Christians and Jews
http://www.jcrelations.net/en/

Sacred Heart University Center for Christian-Jewish Understanding
http://www.sacredheart.edu/pages/122_center_for_christian_jewish_understnding.cfm

SIDIC Rome
http://www.sidic.org/en/default.asp

Vatican: The Holy See
http://www.vatican.va/

King Hussein of Jordan. The Pope is being hosted in Jordan by King Hussein. The relationship with neighbouring states in the region impacts significantly on meeting many of the challenges outlined in the essays in this book. Courtesy of Helene C. Stikkel.

Challenges

Julia Chaitin

reflects on the power of the past and the need to listen and work together.

The past, as we know, is an inseparable part of us; it ties us to the histories of our family, our nation and our people. The past is etched in our genes, helping make us who we are, or what we might become. It contains potentials for making us great singers or leaders, or for hating others because their religion or ethnicity differs from ours. The past not only affects our physical health, such as whether we are at high risk for heart disease, but also our psychological health, such as whether we will carry within us scars of trauma experienced by our great grandparents, grandparents or parents, who were victimized by others, or whether we will harm others, as perhaps our elders did. The past can steer us toward destructive ends, but also provides roots for development and new beginnings. The past does not determine what our futures ***must*** be, but it often has a clenching hold on us from which we must struggle to be free.

"The past not only affects our physical health... but also our psychological health, such as whether we will carry within us scars of trauma experienced by our great grandparents, grandparents or parents, who were victimized by others, or whether we will harm others, as perhaps our elders did."

We Jewish-Israelis love to invoke our pasts. Every year, during our holidays and holy days, we 'remember' our escape to freedom from ancient Egypt where we were enslaved; our dispersal in the Diaspora after the destruction of the Second Temple, and our expulsion from Christian Spain in 1492. The Holocaust, our ***most*** traumatic past, is part of everyday Israeli discourse – we are constantly reminded of the horror, and how the ***only*** way to ensure our survival is by remaining militarily strong. Our numerous Israeli wars have supported this notion, and they, too, are repeatedly remembered and commemorated.

Our past makes living securely in the present and envisioning a trauma-free future difficult. Too often, we Jewish-Israelis (re)act to events as though we were still living in that past. Our collective memory, reinforced by our fear-based discourse of our past, colours the way we view all 'others'. And so, we do not separate Palestinians from those who persecuted us and nearly succeeded in destroying us long ago. We conflate the Palestinians with past perpetrators who held great power over us when we were stateless, unwanted in our Diaspora 'homelands'.

Due to fear of annihilation, we perceive Qassam and Grad rockets (which ***have*** killed people, and terrorize and harm hundreds of thousands of innocent people living within their range), as an existential threat. In our legitimate fear of these immoral attacks, we 'forget' that we have one of the strongest armies on earth, that has harmed millions of Palestinian people who, like us, have done no wrong. We 'forget' that this conflict has two sides that are suffering. And while we are acutely aware that Palestinians must bear their responsibility for keeping this war going, we 'forget' that we must bear our heavy responsibility as well.

By not untangling these different conflicts/persecutions, we engage in poor decision-making and become enmeshed in a highly emotional cycle of fear and hate. Instead of employing higher-level mental capabilities to find a sustainable resolution to this conflict, we react from our 'hot' emotional system that is triggered by fear and that responds with anger and aggression. We believe that ***all*** Christians and Muslims are against us. We hold the skewed perception that our neighbours are ***only*** evil and will ***never*** accept us as partners in this land. This leads us to build separate roads and to erect walls that create ghettos not only for them, but for us as well (albeit, larger ghettos with fewer restrictions). It leads us to legislate laws that prohibit us from being able to cross the borders and meet over coffee. This fear-based conflation leads us to separate, yet ever-connected existences that are consistently re-rooted in deindividuation and dehumanization of the other.

"... for once people share the tales of their lives with their 'enemy', a depth of understanding becomes possible that had been previously hidden by rhetoric and misunderstandings."

This destructive cycle is etched into our personal, familial and collective lives. We Jewish-Israelis see ourselves as the perpetual victims, who continually live in a danger zone. As characteristic of people suffering from post-traumatic symptoms, we remain hyper-vigilant, always on the look-out for the enemy, whose only wish is to drive us into the sea or disperse us among the nations of the world, making us into unwanted wanderers on this earth.

We have become human self-fulfilling prophecies, which further entrap us in the vicious cycle of fear, hatred and war.

If this is our 'legacy', how do we build bridges of co-existence with the Palestinians? How do we move from fixation on victimization toward a complex understanding of ourselves and our 'others' that holds the potential for a more peaceful, less frightening future? How do we move from distrusting all others who are not 'us', to viewing them as potential co-creators of this future?

The key to this change is rooted in the human mind, spirit and soul. All people possess innate needs and drive to create community and to be part of a larger collective that gives meaning and purpose to life. Aggression is only half the picture of humanity; the needs to connect, to create and grow are also part of who we all are, regardless of the haunting realities we have lived. The question, therefore, is what actions can facilitate the movement and growth we so badly crave?

The answer is through dialogical communication; people-to-people processes rooted in justice and equality; and tenacity, especially during the darkest of times.

When considering communication, we find that people talk – a lot; however we rarely listen. We engage in numerous and complex verbal and non-verbal behaviours, but this communication is often poorly disguised monologue, as we tend to be caught up in what we are saying or in mentally phrasing the biting response to the other's 'nonsense'. We are veteran, yet failed, communicators, with little experience of truly being in dialogue.

Dialogue that addresses the crux of the conflict between Palestinians and Israelis in honest and brave ways is crucial for conflict resolution and reconciliation, especially given that we two peoples have been caught up in rhetoric, not conversation, for decades. One powerful kind of dialogue that can cut through the strongest barriers of hate and fear is the dialogue of personal storytelling and reflection. This is a dialogue that empowers both speakers and listeners, for it encourages confrontation with the most difficult of issues in a way that supports joint honesty, complexity, sharing, reflection, growth and creativity. It is a dialogue that offers the hope of eventual acceptance and forgiveness, for once people share the tales of their lives with their 'enemy', a depth of understanding becomes possible that had been previously hidden by rhetoric and misunderstandings.

When Israelis and Palestinians speak with one another about their day-to-day experiences, and reflect on the meanings these experiences have for them, they begin to reach new perspectives on this 'intractable' conflict that evade communication that is stymied in positions and interests. By offering Israelis and Palestinians opportunities to share the stories of their lives, the 'other' becomes more of a person, less of an enemy; the 'other' becomes a potential neighbour, not ***only*** an 'occupier' or 'terrorist'. Dialogue may 'only' begin as words, but it has the power to become new ways of living. Dialogue cannot ultimately solve the Palestinian-Israeli conflict, but it is essential for its true resolution.

For such dialogue to succeed on the social, as opposed to purely interpersonal, level, it needs to occur in widespread, long-term people-to-people grassroots endeavours. This means that we Jewish-Israelis must meet, again and again and again, with our Palestinian neighbours, in joint activities that have relevance for both peoples. We need to repeatedly see that there ***are*** people on the other side who are partners in this process, who do not yearn for our destruction, and who are committed to joint peace-building actions. These people-to-people processes must strive to engage as many people as possible: old and young, men and women, religious and secular, right-wing and left-wing,

Questions

1. What specific roles can the Roman Catholic Church play in furthering peace initiatives between Israelis and Palestinians?

2. How can the Roman Catholic Church, with Pope Benedict XVI at its helm, build bridges of peace between Catholics and Jewish-Israelis?

3. Is there a way to get past the animosities of the past between Jews and Catholics? What are the obstacles and what are possible ways for overcoming these challenges?

4. How can civil society and grassroots initiatives further dialogue between Jews and Catholics, in Israel and abroad?

professionals and labourers, rural and urban dwellers, everyone. We need to create many opportunities to bring people together in endeavours that speak to their needs, promise full involvement and no manipulation. We need to harness the many civil society organizations that exist, to work together, and to offer counter solutions to the military 'solution' that has so miserably failed us.

Finally, in order to put our pasts to rest, and to co-create this new reality, we need tenacity and inner strength not to give up, even during military operations and terror attacks, and changing Israeli and Palestinian Governments that lack the courage to take the necessary steps toward a just peace. We need resolve, but we cannot do it alone.

Your Eminence, we need your help. We need you to put out the clear call to Roman Catholic leaders and followers throughout the world to directly support us in these endeavours, so crucial for our survival. We need you, Your Eminence, to commit the Church to working together with us on these initiatives so that we ALL – Christians, Jews and Muslims – can become freed from our dark pasts and become human self-fulfilling prophecies of peace.

For Further Reading

D. Bar-On, ed. *Bridging the Gap: Storytelling as a way to work through political and collective hostilities.* Hamburg: Korber-Stiftung, 2000.

I. J. Bickerton & C. L. Klausner. *A History of the Arab-Israeli Conflict, (5th Edition).* Prentice Hall, 2006.

M. Buber. *I and Thou.* New York: Touchstone, 1996.

M. B. Rosenberg. *Speak Peace in a World of Conflict: What You Say Next Will Change Your World.* Encinitas, CA: Puddledancer Press, 2005.

Julia Chaitin holds a Ph.D. in Social Psychology from Ben-Gurion University of the Negev. Her research focuses on the psychosocial impacts of the Holocaust and the Palestinian-Israeli conflict. She is a Senior Lecturer in the Social Work department at the Sapir College in Israel, a programme developer at the Negev Institute for Strategies of Peace and Development and a member of Other Voice – a grassroots initiative calling for a non-violent resolution to the war in the Sderot/Gaza region.

Shlomo Breznitz

discusses human decency, the problem of memory and the need for a little less ego.

Several years ago, I had the privilege of meeting John Paul II on the occasion of his visit to Jerusalem. It was his wish to meet six Holocaust survivors and I was fortunate to be among them. I knew that the choice fell on me because I had been saved by Sisters of St Vincent who operated an orphanage in a remote town in Slovakia. It was a small gesture to make the papal visit to Yad Vashem a touch easier. His actions and personality earned him this token reprieve when facing the darkest period of human history.

I often think of Sister Agatha, the Mother Superior of the orphanage, who so courageously protected me, my sister and a few other Jewish children from certain death. The more I dwell on the mystery of the human psyche, the more convinced I am that the wellspring of her courage was not her religious belief, but rather her basic human decency. I wish it was the other way around, for in that case, instead of the fortunate few, hundreds of thousands would have been saved. Religious belief, after all, is much more prevalent than deep human decency.

Not only is it more prevalent, but much less dependable. After all, history is filled with religious wars and atrocities pursued in the name of religion. The promise of paradise after death does not necessarily lead to a life based on moral codes. Your Eminence, you are visiting a country plagued by terror, feeding on suicides that presumably lead to bliss after death. Typically, in the act of blowing up innocent people, the perpetrators shout: "God is great!"

So how can people of good will think of ways that enhance human decency? Is there a route that promotes tolerance among different nations, races and religions? If so, then our joint task is clear.

I cannot presume to have the key to this most important of riddles. Nor do I expect to find it, or assume that it exists. All I can hope for is the very

Questions

1. Why is religious belief so powerful?

2. How can people of good will think of ways that enhance human decency?

3. Is there a route that promotes tolerance among different nations, races and religions?

first hesitant step in that direction. And that step consists in the realization of our vulnerability as a species and its unfortunate consequences. It is so easy to make us angry. It is so easy to remove the thin veneer of civilized behaviour to unleash the most primitive and bestial impulses in most of us. A small slight can cause an injury that will be remembered for years. An injustice, whether real or perceived, can feed the hate of generations.

As individuals and groups, we remember too much for too long. The chances of an Israeli-Palestinian rapprochement would have been much better were it possible to wipe out most of our collective memories. They serve as a justification for retaliation for past grievances only too often. In the Jewish-Christian context, the memory of the Spanish Inquisition and countless pogroms throughout Europe over the centuries are deviously countered by the still often heard claim that Jews killed The Son of God himself. It is thus the same memory that needs to be cherished in order to learn the lessons of the past, that invariably restricts our vision of the future.

We have to accept this vulnerability as an immutable given. Consequently, the only option left for us is the need to prevent the occasions that can provoke the aggressive impulse. This prescribes the way we use language, the way we report crime, the way we talk about the other. In short, we need a programme based on an ever-present admission of our own weaknesses. Such a programme rests, in addition to a comprehensive educational effort, on specific legislation. We need wise, self-imposed limits on expressing everything we feel like saying in the way we feel like saying it. Pushing free speech to the limits, all the while assuming – nay, falsely hoping – that irrespective of its implications we would always be able to act rationally and maturely, simply does not work. We cannot rely on our rationality or maturity when stimulated by emotional content. Thus, we need laws and regulations that will keep it in manageable forms.

However, the most difficult part of the work we have to do ourselves, each one of us in the confinement of our internal dialogues with ourselves. If we could only learn to forgive more easily, we would all be much safer. If we could only muster the strength to admit our own shortcomings as a basis for judging others, our chances of providing a truly civilized community would be much better. A little less ego would do us all much good.

Our world is sufficiently haphazard and treats us unjustly as a standard modus operandi. Why was I lucky enough to survive the Holocaust when millions of children died? That in its own right should be enough to put us in a frame of mind of greater humility. We are not as important as we think, and besides, we are all going to die some day. If this knowledge could become the cornerstone of our philosophy, the terrible lessons of history would not have been wasted.

For Further Reading

Shlomo Breznitz. *Memory Fields*. New York: Alfred Knopf, 1992.

Carol Rittner & Sondra Myers, eds. *The Courage to Care: Rescuers of Jews during the Holocaust*. New York: New York University Press, 1986.

Jonathan Sacks. *The Dignity of Difference: How To Avoid the Clash of Civilizations*. Continuum, 2003.

Shlomo Breznitz was born in Bratislava and survived the Holocaust hiding in a Catholic orphanage. After the war, he moved to Israel. Dr Breznitz was the Founding Director of the R.D. Wolfe Centre for Psychological Stress, Haifa University, where he also served as the Rector and President of the University. He is now President of CogniFit, a company developing brain fitness software.

Edward Kessler

explores Jewish and Christian scriptural exegesis as the starting point for living faiths.

The title of this letter, *A Different Future: Can Jews and Christians Learn from History?*, is important because, in the words of Martin Luther King, "We are caught in an inescapable network of mutuality. Whatever affects one directly affects all indirectly." Jews and Christians are, in my opinion, inextricably linked. I suggest that the traumatic history of Jewish-Christian relations is illustrative of much of human history. Perhaps it is too bold a claim, but I hold the view that if Jews and Christians can successfully build '*a different future*', our work together will help nurture the tender shoots upon which the peace of the world may depend.

"I hold the view that if Jews and Christians can successfully build 'a different future', our work together will help nurture the tender shoots upon which the peace of the world may depend."

Can we learn from history? Or, in other words, can an uneasy historical relationship between Christians and Jews ever be redeemed?

Many Christian theologians, including yourself, have turned to the Apostle Paul, who stated that God has not forsaken the people of Israel (Romans 11:25-6). As a result, the call for Christianity to abandon its historical religious animosity and misleading caricature of Judaism has been overwhelming. These are now admitted to be wrong and their full and public rejection was required before the possibility of dialogue might exist. Thus, before dialogue could really begin with Judaism, Christianity needed to shift from what was, for the most part, an inherent need to condemn Judaism to one of a condemnation of Christian anti-Judaism. This process has not led to a separation from all things Jewish, but in fact to a closer relationship with "the elder brother". In our times (*nostra aetate*), we are witnessing the occurrence of a demonstrable shift from a Christian monologue about Jews to an instructive (and sometimes difficult) dialogue with Jews. A monologue is being replaced by a dialogue.

In the earlier stages of dialogue in the 20th century, Christian re-acquaintance with Judaism resulted primarily in an increased awareness of

Questions

1. To what extent do Jews and Christians share the same Bible?

2. What is the significance of the fact that Christian commentators such as Jerome and Nicholas de Lyra approached Jewish commentators in their biblical studies?

3. What benefits are there today for Christians and Jews when they study scripture and biblical commentaries together?

the Jewish origins of Christianity – that Jesus was born, lived and died a Jew; that the first Christians were Jews. However, more recently, there is a growing realization that for nearly 2,000 years – not only the first 100 years – living Judaism has interested Christians and has influenced Christianity in one way or another.

The issue from a Jewish perspective is more complicated. At first glance, there is no theological imperative to view the relationship with Christianity as more special than the Jewish relationship with any other faith group. This view is reinforced by the popular assumption that the influence was wholly one-way: Christianity did not influence Judaism; rather, Judaism influenced the development of Christianity.

However, this is inaccurate because Christianity influenced Judaism in many ways. It is well known that after Christianity became the official religion of the Roman Empire, the position of the Jewish communities became increasingly precarious. However, it is not so well known that the rabbis allowed, consciously or not, Christian ideas and interpretations to enter into Jewish thought and life. This happened because dialogue was part of the mainstream of Jewish life.

One example of the Christian influence on Rabbinic Judaism can be seen in exegetical encounters, which took place between Jewish and Christian interpreters. These encounters took place on the basis of a shared textual tradition – the Hebrew Bible – even though each faith community interpreted these writings in different ways. The rediscovery of this interaction will prove significant to Jewish-Christian dialogue.

If Jews and Christians examine post-biblical interpretations, they will discover a shared emphasis on the importance of certain biblical texts, as well as a willingness to be open to, and influenced by, some of each other's teachings. The exegetical encounters, which took place so long ago, can point the way forward.

One example can be seen in the interpretations of the *Akedah*, the Binding of Isaac (Genesis 22). The story of Abraham's attempted sacrifice of Isaac is one of the most well known stories of the Bible. The focus of the biblical story concerns Abraham's relationship with God and how his faith in, and commitment to, God is demonstrated by his willingness to sacrifice his long-awaited son at God's command. Little attention is given to Isaac.

Both the rabbis and the Church Fathers reflected a great deal on the story. In the rabbinic writings, Isaac is no longer portrayed as a peripheral figure but becomes equal, if not superior, to Abraham. The rabbis portray Isaac as the willing martyr who volunteers to give up his life for his people. Indeed, such is the merit of Isaac's action, (*zecut avot*), that Israel benefits from his actions in the future.

The rabbinic portrayal of Isaac parallels a number of aspects of the Christian understanding of Jesus. Like Jesus, Isaac was willing to give up his life.[1] Like Jesus, Isaac was not forced by human hand to carry the wood for the burnt offering, but carried it freely. Like Jesus, Isaac was not forced to offer himself as a sacrifice, but willingly gave himself up to his father.[2] Like Jesus, Isaac was described as weeping bitterly when told by Abraham that he was to be sacrificed.[3] Like Jesus, Isaac shed blood.[4] Like Jesus, Isaac is depicted at the gates of Hell (*gehinna*).[5] In a similar way to Paul's assertion concerning baptism, the *Akedah* was described as atoning for all, Jew and non-Jew.[6] Finally and perhaps most remarkably, Isaac is described as having died and having been resurrected.[7]

There is one other example: "'And Abraham placed the wood of the burnt-offering on Isaac his son.' Like a man who carries his cross (*tzaluv*) on his shoulder."[8]

The reference to a cross is clearly influenced by the Christian description that Christ carried his cross to the crucifixion. The rabbi who offered this interpretation decided that the comparison between Isaac carrying the wood and a man (Jesus) carrying a cross to his execution was valuable. The editors/redactors of Genesis Rabbah concurred since they did not censor the comparison in the final redaction.

Thus, Jewish interpretations of Isaac at the *Akedah* cannot be understood properly without reference to the Christian context. Indeed, they are more easily understood when viewed as illustrating an exegetical encounter, since the rabbis were not only aware of Christian exegesis but were influenced by it.

These exegetical encounters between Jews and Christians in bygone times should inspire Jewish-Christian dialogue in the future. Since the writings of the rabbis and the Church Fathers provide the cornerstone for Christianity and Judaism today, a study of Jewish and Christian biblical interpretation should become a pillar of Jewish-Christian dialogue in the future.

A study by Jews and Christians will highlight a number of similarities between Jewish and Christian approaches to Scripture, such as an insistence on the harmony of Scripture and an emphasis on the unity of the text. Consequently, Jewish and Christian interpretations were understandable to many adherents of both religions. This overlap existed, not only at the beginning of Christianity but continued over many centuries. Thus, it is not surprising that Christian exegetes, such as Origen and Jerome in the patristic period, or Nicholas of Lyra and Aquinas in the medieval period, turned to Jewish contemporaries for help in their translation and understanding of biblical texts.

Discussion between Christians and Jews was centred upon the interpretation of Scripture. Their interpretations can be likened to an electric cable or plug, which has a number of wires, each of them isolated, but together capable of conducting spiritual and creative energy of great intensity. When the different biblical interpretations are brought together, a connection is

For Further Reading

R. Brooks and J. J. Collins, eds. *Hebrew Bible or Old Testament? Studying the Bible in Judaism and Christianity*. Notre Dame, IN: Univ. of Notre Dame Press, 1990.

M. Hirshman. *A Rivalry of Genius. Jewish and Christian Biblical Interpretation in Late Antiquity*. Albany, 1996.

E. Kessler. *Bound by the Bible: Jews, Christians and the Sacrifice of Isaac*. Cambridge, 2004.

H. Reuling. *After Eden: Church Fathers and Rabbis on Genesis 3:16-21*. Leiden: Brill, 2006.

made; when left independent, they remain isolated; combined, they provide light; left alone, their contribution is limited. My suggestion is that an understanding of **both** Jewish and Christian interpretations of the Bible can serve to increase the intensity of that light. This means that Christians and Jews can help each other to reach a deeper meaning of the biblical text when they consider each other's biblical interpretations.

"Nothing is better, I think, than for Christians to study Jewish texts and vice versa."

Nothing is better, I think, than for Christians to study Jewish texts and *vice versa*. Christians will recover the reverence the first Christians entertained towards the Scriptures. Only then shall we truly begin to discover the significance of a shared textual tradition.

The serious study of Judaism as a living faith and its relationship with Christianity are an essential non-marginal part of Christian formation today. A Vatican directive states, "Christians must strive to acquire a better knowledge of the basic components of the religious tradition of Judaism; they must strive to learn by what essential traits the Jews define themselves in the light of their own religious experience."

I offer one specific proposal based on the view that the Bible is a good place to start. Let us together develop a new series of biblical commentaries, which consists of profound and insightful interpretations offered by Christians and Jews over many centuries. Let us make Jewish and Christian biblical interpretation accessible to both our communities and let us bring the Bible back into the synagogue and church in a way that is sensitive to the Jewish-Christian relationship. Let us remind our communities that dialogue should be at the forefront of our religions.

Notes

1. Lamentations Rabbah Proem 24.
2. Fragmentary Targum 22:10.
3. Midrash Composed under the Holy Spirit, p. 65.
4. Mekhilta de Rabbi Ishmael, Pisha 7.
5. Song of Songs Rabbah 8:9.
6. Leviticus Rabbah 2:11 and Gal 3:28.
7. Pirkei de Rabbi Eliezer 31.
8. Genesis Rabbah 56:3.

Edward Kessler is Director of the Woolf Institute of Abrahamic Faiths and Fellow of St Edmund's College, Cambridge. Dr Kessler is a prolific author; his publications include *Bound by the Bible: Jews, Christians and the Sacrifice of Isaac*, (2004); *A Dictionary of Jewish-Christian Relations* (2005); and *What do Jews Believe?* (2006).

Deirdre Mullan

asks Benedict XVI for what purpose he *remembers the Holocaust.*

I write this letter during the UN Year of Reconciliation, at a time of planetary insecurity and hopelessness, and also at a time of immense possibility.

I also write as a concerned member of our Roman Catholic Church because I believe that Church teaching about antisemitism has never seriously left bookshelves or been filtered to the altars or pews of many of our churches.

Why do I say this? For many years, I have listened to and observed what many church-going people say about our Jewish brothers and sisters, both in jest and in serious conversation. As we both know, unfiltered and unchecked speech can become the norm and belief system of any group. I relate two incidents, separate yet similar, which confirm my beliefs.

In early January 2009, I visited the Galilee and a small synagogue built by the Jews who used to live in Derry, my home city in the north of Ireland. The major industry of the kibbutz where the synagogue is located is making furniture for synagogues and some churches. Excited at seeing first-hand this part of my city's untold history, I told a priest friend about the synagogue. His comment startled me, "I hope they sell none of their furniture." When I challenged him, he laughed off my comment. His attitude came just weeks before comments on the Holocaust by the British-born Bishop Richard Williamson, denying the full extent of the *Shoah*: "I believe there were no gas chambers" and "only up to 300,000 Jews perished in Nazi concentration camps, instead of 6 million."[1] It confirmed my beliefs that we have never fully engaged with this prejudice.

Your predecessor Pope John Paul II, on a visit to Yad Vashem, reminded the watching world: "I have come to Yad Vashem to pay homage to the millions of Jewish people who, stripped of everything, especially of their human dignity, were murdered in the Holocaust... We wish to remember. But we wish to remember for a purpose... As Bishop of Rome and Successor

Questions

1. How have our churches, mosques and synagogues remembered and challenged hatred as an integral part of their doctrine and theology?

2. How are the teachers of the faith in all traditions – bishops, priests, imams, rabbis and nuns – dealing with blatant racism and hatred in our midst?

3. Why did so many people take to the streets to protest about Israeli behaviour in Gaza, but at the same time ignore the suffering of the peoples of Zimbabwe/ Democratic Republic of the Congo or India?

of the Apostle Peter, I assure the Jewish people that the Catholic Church, motivated by the Gospel law of truth and love and by no political considerations, is deeply saddened by the hatred, acts of persecution and displays of antisemitism directed against the Jews by Christians at any time and in any place... Let us build a new future in which there will be no more anti-Jewish feeling among Christians or anti-Christian feeling among Jews, but rather... mutual respect..."[2]

Reflecting on the comments of Pope John Paul II, who said, "We wish to remember for a purpose," I ask you as the current Bishop of Rome – for what purpose do you intend to remember the Holocaust and to encourage us Roman Catholic Christians to remember? Surely it is not just to mark a historical event, important as that may be, but, as Pope John Paul II encouraged, to "build a new future", a future rooted in friendship with the Jewish people and, I would suggest, friendship with all people of good will, whatever their religion, race, colour, creed, sexual orientation or nationality. As the Bishop of Rome and the successor to St Peter, not just Roman Catholics, but the whole world needs your leadership in helping us to remember the Holocaust for that purpose, too.

Notes

1. Bishop Richard Williamson, interview on Swedish Television, as reported in the *Irish News*, 23 January 2009.
2. *The Visit of Pope John Paul II to Yad Vashem, Jerusalem* (Jerusalem: Yad Vashem), pp. 14-16.

For Further Reading

H. Fry, R. Montagu & L. Scholefield. *Women's Voices: New Perspectives on the Christian-Jewish Dialogue.* Canterbury: SCM Press, 2005.

Daniel Jonah Goldhagen. *A Moral Reckoning.* New York, 2002.

Rabbi Michael Lerner. *Healing Israel/Palestine.* Tikkum Books, 2003.

Neale Donald Walsch. *The New Revelations.* Atria Books, 2002.

Deirdre Mullan, RSM, a Sister of Mercy from Ireland, is the Director of Mercy Global Concern at the United Nations in New York. Dr Mullan is a member of the Social Development Committee, the Israel/Palestine working group and the working group on Women and Girls at the UN. She has lectured extensively in the USA, Canada, Ireland, England, Australia, South Africa, Kenya and New Zealand.

Dalia Ofer and Nili Keren

reflect on 'flooded' memory, Jewish history, Christian Europe and the future of Israel and Palestine.

We are two Israeli historians of the Holocaust and educators who would like to express their appreciation of, and satisfaction with, your upcoming visit to Israel. Your future visit follows the unforgettable visit of your predecessor, His Holiness Pope John Paul II, which reached its climax with his written prayer at Yad Vashem on 26 March 2000:

> God of our fathers,
> You chose Abraham and his descendants
> to bring Your name to the nations.
> We are deeply saddened
> by the behavior of those
> who in the course of history
> have caused these children of Yours to suffer
> and asking Your forgiveness
> we wish to commit ourselves
> to genuine brotherhood
> with the people of the covenant.

We view your sacred pilgrimage as a further step in the fruitful dialogue between Israeli Jews and the Roman Catholic Church. We therefore take this initiative to share with Your Holiness some of our thoughts and concerns in relation to Jewish history in Christian Europe, the Holocaust and the State of Israel.

We begin by acknowledging a sad fact: Israeli education pays little attention to the study of Christianity or Islam. Therefore, many Israelis shape their attitude toward the Roman Catholic Church out of ignorance. This is probably

"We begin by acknowledging a sad fact: Israeli education pays little attention to the study of Christianity or Islam."

Questions

1. Are the expressions of Holocaust denial by Bishop Williamson and some confreres considered by the Church as private expressions, or do they reflect common opinions which influence the community of believers?

2. Does the Catholic Church see itself obligated to the findings of historical research in general and of Jewish-Christian relations in particular? To what extent?

3. Does the Church define its attitude to the State of Israel vis-à-vis its position as the Jewish state, or the state of the Jewish people, or as a normal sovereign state without any religious/ national context?

4. How does the Catholic Church conceive its role in the creation of mutual understanding between the three major monotheistic religions? What is the Church's role in getting the leaders of these three religions to work together for the benefit of millions of human beings?

also true in Islamic and Roman Catholic education vis-à-vis the two other religions. Consequently, many mutual prejudices and stereotypes prevail among the three groups.

We shall relate with great humility to the Holocaust period and its aftermath. As mentioned above, we are both historians and educators, but neither the Church nor the Holy See during the Holocaust is our main field of research.

When studying Jewish history, Israeli students confront the sad reality of lengthy periods of sour relations between Christians and Jews. Our students learn that popes protected Jews from kings and barons who exploited them and defended Jews from ignorant mobs that constantly robbed and killed them. However, popes were also among the instigators of violence. Young Israelis often hear recollections of grandparents, or read in memoir literature, about the religious ecstasy of mobs during Easter processions that often ended with attacks on Jews.

The Jews' collective memory is flooded with anti-Jewish events that originated in laymen's and priests' interpretations of the role of the Jews in Christian societies and states.

How does the Roman Catholic Church relate today to such historical events and does it encourage the study of sound historical investigations and findings?

Jewish historians review these issues critically and expose in their accounts the negative attitudes of Jews toward Christianity and Christian society. Examples are Israel Yuval, *Two Nations in Your Womb: Perceptions of Jews and Christians in Late Antiquity and the Middle Ages*[1] and Avraham Grossman, *Pious and Rebellious: Jewish Women in Medieval Europe.*[2]

Following the benighted days of the Holocaust, the attitude of the Church toward the Jews became an even more painful issue and a central component in the attempts that were made to understand the massive participation of Christians in the killing of the Jews. One is constantly disturbed by the question of the impact of the long years of anti-Jewish teachings and preaching by the Church on Christians' indifference to the annihilation of the Jews. How central to the simple Christian ('the man in the street') was the idea that the Jews deserved the 'death penalty' and that, therefore, they could justify the Nazi persecution and the Final Solution?

The question becomes even more complicated when we relate directly to Pope Pius XII. We have read the conflicting accounts about this pontiff. We have learned about the prodigious actions of high and lower clergy of the Roman Catholic Church in France, the Netherlands, Belgium, and Central and Eastern Europe to intervene on behalf of Jews and prevent their deportation. All of these clerics turned to the Vatican. They received all sorts of responses but, like many others in occupied Europe and in the free world, waited for an official declaration from the Pope.

In his important address at Christmas 1942, Pope Pius XII sent a political and moral message. He spoke of the suffering and pain of thousands in the world war. He mentioned the torn homes, the mourning wives, the mothers, and the deserted and defenceless children. He discussed the cruelty and suffering of those days. But he uttered only one phrase that related to Jews:

"The hundreds of thousands of persons who, without any fault on their part, sometimes only because of their nationality or race, have been consigned to death or to a slow decline."

Pius XII was well informed about the mass killings and gassings in the labour and death camps.

Historians have offered numerous explanations for the Pope's ambiguous choice of words concerning the Jewish victims in his address. They attribute the fact that the Pope did not directly mention the Jews to complex political factors. Few major researchers, however, believe that these bishops and clergy who waited for the message doubted that the Pope had the Jews in mind.

Michael Phayer found German sources indicating that the German officials also had no doubts that the Pope was referring to the mass killing of Jews.[3]

We wonder, however, whether this indirect reference to the Jews was clear enough for simple Catholic men and women. December 1942 was the most dreadful period in the war. Desperate battles in Leningrad and Stalingrad were taking place and the USSR was fighting on the 'good' side. Hundreds of thousands of soldiers and innocent civilians lost their lives. The spiritual message of the Pope's address was complex due to the political and military reality. The message concerning Communism and religion was straightforward, sharp and crystal-clear, but what about the fate of the Jews? Could an ordinary Catholic understand that his/her highest religious authority was denouncing the killing of the Jews and encouraging him or her to favour the obstruction of such actions and, perhaps, to make efforts to rescue Jews?

"Could an ordinary Catholic understand that his/her highest religious authority was denouncing the killing of the Jews and encouraging him or her to favour the obstruction of such actions and, perhaps, to make efforts to rescue Jews?"

John Morley, in his classic *Vatican Diplomacy and the Jews during the Holocaust, 1939–1943,* wrote:

> If the Vatican did not allege that it was unique in being a combination of religious, moral and temporal interests, then it should not be expected to have reacted any differently to the Holocaust than other governments. If this uniqueness is denied a priori, then the presumption must logically be that the Vatican, like all institutions and governments, acted always in what it considered its best interests. If that be so, its activity and decisions can hardly be challenged on any other grounds.
> Vatican diplomacy purported to be a model and ideal for all states... By its own avowal, the injustices committed against the Jews, to say nothing of the atrocities, should have been a major source of effort for it during the years 1939–1943.[4]

We in Israel today live in a region where fear and war never subside, especially now as extremists among Israelis and Palestinians alike are gaining force. Therefore, we are deeply disturbed by the moral stand of our political and spiritual leadership. We expect them to constantly and openly condemn all rhetoric of hate and to directly oppose collective guilt, even when Palestinian terrorists raid Israeli towns and suicide bombings occur. We demand that our leadership be devoted to justice and send a clear message of total responsibility for all human lives, a message of compassion and respect for 'the other' – be he friend or foe.

Although we are often disappointed, we have never stopped fighting for the fulfilment of these demands. We express our beliefs in our public activism in the social, political and educational fields.

This is how we wish that the Church and the Roman Catholic pontiff had behaved in the dark days of the past. It is the responsibility of any leadership today to be clear in the moral messages that they transmit.

As educators and researchers, we would like to tell our students that today the Church has translated the decisions of the Second Vatican Council of 1965 (*Nostra Aetate*) into the language of education – that in textbooks, sermons and prayers, in text and subtext alike, Jews are no longer portrayed as murderers of Christ. We hope that the Holocaust and its experience will stand like a pillar of fire, warning against all forms of inhumanity and betrayal of the Almighty. Can we develop confidence that this is happening and that such a trend will develop? We would like to assure our students that the Roman Catholic Church considers Holocaust denial utterly illegitimate and teaches the history of the Holocaust in a sound way. We hope that the facts, events, processes and interpretations are being discussed and internalized and that the Holocaust deniers are condemned. The response of the Holy See to the recent incident involving the British bishop, Richard Williamson, evokes both concern and hope. Can we be confident that the path of hope has been chosen?

We conclude by relating to the attitude of the Church toward the State of Israel as the Jewish state, the state of the Jewish people. In 1993, the Roman Catholic Church established full diplomatic relations with Israel. We Israelis and many Christians, too, viewed this as an acknowledgment of the right of Jews to their state in their historic homeland, the Holy Land. We hope to see progress in this relationship, of the sort that would encourage cooperation in various educational settings such as research, study and further discussions on the past, developing a vision for a safe future.

We hope that within the not-distant future the Land of Israel, the Holy Land, will accommodate two sovereign states – a Jewish state and a Palestinian state. We believe that the Holy See will share with both states the mission of protecting the Holy Places of all religions for the benefit of all the country's inhabitants.

For Further Reading

Victoria J. Barnett. *Bystanders: Conscience and Complicity During the Holocaust*. Westport, CT: Praeger, 2000.

Leonard Grob & John K. Roth. *Anguished Hope: Holocaust Scholars Confront the Palestinian-Israeli Conflict*. Grand Rapids, MI: Wm. B. Eerdmans Publishing Co., 2008.

John Morley. *Vatican Diplomacy and the Jews during the Holocaust, 1939-1943*. Jersey City, NJ: Ktav, 1980.

Notes

1. Israel Yuval, *Two Nations in Your Womb: Perceptions of Jews and Christians in Late Antiquity and the Middle Ages* (Berkeley: University of California Press, 2006).
2. Avraham Grossman, *Pious and Rebellious: Jewish Women in Medieval Europe* (Waltham, MA: Brandeis University Press, 2004).
3. Michael Phayer, *Pius XII, The Holocaust and the Cold War* (Bloomington: Indiana University Press, 2008).
4. John Morley, *Vatican Diplomacy and the Jews during the Holocaust, 1939–1943* (New York: Ktav Publishing House, 1980), p. 16.

Dalia Ofer has served as the Head of the Vidal Sassoon Center for the Study of Antisemitism and Racism and also chaired the Institute for Contemporary Jewish Studies, both in the Hebrew University of Jerusalem. She has written books dealing with illegal immigration to Palestine and has contributed a great deal to research on gender and daily life during the Holocaust. One of Dr Ofer's main concerns is Holocaust education.

Nili Keren is a historian and has written many articles on Holocaust education, as well as two textbooks for Israeli and non-Israeli college students. She is the senior lecturer on the Holocaust in the Kibbutzim College of Education in Tel-Aviv. Dr Keren is also the academic advisor of Massuah, the International School for Holocaust Studies in Kibbutz Tel-Itzhak.

Henry F. Knight

suggests that we should 'know before whom we stand' as Jews and Christians in the aftermath of the Shoah.

One of the artefacts on display at the United States Holocaust Museum in Washington, DC is a disfigured lintel that once adorned the ark of a synagogue in Nenterhausen, Germany. Carved across the top in Hebrew text are the words, Know before whom you stand (דע לפני מי אתה עמד). The lintel and these words overlook a glass display case that houses Torah scrolls that were defiled during the November pogrom of *Kristallnacht*.

> *"No statement, theological or otherwise, should be made that would not be credible in the presence of the burning children."*

©USHMM

Rabbi Eliezer's instructions to his students centuries ago recorded in the Talmud[1] have fed Jewish communities throughout the world, linking study with prayer and guiding the lives of Jews of every nationality. Often those words are carved above the arks in synagogues and temples, guarding the space that houses the sacred words of Torah. On 9-10 November 1938, those words were cut and gouged, most likely by a bayonet. The word *lifnei*, constructed from the Hebrew word for *face*, was horribly disfigured – literally and physically defaced. Its message, especially now, is profound. Since every human being bears God's image, God and God's children have been tragically, catastrophically assaulted.

Rabbi Eliezer's words continue to reach out across the generations to teach new congregations. His words hold, like a Kiddush cup, the responsibilities Jews have to God and one another, binding them to each other and to all that they honour as sacred in their lives. Just as easily, they could bind post-*Shoah* Christians like me. Those ties, like those very words, were betrayed on *Kristallnacht*. They were desecrated, along with the trampled Torah scrolls now on display in the Holocaust Museum in Washington. Know before whom you stand.

Rabbi Irving Greenberg, a prominent Holocaust scholar and theologian, has captured the depths of this crisis with his criterion for post-Holocaust faithfulness: "No statement, theological or otherwise, should be made that would not be credible in the presence of the burning children."[2] Greenberg's words are instructive. As a post-Holocaust Christian, I have learned to pray with the psalmist: "May the words of my mouth and the meditations of my heart be acceptable in your sight, O God, my rock and my redeemer." And from Greenberg I have learned to add, "May they be credible in the presence of the burning children." To say ***Amen*** to that amended and compounded prayer is to know before whom I stand.

"Over a million children under 12 were murdered by the Nazis or by their collaborators. Thousands were tortured... Their suffering challenges Christian assertions that Jesus has known every dimension of human misery."

Artist Samuel Bak has given this post-*Shoah* summons visual power in his renderings of the iconic Warsaw ghetto boy. Wearing shorts, knee-high socks, a hat and a fine, buttoned coat, a young boy is standing in a crowd as a nearby soldier holds the child at gunpoint. Both hands are raised as if he were a criminal under arrest. Bak renders a version of this child in numerous paintings, often depicting his upraised hands pierced by nails. The symbolism is inescapable. A Jewish child is being crucified.

Samuel Bak, Study I, 1995, Pucker Gallery

To stand before Bak's little boy is another way to know before whom we stand. Indeed!

Christians must be careful before this image. It would be tempting to

Questions

1. How does the Holocaust challenge Christians to re-examine critical features of Christian identity, particularly with regard to traditional Christian attitudes toward claims made by Jewish identity?

2. What assumptions made by Christians and Jews about each other, and their relationships with each other, need to be re-examined in the light of the Holocaust?

3. Is supercessionism an essential feature of Christian identity? If so, how does Christianity deal with supercessionism's resistance to difference? If not, how might Christianity deal with this legacy of its history and ground its respect for difference?

4. How is supercessionism a lingering, if not fundamental, problem for Christianity as well as for individual Christians who pursue reconciliation with Jews and Judaism?

5. How might a preoccupation with matters of purity contribute to (and perhaps exacerbate) supercessionist attitudes and foster negative regard toward those who are perceived by one's tradition as truly other?

project the crucified Christ onto crucified Jewish children. However, that would be another violation of those children and an inversion of Greenberg's searing hermeneutical principle. The power of these juxtaposed images works in the other direction. Over a million children under 12 were murdered by the Nazis or by their collaborators. Thousands were tortured. None were given a choice about how they might live their lives. Their suffering challenges Christian assertions that Jesus has known every dimension of human misery. He chose his cross. He offered up his life. The children did not. Not all suffering is encompassed by the anguish of Golgotha! Emil Fackenheim's thoughtful commentary underscores the importance of this recognition:

> Christians have always known how to acknowledge sin, including the sin of crucifying Christ all over again. However, the crucifixion of Christ-in-general is one thing; quite another is the crucifixion-in-particular of six million human beings, among them the helpless children, their weeping mothers, and the silent *Muselmänner*.[3]

We who lift high the cross stand in the presence of a heinous act that we cannot diminish by forcing the suffering of others to fit our interpretive needs. Are we really prepared to know before whom we stand?

I am summoned by Bak's crucified, Jewish child just as surely as I am summoned by the man from Nazareth who has been for me and my faith tradition our burning bush. Both figures call me out of myself to regard the other who stands before me with compassion and care. The Jewish man who stands at the centre of my life and the wounded child who approaches from the shadows each call me into mutual responsibility for the life we share. Together, yet in distinctive ways, they call me out of my zones of comfort, into an ever-expanding sense of life. That summons, in both Jewish and Christian forms, was fundamentally violated during the night of *Kristallnacht*, and more catastrophically during the long night that followed.

Facing that violation is no simple matter. As a Christian living in the aftermath of the Holocaust, I must face a dark side of my own history. What happened could not have happened without centuries of Christian contempt and persecution propagated against the Jewish other before whom, over against whom, Christian identity has too often been formed. In her book *The Curse of Cain*, Regina Schwartz describes the consequences of an identity formed, in part, by using a negative, yet significant other, over against whom one shapes one's sense of identity and truth. The *Shoah* provides haunting testimony regarding the ways in which an identity formed in this manner violates the other it requires for its own differentiation. To stand before this history is difficult, but necessary, if we who face the Jewish others in our lives are going to do so in full knowledge and respect for those who stand before us and the One before whom we all stand.

Rabbi Eliezer's words were originally offered as a reply to a question put by his disciples about how to live so they might inherit the future life. He answered them, saying, "When you pray, know before whom you are standing and in this way you will win the future world."[4]

Evoking the traditional posture for Jewish prayer, standing, Rabbi Eliezer was imploring his followers to know well the One to whom they prayed. And yet, his way of putting the matter suggested that any time we stand before another can be a moment of prayer. Likewise, any other before whom we stand provides an opportunity to face the One to whom we pray.

In the aftermath of the *Shoah*, Irving Greenberg reminds us that the dignity of every human being is secured by remembering that each of us reflects God's countenance to the other.[5] Therefore, each act whereby human beings stand respectfully before another person is a sacred act. When we face the other, who reflects in his or her image the loving presence of God, we stand before the One who gives us life. In the aftermath of the *Shoah*, Rabbi Eliezer's words are *limned*, charged, like the white fire of midrash. They are rich with promise and the summons to responsibility. Know before whom you stand. Indeed.

According to Emmanuel Levinas, the human face is the fundamental datum of our embodied existence.[6] Levinas, a survivor and witness to the atrocity that befell his people, reminds us that the human face speaks to each of us with its presence, calling us to be present in return. Its appearance can be a theophanic moment, another burning bush, declaring, "Here I am" and asking at the same time, "Where are you?" But we must have the eyes to see and the heart to comprehend that moment – a moment that is as true from the beginning as it is now, and was in its violation. In other words, the human other can be a sacramental presence, to use a more Christian metaphor, if we dare to pay attention. Indeed, the face of the other may serve as a sign of post-Holocaust, interfaith respect.

We Jews and Christians can be bound together in covenantal regard for the other without subsuming the other, nor his or her commitments, by devoting ourselves to covenant life while respecting the particular covenants in which that life is manifest. We encounter this dynamic in the witness of married life when children of loving homes choose to establish their own covenants of love and devotion for one another. They are, to use St Paul's metaphor, grafted into married life, covenant life, not someone else's specific relationship. In other words, debate about singular or parallel covenants can refocus on how each of our traditions binds itself to the other and thereby embrace God's covenantal wager with life that we know as creation. Indeed, the human face, in its particularity, can serve as a Levinasian "sacrament of the other," calling each of us to know before whom we stand. In the shadows of the Holocaust there is still much for each of us to learn.

For Further Reading

Richard Harries. *After the Evil: Christianity and Judaism in the Shadow of the Holocaust*. Oxford University Press, 2003.

David Patterson and John K. Roth, eds. *Fire in the Ashes: God, Evil, and the Holocaust*. University of Washington Press, 2005.

Regina M. Schwartz. *The Curse of Cain: The Violent Legacy of Monotheism*. University of Chicago Press, 1998.

Clark M. Williamson. *A Guest in the House of Israel: Post-Holocaust Church Theology*. Westminster John Knox Press, 1993

Notes

1. Berachoth 28b.
2. Irving Greenberg, "Cloud of Smoke, Pillar of Fire: Judaism, Christianity, and Modernity after the Holocaust" in Eva Fleischner, ed., *Auschwitz? Beginning of a New Era* (New York: KTAV, 1977) p. 23.
3. Emil Fackenheim, *To Mend the World: Foundations of Future Jewish Thought* (New York: Schocken Books, 1982) p. 281.
4. Berachoth 28b.
5. Greenberg, op.cit. p. 42ff.
6. Emmanuel Levinas, "Ethics As First Philosophy" in *The Levinas Reader* ed. by Seán Hand (Oxford: Basil Blackwell, 1989) pp. 82-84. See also Levinas, "The Pact" in the same publication, pp. 224-226, for an elucidation of the face as a symbol of our covenantal regard for life.

Henry F. Knight is the Director of the Cohen Center for Holocaust Studies at Keene State College, Keene, New Hampshire, USA. A United Methodist minister, Knight is the author of *Confessing Christ in a Post-Holocaust World* (Wipf and Stock, 2006) and *Celebrating Holy Week in a Post-Holocaust World* (Westminster John Knox, 2005) as well as chapters in volumes produced by the Steven S. Weinstein Holocaust Symposium.

Abdal Hakim Murad

says that we must not remember the past at the expense of the present or the future.

Peace be upon you, and the mercy of God.

The Holy Koran says of Christian clergy that "they are not puffed up with pride" (5:82). Christ himself, in the Scriptures, appears as the essence of humility, referring to himself as a servant of his Lord (Koran 19:31; Matthew 19:17). Looking to the Holy See, the world's Muslim peoples know that in the Sovereign Pontiff they will see a servant, who carries numberless burdens on behalf of those in the world who carry burdens themselves. His solidarity is with the poor and dispossessed; "God has filled the hungry with good things, and the rich He sent away empty" (Luke 1:53).

"...the world's Muslim peoples know that in the Sovereign Pontiff they will see a servant, who carries numberless burdens on behalf of those in the world who carry burdens themselves."

Such are God's prophets and messengers, and their true vicars. Their ministry is always against the complacent culture of the age, of power, money and privilege. Courageously courting unpopularity, they unflinchingly uphold the rights of those the world has wronged.

Sixty years in the past, and for many centuries before, the Jewish people were singled out for a persecution that is historically unique, both in its persistence and in the strength of the conviction which drove it. The Church, *semper reformanda*, has had the courage to turn that page, through the great declarations of Vatican II, and in subsequent allocutions and papal addresses. So great a change cannot be accomplished without mishaps, misunderstandings and controversy. But it is evident that the page has been turned.

Despite this new beginning, a pilgrim who stands at Yad Vashem is compelled to remember a past which bears witness to the sinfulness of earlier generations of godless and God-fearing laity and clergy. He or she cannot leave without remembering the God who is with the poor and despised, and is angered at their persecutors. The vengeance of Heaven against tyrants and oppressors, sometimes visited upon them in this world, but promised to come at the hands of Christ at the close of history, should make us all fearfully search our consciences, for Heaven's judgment is severe.

Perhaps Europe's punishment for its crime has taken the form of the withdrawal of faith from the hearts of its people. The secularity which you lament in today's Europe is surely the consequence, at least in part, of the sense that a wickedness has been committed which makes the God of love seem very distant indeed, and perhaps even absent. To heal Europe, and to heal Germany above all, the pontiff must look the *Shoah* in the eye, and reaffirm the Prophetic truth that spiritual leaders must always speak out on behalf of the hated, the poor and the persecuted. Perhaps, if this is fully done, God's punishment of the hearts of Europe will abate, and the cradle of Christianity will return once more to faith.

But the halls of Yad Vashem recall another wound, which also cries out to be healed. Beneath its foundations lie the Palestinian fields and houses of Ayn Karam, whose people now suffer in exile. Nearby, a Museum of Tolerance is to be built on West Jerusalem's main Muslim cemetery, and the bones are already being excavated and removed. Among them are the remains of the city's Muslim saints, and even companions of the Holy Prophet himself. The agony of Palestine continues to increase.

"At Yad Vashem, we must not remember the past at the expense of the present, or the future."

The mind of a true follower of God's solidarity with victims is thus torn. The museums call crimes to mind and urge a healing. But beneath, forgotten by too many, are the more recent victims of a tragedy which continues to unfold. It is, perhaps, the most difficult and painful tragedy of our present generation.

At Yad Vashem, we must not remember the past at the expense of the present, or the future. The present is visible, in the grim concrete walls and watchtowers built across the Holy Land to exclude an angry rival ethnic group. The resemblance between those hideous wounds on the landscape and the architecture of Yad Vashem itself is sobering. If the latter recalls the death camps and the logic of ethnic rejection, then so does the wall.

Richard Falk, the UN Special Rapporteur on human rights in the Palestinian territories, has concluded that in some respects, Israel's treatment of the Palestinians resembles the behaviour of Nazi Germany. As a Jew, he feels that he cannot remain silent when policies of ethnic exclusion and cruelty are once again damaging the peace and right order of the world. His predecessor, the South African jurist John Dugard, was struck by another, no less tragic parallel, comparing Israeli policies to apartheid. Of Israel's actions, he wrote: "Can it seriously be denied... that the purpose is to establish and maintain domination by one racial group (Jews) over another racial group (Palestinians), and systematically oppressing them?"

Your Holiness is aware that across the globe, people of conscience, including steadily growing numbers of faithful Christians and Jews, regard

Israel's treatment of its subject Christian and Muslim populations as a tragic recollection of some of the twentieth century's darkest episodes. In 2003, an opinion poll suggested that 60 per cent of Europeans believe that the State of Israel is the greatest threat to world peace. This European verdict reflects a groundswell of human anger around the globe, where people of every faith and even of no faith, cry out with increasing insistence: Never again!

This hatred of Israel's behaviour is shared by many of the most godly Jewish believers. At the creation of Israel, the Holocaust survivor Rabbi Joel Teitelbaum lamented the atheism of the State's founders and their mockery of the ancient rabbinical wisdom. "The heretics," he writes, "have made all kinds of efforts to violate the oaths, to go up by force and to seize sovereignty and freedom by themselves, before the appointed time. And it is no wonder that the Lord has lashed out in anger." Like many of the faithful Orthodox, he knows that to break the promise not to return violently before the Messianic age may open the gates of Divine wrath.

In our own time, Rabbi Mair Hirsh, spokesperson of the Naturei Karta in Jerusalem, maintains this brave tradition of prophetic dissent. Crying out against all ungodly tribalism and racial pride, he writes (9 February 2009):

> Judaism is a religion and spirituality. Turning Judaism on its head, transforming this holy religion into a materialistic nationalism, with a singular earthly goal of land conquest and military prowess, void of Godliness, is exactly what the State of 'Israel' is about. Attempting to leave exile and all the other cardinal crimes associated and committed by Zionism and its 'State', such as the theft from, subjugation and oppression of, the Palestinian people, the continuous attempts to uproot the Torah and oppress the Torah-true Jews, etc., are to us religious Jews the worst tragedy.
>
> Orthodox Torah-true Jews are humiliated and pained by the terrible crimes that Zionism and its 'State' are committing. The humiliation is compounded, when this is being done in the name of 'Israel', the name that Zionism has appropriated from the Jewish religion. The terrible atrocities committed in Gaza in the recent weeks, should be an awakening call to all Jews true to the Almighty and His religion, to totally disassociate themselves from this godless illegitimate entity.
>
> We pray for the speedy and peaceful dismantlement of the entire State of 'Israel'. Our yearning and prayers are ultimately for the revelation of the glory of the Almighty, when all nations will serve Him, in harmony and joy. Amen.

Your Holiness, the Prince of Peace whom you serve, would commend these words. Israel, living by the sword, is in grave peril of dying by the sword.

Questions

1. Is the anti-Zionist position of early twentieth-century popes still binding upon Catholics?

2. Is the Holocaust of the 1940s a more urgent question for the Church than the present-day clash between Israel and the Palestinians?

3. Should the Catholic Church oppose Israel simply for the sake of gaining popularity in the Third World?

4. Can we judge Zionism before witnessing its final outcome?

The belief that she will forever defeat her enemies who crowd in on every side, and that she can eternally frustrate the Palestinian will to return home, is not founded in reason, the laws of history or scriptural promise. We must strive to ensure that the wisdom of the traditional rabbis, with its deep faith in God, guides the growing anti-Zionist feeling of the world. Thus will it be ethical and pro-Jewish, as well as fearlessly upholding the legitimate rights of the Christians and Muslims who live in the holy places.

In its wisdom, the Holy See responded negatively to Zionist aspirations when these were first made known. The British Chief Political Office in Palestine observed, in 1919, that "the Vatican is violently opposed to Zionism." The righteous concerns of the popes seem far-sighted and prophetic indeed, as we survey the present risks to Jews, Muslims and Christians in the suffering land of Christ's birth.

But the Vatican does not only have an absolute duty, recalled at Yad Vashem more than anywhere else, to speak against the forces of established power and privilege, to ensure the long-term safety of the Jewish people, through the peaceful dismantling of Zionism. It will also not forget the Muslim world, a fifth of the world's population, which yearns for Jerusalem as for an estranged bride. Israel's treatment of the Palestinians is seen as the icon of a larger fact of global inequality. If the Church sides, as Christ did, with the poor, the refugees and the victims of occupation, the Muslim world will surely hail the Church as an authentic servitor of God's truth.

May the God of Abraham constantly bless you and guide you to what is most pleasing to Him.

For Further Reading

Kenneth Cragg. *Palestine: the Prize and the Price of Zion*. London: Cassell, 1997.

Richard Falk. "Slouching towards a Palestinian Holocaust", www.transnational.org/Area_MiddleEast/2007/Falk_PalestineGenocide.html

Norman H. Gershman. *Besa: Muslims who Saved Jews in World War II*. Syracuse: Syracuse University Press, 2008.

Peter Stockton. *Transcending Jerusalem*. www.transcendingjerusalem.com

Abdal Hakim Murad (Tim Winter) is University Lecturer in Islamic Studies in the Faculty of Divinity, University of Cambridge. He has worked extensively in interfaith relations, editing *Abraham's Children* (2006) with Bishop Richard Harries and Rabbi Norman Solomon. In 2008 he published, as editor, the *Cambridge Companion to Classical Islamic Theology*. He is also a well-known preacher and imam in Britain's Muslim community.

Saliba Sarsar

hopes the 'barbed wire and demons' can be extracted from our brains and a rich mosaic of faiths can be created.

As children of a caring and loving God, we are called upon to use our voice and touch to be servant leaders, to heal the world. Our involvement, if we so choose, requires us to understand and respect "the Other," while knowing well not only our common beliefs and values, but also the different or the unique among them.

Seeing ourselves as belonging to the universe, with rights and obligations, is what faith is all about. Hence, we need to engage our faith by embracing humanity, by finding common ground through enhanced dialogue and sharing.

"...we need to engage our faith by embracing humanity, by finding common ground through enhanced dialogue and sharing."

Our engagement is essential as we reflect on the horrors and oppression of prior centuries – notably the Crusades, the Inquisition and the Holocaust or *Shoah* – and grapple with humanity's current pain and suffering in the Holy Land and elsewhere around the world.

While we must always remember the Holocaust and similar tragedies, like barbed wire and demons, these must be extracted from our brain. This intentional act, in addition to its healing powers, is critical as it enables us to reconstruct human discourse after trauma and build hope for our future.

This reconstruction and building are doable, particularly through the agency of faith. "The surest way to the heart of a people," Huston Smith argues, "is through their faith."[1]

Thinking of the Holy Land, the main responsibility falls on the shoulders of those belonging to the three Abrahamic faiths – Judaism, Christianity and Islam. Like stained glass windows, these project colours and forms, soon forming a mosaic richer than what each can provide independently. If they offer the world anything, it is God's centrality in their lives and the gift of sharing – their beliefs and values, their wisdom.

The Abrahamic faiths, like most other traditions, teach the Golden Rule. Jews recite with Hillel: "What is hateful to you, do not do to your neighbour.

Questions

1. Is denial of the Holocaust and other genocides a result of outright ignorance, or a sad commentary on our inability to face the truth, shoulder responsibility and demonstrate solidarity with our fellow human beings? What are the remedies?

2. What is common and what is unique between Judaism and Christianity and between Jews and Christians? Explain and use specific examples.

3. How can Jews and Christians bridge the divide between them and bring about more meaningful, sustained dialogue and sharing of beliefs and values with each other on the one hand, and between them and other religions, including Islam, on the other?

4. What must Jews and Christians do to advance forgiveness, reconciliation, justice and peace in the Middle East in general, and in Israeli-Palestinian relations in particular?

This is the whole Torah; all the rest is commentary" (Hillel, Talmud, Shabbat 31a). Christians recite with Jesus: "In everything, do to others as you would have them do to you; for this is the law and the prophets" (Matthew 7:12). Muslims recite with Muhammad: "No one of you truly believes until you wish for others what you wish for yourself" (13th of the 40 Hadiths).

Yet the Golden Rule has more often than not been forgotten or ignored, with dire consequences for all. Most Christians were not as articulate as they should have been during the Holocaust. Today, not all Christians and Jews are in tune with "the Other." Some Christians still harbour ill thoughts against Jews, while others believe that the treatment of Palestinians by Israel – read the Jewish state – is oppressive and unjust. Some Jews are suspicious of Christian designs over Jerusalem and Eretz Israel and are opposed to Jewish-Christian cooperation and dialogue, let alone doing so with Muslims. As Roman Catholic Patriarch Emeritus of Jerusalem Michel Sabbah has explained, "...there is still a religious immaturity in our societies where the acceptance and respect of the other are concerned... There are always elements of extremism or ignorance that carry with them the negative things of the past and that do not cease to be a source of distrust, of suspicion, and of fear, and, thus, of aggressiveness against their fellow citizens who have a different religion."[2]

Even though the links between the Jewish and Christian worlds have not always been strong, relations between Christians and Jews have generally improved during the past few decades. The Roman Catholic Church's unequivocal repudiation of antisemitism in the 1965 Second Vatican Ecumenical Council's declaration, *Nostra Aetate*, and the 1993-94 Accords between the Holy See and the State of Israel are positive expressions. The same is true of the German Lutheran and Reformed Churches that acknowledge the Jewish claim upon the Land of Israel, but distinguish between God's promise of the land and the State of Israel. *Dabru Emet* ("Speak [the] Truth"), the enlightened statement on Christians and Christianity, issued in September 2000 and signed by over 220 rabbis and intellectuals from all branches of Judaism, signalled a significant step forward. Even Presbyterians in the United States voted in 2006 to reverse a 2004 divestment policy and to withdraw their condemnation of the separation barrier between Israel and the Palestinians. Despite the conflict between Palestinians and Israelis, Christians and Jews in Israel have been in dialogue to understand each other and to work for coexistence. Christians, Jews and Muslims have been in contact as well, as evidenced by the work of the Council of Religious Institutions in the Holy Land.

Through increased knowledge of beliefs and values – especially in terms of the articles of faith (e.g., God, angels, and humans; belief in revelation; Divine providence and just reward) and believers' obligations (e.g., toward God and toward other humans) – and of divergent views over theological matters (e.g., the Holy Trinity and resurrection), Jews and Christians can engender increased awareness, tolerance and sharing. The Divine Presence in Creation and in every human being means that when humanity engages "the Other," it is actually encountering God. God's message of compassion, forgiveness, justice, love and peace provides sure paths which humanity can follow in relating to "the Other". The paths lead to good deeds and to salvation.

This bridging of the divide enables us to revisit our own and the other's teachings and practices. Speaking of the benefit of interreligious dialogue and sharing, Rabbi David Rosen states, "As we free ourselves of the shackles and heal ourselves of the wounds of past persecution and conflict; and as we enjoy the fruits of cooperation and mutual esteem, we can learn much from Christian teaching... to recover, reaffirm, and deepen, in our own understanding and expression of these fundamental Jewish concepts and teaching."[3] The same may be expressed by a Christian, explaining the learning and transformation that come from interacting with Jews and Judaism.

What must we do as people of faith? How can we become part of the solution, not the problem?

No matter how angered or disengaged we are or might become, no matter how we feel about Church-Israel or Israeli-Palestinian relations, we must always shun the culture of exclusion, racist mythology and death. The opportunity must never be given for the indescribable and the undiscussable to occur again. We must commit to *tikkun olam*, the Jewish principle that obligates each of us to leave our world more whole than we found it. We must commit to repairing the world, as Jesus did, by providing justice for the oppressed, by calling for an end to violence, and by tending the garden.

We must learn to listen, alertly, deeply. Smith writes, "Those who listen work for peace, a peace built not on religions or political hegemonies, but on mutual awareness and concern. For understanding brings respect, and respect prepares the way for a higher capacity which is love."[4]

A new system of education is essential, one that embodies ethical and humanistic qualities, as well as the qualities of socially responsible leadership and the common good. As Patriarch Sabbah writes, "The new generations in all the religions must hear it said: the other who belongs to a different religion is not the enemy or the stranger. He or she is a brother, a sister, whom we must love and with whom we must collaborate and build society."[5]

What better place for dialogue and sharing than Jerusalem? Jerusalem – my city, our city – is "the image of the new creation and the aspirations of all peoples..." (Rev 21:4). Like any other city, it is also home to multitudes of people – Jews, Christians and Muslims; Israelis and Palestinians – wishing to live and prosper. Their conditions in Jerusalem and its environs have been less than ideal. They deserve a better life.

Jews and Christians, as they dialogue and share, must extend themselves to help resolve not only what is dividing them, but also the Question of

For Further Reading

Karen Armstrong. *Jerusalem: One City, Three Faiths*. New York: Ballantine Books, 1996.

Gerald Krell & Meyer Odze. *Three Faiths, One God: Judaism, Christianity, Islam*. A documentary film at www.threefaithsonegod.com.

David Rosen. "Learning From Each Other: Reflections of a Jew, http://www.jcrelations.net/en/?item=2885 and "Pope Benedict XVI, Child of Abraham," *http://www.beliefnet.com/Faiths/Christianity/Catholic/2005/04/Pope-Benedict-XVI-Child-Of-Abraham-aspx.*

Saliba Sarsar and Yehezkel Landau. "Reclaiming Dignity and Hope." *Middle East Times*, 25 September 2006, http://www.metimes.com/Opinion/2006/09/25/commentary_reclaiming_dignity_and_hope/1298/

Jerusalem and the larger issues obstructing Israeli-Palestinian accommodation. This includes reaching out to co-religionists, including Christian and Muslim Palestinians, as well as to secular authorities, urging them to pay closer attention to the significance of interfaith and interreligious dialogue and its contributions to peacemaking and peace building. Such an approach will go a long way to heal the wounds of history and what is ailing the peoples of the Holy Land.

Your Holiness, as you tour the Holy City, remember to recite a special prayer for continued dialogue, sharing and reconciliation, in addition to peace. As you converse with leaders from all walks of life, urge them to discover anew the meaning of creation and Divine grace, to repair the world. If these do not happen in Jerusalem, where can they happen? If not now, when?

Jerusalem is the perfect place for joining sanctity with conscience, holiness with hope. It is best for expressing our voice and touch, for enabling positive actions, dialogue and sharing.

Notes

1. Huston Smith, *The World's Religions* (New York: HarperCollins Publishers, 1994), p. 13.
2. Patriarch Michel Sabbah, *Faithful Witness: On Reconciliation and Peace in the Holy Land*, edited and with an Introduction by Drew Christiansen and Saliba Sarsar (Hyde Park, NY: New City Press, 2009), p. 186.
3. David Rosen, "Learning From Each Other: Reflections of a Jew," Address at Fordham University, 28 October 2003, http://www.jcrelations.net/en/?item=2885.
4. Huston Smith, op.cit. p. 249.
5. Patriarch Michel Sabbah, op.cit. p. 186.

Saliba Sarsar, born and raised in Jerusalem, is Professor of Political Science and Associate Vice President for academic program initiatives at Monmouth University, USA. Dr Sarsar's research has focused on Jerusalem, peace and Palestinian-Israeli relations. His latest edited work (with Fr. Drew Christiansen) is *Michael Sabbah: Faithful Witness – On Reconciliation and Peace in the Holy Land*, New City Press, 2009.

President Shimon Peres. During his visit to Israel, the Pope is being hosted by President Peres. Israel is an independent nation state formed after the Second World War. However, the Holocaust continues to cast a shadow over Jewish identity, as it does over the relationship between Jews and Christians.
Courtesy of World Economic Forum.

Holocaust

Isabel Wollaston

discusses Yad Vashem and the 'hot' topics in Christian-Jewish relations today.

When you visit Israel in May 2009 and go to Yad Vashem, it will be a more controversial occasion than that of your predecessor in March 2000. There, you will encounter a very different site than did Pope John Paul II, following extensive redevelopment under the Yad Vashem 2001 Masterplan.

The 2001 Masterplan acknowledged that Yad Vashem (founded in 1953) required extensive redevelopment to cater for the number and needs of visitors, to reflect contemporary scholarship and draw on current pedagogy and museology. Redevelopment included a new entrance plaza and Visitors' Centre (2003), and museum complex (2005), incorporating a new Holocaust History Museum (HHM), Holocaust Art Museum, Exhibitions Pavilion, Learning Centre, Visual Centre and Synagogue. According to Moshe Safdie, architect of the new complex, this entrance plaza was designed as "an aqueduct-like structure that would separate the sacred site from the surrounding city".[1] It therefore embodies both an assumption that Yad Vashem constitutes, in some senses, sacred space (hence the request that men cover their heads in parts of the site, notably the Hall of Remembrance and Synagogue), and an Israeli perspective on the Holocaust (most evident in the final sections of the HHM, including a viewing platform as visitors exit the exhibition, and in the quotation chosen for the entrance plaza: "I will put My breath into you and you shall live again, and I will set you upon your own soil" [Ezekiel 37:14]).[2]

"... Yad Vashem constitutes, in some senses, sacred space... and an Israeli perspective on the Holocaust..."

Publicity material suggests that visitors should spend 1½ to 2 hours in the HHM and proposes two routes round the museum complex and memorials, one that takes 3, the other 4-5 hours. However, when you visit Yad Vashem, your visit is likely to be relatively brief, focusing on the Hall of Remembrance and avoiding the HHM. Why? Because of controversy over a caption[3] and photograph of Pope Pius XII in the exhibition.

This controversy hit the headlines in April 2007 with a report that Monsignor Antonio Franco, the Vatican's ambassador to Israel, would boycott the national ceremony at Yad Vashem on *Yom hashoah* in protest[4]: "I consider this picture in that place and the caption that accompanies it unfair and something that disturbs my feelings and the feelings of Catholics all over the world.'[5] Although he subsequently attended the ceremony, Franco's initial stance prompted strong reactions, for and against. The initial article quoted Yad Vashem's insistence that "the Holocaust museum presents the historical truth on Pope Pius XII as it is known to scholars today," and Itzhak Minerbi's view that the caption was "neutral", reflecting "the very minimum" that could be said. Conversely, Sister Margherita Marchione deemed the caption "unjust" and "contrary to the truth", and called on Yad Vashem to honour Pius as a Righteous Gentile.[6] Between these positions was that of British historian Martin Gilbert, who commented, "I could understand that caption 10 or 15 years ago, but... it's just too much of a distorted shorthand," but Gilbert also supported Yad Vashem's call for the Vatican to allow scholars full access to its archives.[7] The controversy gained further impetus in October 2008 when Father Peter Gumpel, realtor for the cause for beatification of Pius XII, called the caption a "historical falsification" and such "a scandal for Catholics" that it would preclude any papal visit to Israel.[8] These comments prompted Father Federico Lombardi, director of the Vatican Press Office, to insist that whilst he hoped the caption would be "the subject of a new objective and in-depth consideration on the part of museum officials", it was not a "determining factor" in deciding whether or not there would be a papal visit to Israel in the near future.[9] This controversy provides further evidence that Pius' 'silence' during the Holocaust, and his possible beatification/canonization,[10] are amongst the most incendiary issues in Catholic-Jewish relations. It is unlikely that supporters or critics of Pius will heed Lombardi's call for them to desist from attempting to pressurize you, as the Pope, on the issue.[11]

Controversy over Pius XII first became widespread with the 1963 premiere of Rolf Hochuth's play *Der Stellvertreter* (*The Representative*),[12] and prompted the Vatican to release the 12 volume *Actes et Documents du Saint Siège relatifs à la Seconde Guerre Mondiale* (1965-1981). The 'Pius wars' have continued unabated since the publication of the Vatican's Commission for Religious Relations with the Jews, *We Remember: A Reflection on the Shoah* (1998) and John Cornwell's *Hitler's Pope: The Secret History of Pius XII* (1999).

Given this context, it is unsurprising that Yad Vashem addressed the subject in the HHM. However, the caption should be understood in relation to the exhibition's overall aims and its general treatment of Christianity in relation to the Holocaust. Yad Vashem stresses that the new museum complex's main focus is on Jews as primary victims of the Holocaust, and as subjects rather than objects: it seeks to demonstrate how different Jews in a range of

Questions

1. To what extent, if at all, does Yad Vashem represent sacred space or some kind of holy site and/or a place of pilgrimage?

2. How is Christianity represented at sites such as Yad Vashem? Should museums on the Holocaust represent Christians as all of the following: perpetrators, collaborators, victims, resistors, rescuers and bystanders?

3. Should the authorities at Yad Vashem consider withdrawing and/or revising the wording of the caption on Pope Pius XII?

4. How are Jews and Judaism represented at Yad Vashem? Is there sufficient sensitivity to the diversity of Jewish life before and after the Holocaust, and to the specific concerns and needs of religious Jews?

contexts responded. It aims to provide an accurate historical overview, reflecting current historical research, whilst also placing "the individual at the centre. We're telling the story through the eyes, the mouths, the feelings of the individual. Eye to eye. Person to Person."[13] Historians sought to identify who features in various photographs and the story behind particular artefacts, with the exhibition telling c. 90 personal stories. It is also why the Hall of Names is part of the HHM. Limited space is devoted to the experience of non-Jewish victims of the Nazis and their collaborators, with most attention paid to the fate of Romanies (Gypsies) and the mentally and physically handicapped.

The first gallery in the exhibition focuses on Christian anti-Judaism and antisemitism, noting that "from its inception, Christianity was ambivalent towards Judaism",[14] but then acknowledges that "a new type" of modern antisemitism emerged, based on social Darwinism and racism, upon which Nazi antisemitism was based. The effect is somewhat undermined by a film which stresses that "from its beginning Christianity cultivated hatred for the Jews," implying a seamless progression from Christian anti-Judaism to the Holocaust. However, the role of the Churches in opposing the Euthanasia Programme is noted in a later section on 'Non-Jewish victims of persecution and oppression' and considerable attention is paid to the Righteous Among the Nations, both in the HHM and via memorials in the grounds. Dan Michman, a senior historian at Yad Vashem, believes that the exhibition offers a balanced view, one that is critical but also "makes plentiful reference to the rescue of Jews by Catholics and representatives of the Vatican in Europe".[15]

The story Yad Vashem tells about Christians and Christianity is complex, but one that is a sidebar to its real focus: the ways Jews reacted to events during and immediately after the Holocaust. There is an impressive attempt to emphasize the diversity of Jewish communities, both prior to and during the Holocaust[16] and to personalize this via text, image, artefact and video testimonies. The use of Yad Vashem's extensive collection of Holocaust art at key points in the exhibition is particularly well judged. The HHM provokes questions and overwhelms (by sheer weight of information, as well as because of the difficulties of viewing it in any detail whilst jostled by large numbers of visitors). Viewing the exhibition as a European and/or a Christian can be unsettling given some of the judgments and provocative questions explicit and implicit within it. The addition of the Learning Centre, Visual Centre, new Museum of Holocaust Art and Synagogue is particularly welcome – if the visitor has time to visit them. In the grounds there is a range of memorials embodying the many different ways in which it is possible to remember, memorialize and interpret the Holocaust. It is a shame that some of the more reflective and provocative examples, such as Nandor Gild's *Memorial of Victims of the Concentration and Death Camps*, Ilana Gur's

"The story Yad Vashem tells about Christians and Christianity is complex, but one that is a sidebar to its real focus: the ways Jews reacted to events during and immediately after the Holocaust."

Hope, Lea Michelson's *Silent Cry* and Nathan Rapoport's *Job* are not marked on the map in the new Visitors' Guide. The latter, in particular, is a challenging example of a post-Holocaust Jewish reading of a biblical figure, and could provide an interesting focus for discussion amongst visiting Christian groups, or for dialogue between Jews and Christians visiting the site together.

Yad Vashem, and its caption on Pius XII, encapsulates many complex, 'hot' topics in Christian-Jewish relations today, such as the relationship between Christian anti-Judaism and Nazi antisemitism; the role of Churches and individual Christians during the Holocaust; what, if anything, is unique about the Holocaust, both in relation to non-Jewish victims of the Nazis and their collaborators, and other genocides; the dangers of 'Christianizing' the Holocaust versus a readiness to criticise and a tendency to narcissism in easy assumptions that we would have acted differently or better; the 'lessons' we draw from the Holocaust and their practical ramifications for ourselves and others; the 'etiquette' of dialogue and the extent to which we are entitled to make demands on each other.

Your Holiness, it is a great shame that when you visit Yad Vashem, it will be amidst a swirl of controversy, with little time to pause and reflect on what you see, assuming you even see much of it (it is unlikely that you and your entourage will have the time available that Yad Vashem itself suggests is required). Yet, given current circumstances, the fact that you are visiting Yad Vashem at all is sufficient, if only for its symbolic value, not least in keeping channels of communication open about these very delicate and difficult issues.

Notes

1. Moshe Safdie, "The Architecture of Memory" in Yad Vashem, *Moshe Safdie – The Architecture of Memory*: 92-101, 96.
2. Tom Segev provocatively suggests that "the message at Yad Vashem is Israel should exist, Israel should be strong, as victims we can do no wrong," a view he criticises as a "narrow Israeli interpretation of the Holocaust". See Chris McGreal, "This is ours and ours alone," *Guardian*, 15 March 2005.
3. The full caption reads: "Pius XII's reaction to the murder of the Jews during the Holocaust is a matter of controversy. In 1933, when he was Secretary of the Vatican State, he was active in obtaining a concordat with the German regime to preserve the Church's rights in Germany, even if this meant recognizing the Nazi racist regime. When he was elected Pope in 1939, he shelved a letter against racism and antisemitism that his predecessor had prepared. Even when reports about the murder of Jews reached the Vatican, the Pope did not protest either verbally or in writing. In December 1942, he abstained from signing the Allied declaration condemning the extermination of the Jews. When Jews were deported from Rome to Auschwitz the Pope did not intervene. The Pope maintained his neutral position throughout the war, with the exception of appeals to the rulers of Hungary and Slovakia towards its end. His silence and the absence of guidelines obliged churchmen throughout Europe to decide on their own how to react."
4. Etgar Lefkovits, "Vatican to Skip Yad Vashem's ceremony," *Jerusalem Post*, 12 April 2007. The issue of the caption was also raised in 2006 by the previous nuncio, Archbishop Pietro Sambi, without prompting public debate.
5. Quoted in Conal Urquhart, "Papal Envoy's u-turn on memorial," *Guardian*, 16 April 2007.

For Further Reading

Joseph Bottum and David G. Dalin, eds. *The Pius War: Responses to the Critics of Pius XII.* Lanham: Lexington Books, 2004.

Phillip A. Cunningham, Norbert J. Hoffmann, S.D.B., and Joseph Sievers, eds. *The Catholic Church and the Jewish People: Recent Reflections from Rome.* New York: Fordham University Press, 2007.

Bella Gutterman and Avner Shalev, eds. *To Bear Witness: Holocaust Remembrance at Yad Vashem.* Jerusalem: Yad Vashem, 2005.

Carol Rittner and John K. Roth, eds. *Pope Pius XII and the Holocaust.* London: Leicester University Press, a Continuum Imprint, 2002.

Yad Vashem. *Moshe Safdie – The Architecture of Memory.* Baden: Lars Müller Publishers, 2006.

6. See her article, "Pius XII and Yad Vashem," http://www.catholicleague.org/printer.php?p=rer&id=43
7. Edward Pentin, "Distorted Shorthand" (12 May 2007), http://www.insidethevatican.com/phprint.php.
8. Gumpel's comments attracted extensive press coverage, e.g. Peter Popham, "The unholy legacy of Pius XII," *Independent*, 20 October 2008.
9. Statement of 20 October 2008, quoted amongst others by www.zenit.org/.
10. In 2000 Pope John Paul II conferred the title of 'venerable' on Pius XII. In 2007 the Congregation for the Cause of Saints voted in favour of a decree that Pius possessed 'heroic virtues', a prerequisite for beatification. Following this, Pope Benedict is studying an extensive dossier on the subject prior to deciding whether or not to sign this decree.
11. See, for example, "Peres urges Pope to ignore row over Pius XII and visit Israel," *Haaretz*, 18 October 2008.
12. Controversy ignited again in 2002 with the release of Constantin Costa-Gavras' film *Amen*, based on Hochhuth's play, advertisements for which centred on the cross and the swastika.
13. Avner Shalev, Chairman of the Yad Vashem Directorate, quoted in Jonny Dymond, "Holocaust Museum's Journey to Light," 15 March 2005, BBC News Channel, http://news.bbc.co.uk1/hi/world/middle_east/4350505.stm.
14. The text goes on to observe that 5th-century Christian theology "determined that the Jews should not be killed, rather, they should be kept in their humiliated status until they accept Christianity. In the Middle Ages, the negative image of the Jews as guilty of deicide became further entrenched. This image led to popular outbursts – blood libels against the Jews, especially in times of crisis. In its theological struggle against Judaism and the Jews, Christianity perpetuated and spread this negative image over the centuries and wherever European Christian culture reached."
15. Adi Schwartz, "The Silence of the Shepherd," *Haaretz*, 24 October 2008. These issues are also addressed from a variety of perspectives in response to the question 'How did Christian denominations respond to the Holocaust?' in Yad Vashem's educational CD-Rom *Eclipse of Humanity: the History of the Shoah*, in interviews that can be accessed by visitors in the Learning Centre.
16. An ongoing criticism of Yad Vashem is that it fails to pay sufficient attention to the specific concerns and sensitivities of religious Jews, e.g. Clyde Haberman, "Jerusalem Journal: in a museum of hell qualms about decorum," *New York Times*, 7 March 1995. Whilst Yad Vashem has made considerable efforts to address these concerns, similar criticisms have been levelled against the HHM, e.g. Jonathan Rosenblum, "Some thoughts on visiting Yad Vashem," *London Jewish Tribune*, 10 November 2005.

Isabel Wollaston is a senior lecturer in the Department of Theology and Religion, University of Birmingham, UK, whose publications include: *A War against Memory? The Future of Holocaust Remembrance* (London, 1996); *Auschwitz and the Politics of Commemoration*, Holocaust Educational Trust Research Papers 1:5 (1999-2000); and "Negotiating the Marketplace: The Role(s) of Holocaust Museums Today," *Journal of Modern Jewish Studies* 4:1 (2005): 63-80.

Gemma Del Duca

reflects on the need for Holocaust education.

Questions

1. Who was Edith Stein? Why was her canonization in October 1998 problematic, especially for the Jewish community?

2. When was the international commemoration of the Holocaust begun and why? Why is Holocaust remembrance still important?

3. Why should Holocaust education be part of the curriculum for those being trained for leadership and teaching roles in the Christian community?

Blessed be your coming to Israel! May your presence and your words further peace and understanding for all the peoples of this Holy Land.

The privilege of writing "a letter to the Pope" brings to mind another letter written in the spring of 1933 by a German Jewish/Catholic woman, philosopher, educator – Edith Stein.[1] Under her patronage, I write as a religious, an American Sister of Charity for over 50 years, a resident in Israel for over 30 years, and for over 20 years committed to Holocaust education through our National Catholic Center for Holocaust Education, Seton Hill University, Greensburg, Pennsylvania.

In her letter to Pope Pius XI, Edith Stein spoke of the brutal, systematic persecution of the Jews of Germany and of the responsibility that "falls on those who keep silent in the face of such happenings". As we know, she also suffered persecution and died in Auschwitz in 1942. Much has happened in the Church since her letter was written. In the aftermath of the Holocaust, the Second Vatican Council brought with it *Nostra Aetate*. This document repudiated the deicide charge, deplored antisemitism, acknowledged the ongoing validity of the covenant with the Jewish people and called for improved Catholic-Jewish relations.

So that now in this letter I thank you, Holy Father, for speaking out recently in a clear and forthright manner concerning the *Shoah*, the Catholic Church's relationship with the Jewish people and your own "unquestionable solidarity with... the recipients of the First Covenant".[2] Your words give courage to Catholics and Jews in Israel and in the world to continue "the laborious journey of listening and dialogue".

Furthermore, your words concerning the teaching power of the Holocaust, as an admonition "against forgetting, against denial or reductionism," urge those of us who are Holocaust educators to continue to engage in new and creative ways with "both the old and new generations" in that "laborious journey of listening and dialogue".

But we, too, like St Edith Stein "dare to speak," to make a request of you, our Holy Father. We need you, your interest, your words, and above all your personal leadership in initiating for the Church universal a comprehensive programme of study, research and education on the *Shoah* for this generation and for future ones. This programme under your leadership would be given priority in Catholic educational institutions, particularly in seminaries, universities and colleges.

You are a powerful witness in the Church of the reality of the *Shoah*. We need your steady, scholarly leadership to implement the teaching of the magisterium from *Nostra Aetate* to the present. We need your active presence with Holocaust education in the Church and for "the laborious journey of listening and dialogue".

With all the colleagues who work in Holocaust education at Seton Hill University, I ask for your blessing.

Notes

1. Letter of Saint Edith Stein, www.ourgardenofcarmel.org/edithLetterToPope.htm
2. Statement made by Pope Benedict XVI, Audience, 28 January 2009.

For Further Reading

Harry James Cargas, ed. *The Unnecessary Problem of Edith Stein*. Lanham, MD: University Press of America, 1994.

Edward H. Flannery. *The Anguish of the Jews*. New York: Paulist Press, 1985.

David Tracy. "Religious Values after the Holocaust: A Catholic View," in Abraham J. Peck ed. *Jews and Christians after the Holocaust*. Philadelphia: Fortress, 1982, pp. 87-110.

Gemma Del Duca, SC, a Sister of Charity, taught history at Seton Hill University and worked in campus ministry at various universities before moving to Israel. She works with the staff at Yad Vashem in Jerusalem as coordinator of the Catholic Institute for Holocaust Studies, under the auspices of the Seton Hill University National Catholic Center for Holocaust Education. Sr. Gemma also serves as administrator of the Isaac Jacob Institute for Religious Law, an institute that supports religious dialogue through lectures, publications and Holocaust education.

Emanuel Tanay

writes on Nostra Aetate *as postscript to an obituary and the toxic consequences of vengeance.*

Should the Catholic Church commemorate the Holocaust? The Holocaust was a tragedy of epic proportions for the Jews. At the same time, it was a history-transforming event for Christianity and Western civilization. I am a Holocaust survivor from Poland, the country that considered itself the outpost of Catholicism. "*Antemurale Christianitatis*" was the Latin term for Poland's special status within the Catholic Church. I am intimately familiar with the teachings of the Catholic Church. I gained knowledge of Catholicism during the time I spent in a novitiate of a Benedictine monastery in Krakow, Poland.

The commemoration of the genocide of the Jews of Europe has had a difficult history. There was a conflict among Jews as to how to commemorate this calamity. Germany selected the most appropriate date, namely the liberation of Auschwitz.

"As a Holocaust survivor and a student of Holocaust history, I am aware of the twin dangers of remembrance: the failure to remember what happened and remembering what did not happen."

As a Holocaust survivor and a student of Holocaust history, I am aware of the twin dangers of remembrance: the failure to remember what happened and remembering what did not happen. In the Jewish community, the heroic struggle for survival is neglected, the suicidal defiance is celebrated.

The dreadful but memorable slogan of Nazi Germany was "The Only Good Jew is a Dead Jew." It should also be remembered that this slogan resonated with millions of people throughout Christian Europe. The outcome was predictable; the genocidal project succeeded and the Jewish culture of Europe was eliminated.

Hatred of the Jews existed before the creation of Nazi Germany in 1933. Catholicism instructed the faithful that the Jews were responsible for the crucifixion of Jesus Christ. Hatred of the Jews has been an integral part of Christianity. The Church isolated the Jews, labelled them as untouchable, declared them disgusting and disgraced. The interactions between Christians and Jews were reduced to commercial transactions. The Jews were prohibited from performing a variety of normal work roles. This was an effective way to dehumanize the Jews.

The genocide of the Jews during World War II was the product of a belief system. That much is beyond dispute. Some people claim that Nazism alone is the belief system responsible for the genocide of the Jews. Any student of history and psychology would find such a contention absurd. Nazi Germany existed from 1933 to 1945. It is unreasonable, from a psychological perspective, to argue that the national character of Germany and of other European countries could be significantly changed in a mere few years.

Germany acknowledged its culpability for the genocide of the Jews. In February of 2009, France formally recognized the nation's role in deporting Jews to Nazi death camps. It has been silent about the failure to condemn mass murder in progress.

Pontius Pilate, the Roman Governor of Judea, was a cruel oppressor of the Jews. His treatment of the Jews resulted in his recall to Rome, where he had to stand trial for cruelty and oppression. Pilate killed himself on orders from Emperor Caligula in AD 39. This is the historical Pilate. The man who presided over the trial of Jesus and gave the order for his crucifixion is portrayed in the Gospels as a tool of the Jews. We are told that he washed his hands of this act, but he ordered it and his soldiers carried it out. As the *Encyclopaedia Britannica* says:

> But it [the New Testament] is preoccupied with concerns of the nascent Christian communities, increasingly making their way among the Gentiles and anxious to avoid giving offense to Roman authorities. Eventually, in Christian tradition, Pilate and his wife became converts, and the latter is a saint in the Eastern Church.

Pilate was portrayed as personally convinced of Jesus' innocence, but he was weak, cowardly, vacillating. He yielded to the pressure of the Jewish crowd. But the only description we have of him by a contemporary calls him "a man of inflexible, stubborn, and cruel disposition... a spiteful and angry person" and speaks of "his venality, his violence, his thefts, his assaults, his abusive behavior, his frequent executions of untried prisoners, and his endless savage ferocity" (Philo, *Legatio*, 301f).

The Church revoked the indictment against the Jews in *Nostra Aetate* after the verdict had been carried out. The Vatican speaks of "dialogue with the Jews". This catchphrase obscures the fact that European Jewry as a cultural entity was destroyed. One cannot "dialogue" with ashes. *Nostra Aetate* is not part of a dialogue but postscript to an obituary. The President of the Pontifical Commission for Religious Relations with the Jews, Cardinal Edward I Cassidy, spoke at a meeting of the international Jewish-Catholic Liaison Committee

Questions

1. Should the killing of six million Jews by Nazi Germany be called the genocide of the Jews or the Holocaust?

2. Nazi Germany killed millions of civilians who were not Jews. What are the reasons to differentiate these murders from the extermination of the Jews?

3. Discuss the statement of Pope John Paul II: "The Church cannot be held responsible for the guilt of its members."

in Prague in 1990. He expressed the need for "*teshuva*" or repentance toward Jews by the Roman Catholic Church. The Church has not adopted that view as an official position.

The Pontifical Commission for Religious Relations with the Jews is an unfortunate designation, because it implies interactions between two partners. It would be useful to have a Commission on the history of the teachings and practices of the Catholic Church in relation to the Jews. The post-Holocaust Vatican has revised the teachings of the Church in relation to the Jews without exploring the history of "the theology of hate".

Talking about relations with the Jews as if the Jews were a living presence denies the reality of the annihilation of the Jewish culture of Europe. The issue is not only relating to the Jews after the Holocaust, but also assuming responsibility for contributing to the annihilation of the Jews of Europe.

On 29 October 1965, more than 20 years after the liberation of the death camps, the Catholic Church took doctrinal notice of the theology of hate. *Nostra Aetate* told the faithful, "[T]he Jews should not be presented as cursed or repudiated by God." *Nostra Aetate* absolves the "Jews of today" of the responsibility for the death of Christ. It advises against placing blame upon "all the Jews then living" for the suffering and killing of Jesus. The reality is that the Romans executed Jesus Christ, in accordance with Roman law.

Many Christian theologians believe that a significant factor in the genocide of the Jews perpetrated by Nazi Germany was the anti-Judaic teaching of the Catholic Church. However, this historical reality is known only in academic circles. I have little doubt that many Christians were horrified by what was done to the Jews in Nazi Germany. I am equally certain that many Christians opposed Catholic and Protestant Churches' support of Nazi Germany, but they did next to nothing to stop the atrocities. The same was the case during the Inquisition and all the other anti-Jewish measures instituted by the Catholic Church against the Jews.

The Catechism of the Catholic Church says, "Among the penitent's acts, contrition occupies the first place. Contrition is sorrow of the soul and detestation for the sin committed, together with the resolution not to sin again." This commitment to repentance would be fulfilled by designating a date for the commemoration of the genocide of the Jews by the Catholic Church.

Many acts are unforgivable; this is certainly true of any genocide. For this reason alone, forgiveness is not an issue in connection with the Holocaust. What matters in human relations is the presence or absence of vengeance. Whenever we harm someone, there is the risk that vengeance will aggravate the harm already done. The victim and the actor suffer the toxic consequences of vengeance. Some people, including most Holocaust survivors, were fortunate not to be afflicted by vengeance. Other people are able to overcome vengefulness.

For centuries, the Catholic Church practised retribution against the helpless Jews for a crime our ancestors did not commit – the crucifixion of

For Further Reading

Michael Berenbaum. *The World Must Know: The History of the Holocaust as Told in the United States Holocaust Memorial Museum*. MA: Little, Brown and Co., 1993.

Martin Gilbert. *The Holocaust: A History of the Jews of Europe during the Second World War*. NY: Henry Holt and Co., 1987.

Martin Gilbert. *The Second World War: A Complete History*. NY: Henry Holt and Co., 1992.

Israel Gutman ed. *Encyclopedia of the Holocaust*. Vol. 3. NY: Macmillan, 1995.

Raul Hilberg. *The Destruction of the European Jews*. NY: Holmes & Meier, 1985.

Raul Hilberg. *Perpetrators, Victims, Bystanders: The Jewish Catastrophe 1933-1945*. NY: Harper Perennial Library, 1993.

Jesus, which was a Roman punishment against a rebellious Jew. The time has come for the Catholic Church to recognize that this unjustified accusation contributed to the genocide of the European Jews. This is a prerequisite for a meaningful dialogue between the Catholic Church and the Jews.

"I have little doubt that many Christians were horrified by what was done to the Jews in Nazi Germany... but they did next to nothing to stop the atrocities."

Emanuel Tanay, Clinical Professor of Psychiatry at Wayne State University in Detroit, is a forensic psychiatrist. He is a Distinguished Fellow of the American Academy of Forensic Science and of the American Psychiatric Society and has taught in the US, Canada and Europe. Dr Tanay has published numerous articles about forensic psychiatry, post-traumatic stress and the Holocaust. He is the author of *Passport to Life: Reflections of a Holocaust Survivor*, an autobiography of his experiences in Europe during World War II and a series of essays about the roots of bigotry and genocide.

Christine E. King

reflects on difference, clarity of conviction and the possibility of peace.

"A western society, known for its culture and civilisation had watched racism, bigotry and nationalism find physical shape in men and women who were willing to torture and murder fellow citizens and neighbours simply for being 'different'."

I once bought a badge from the United States Holocaust Memorial Museum in Washington, DC. I have it still. On it are written just two words: "Never Again". Tragically, since the persecution and murder of millions of innocent people who suffered at the hands of the Nazi state, we have seen political, religious and ideological fanaticism turn into aggression, war, murder and genocide many times. It is particularly bitter and sad to observe, in 2009, the hatred and violence between the State of Israel, home to so many descendants of the Holocaust, and its neighbours.

It seemed, as the Third Reich fell and the world watched with horror as its reality was revealed, that the unspeakable had been spoken and that those words could never be repeated. A western society, known for its culture and civilisation had watched racism, bigotry and nationalism find physical shape in men and women who were willing to torture and murder fellow citizens and neighbours simply for being 'different'.

As the Second World War ended and the regime fell, a world with access to film and the printed word could read and watch, like never before, detailed records of the horrors. It seemed impossible to those who had witnessed such scenes from the liberation of the camps, either on film or in person, that such events, on such a scale, could ever happen again. Sadly, we now know differently. How can this be? How can we change the future? Can we still learn from what happened?

It is sometimes useful to come to the study of the whole picture through individuals. In my own search to understand more of what happened, I came to study the experiences of one small group whose members suffered under the Nazi regime: the Jehovah's Witnesses. I am not a Jehovah's Witness and when I came to this research, like many people, I had stereotypical assumptions about their beliefs and the kind of people they were.

Whilst I still do not share their beliefs, what I learned about their story during these years in Germany and beyond both challenged my stereotypes and humbled me. I believe that there are reflections on their story which need to be considered.

Who were these people and what was their fate during the Third Reich? It was a small group, some mere 20,000 or so in number, who found themselves subject to an official ban on their religious work, to imprisonment and, for some, execution.

How and why did this happen? The Witnesses believe that we are living in the 'last age', awaiting the end of the world as we know it. This current world is under the power of Satan and they are literally 'witnesses' to their God, Jehovah, on the stage of history. Whilst they are law-abiding citizens, their first loyalty is to Jehovah. They see themselves as neutral in the political affairs of Satan's world.

The demand for total loyalty from the Nazi regime was in conflict with the beliefs and practices of the Witnesses as they stood firm to their convictions on political 'neutrality'. Whilst remaining highly moral members of society, they would not enlist, bear arms or work for the state in any way that conflicted with their conscience. This is not a faith where beliefs and practices can be selected at will. This is a total belief system where beliefs drive practice.

By behaving consistently and relentlessly in line with their beliefs, the Witnesses presented a challenge to the Nazi state, which in itself represented a total world view. This was not just another political state; this was the thousand-year Reich. What followed was the clash of two total systems; one using violence, the other using the refusal to engage with violence.

With a ferocity which at face value well outstripped the threat, the state removed civil rights from many Witness workers and arrested and imprisoned members of the group, sentencing them to labour or concentration camps. A number of Witness children were taken from their parents to be brought up in Nazi homes. In the camps the Witnesses still refused to bend the knee and many were tortured and brutally executed for keeping and acting on their faith.

The Witnesses, in spite of manifold humiliations and tortures, according to all the evidence, kept their dignity and kept their faith. They supported each other and they supported others. They demonstrated that the might of arms and of aggression cannot win the moral victory against unbending faith and conviction. Their faith led members of the group, at the risk of their own lives, into a refusal to become engaged in any fighting or violence. They refused to compromise. They were prepared, on an individual basis, to stand up to the all powerful and the seemingly invincible state.

Jehovah's Witnesses would still be seen by many commentators as extreme in their views. Their attitude to the state is seen as potentially dangerous. Their proselytizing is both seen as intrusive and often the butt

Questions

1. What does the stance of the Jehovah's Witnesses during the Third Reich say to you?

2. Is it possible to hold firm views, to differ from the views of your neighbour and yet live in peace?

3. Do people of faith have a special responsibility to broker and promote peace?

For Further Reading

D. Bloxham and T. Kusher. *The Holocaust, Critical Historical Approaches.* Manchester, 2005.

S. Gigliotti and B. Lang eds. *The Holocaust: A Reader.* New Jersey, 2004.

C. E. King. "Jehovah's Witnesses under Nazism" in M. Berenbaum, ed., *A Mosaic of Victims.* New York, 1990.

M. R. Marrus. *The Holocaust in History.* Harmondsworth, 1989.

of jokes. Their teachings are seen as on a spectrum from heresy to simply 'wrong'. Witnesses are sometimes described as 'deluded'.

Yet what allowed the Witnesses to keep firm to their position was the total message of their faith. They believed, as concentration camp inmates, that they had an explanation for a world turned upside down and that there was a clear role for them as 'witnesses' to their God. A belief which might be described as 'absolute' or 'conservative' proved to be a point of moral strength when the chips were down.

Three Reflections

Celebrating Difference

There were German citizens, some of them church members, who saw the rounding up of their Jehovah's Witness neighbours as the proper suppression of heresy. There were few who would stand up for them as the innocent victims of bigotry and persecution. There were few who recognised that the society unable to tolerate old age, disability and difference of faith, race or sexual orientation is both dangerous and potentially unstable.

Clarity of Conviction

At a time when relativism is core to the way many of us think, it may be uncomfortable to look at the story of the Third Reich and see the Witnesses with their non-negotiable position offer a point of powerful opposition. As someone who comes from an academic and relativist tradition, I find it hard to come to terms with the fact that it was the more flexible and eclectic belief systems which shifted and bent to accommodate the Nazi world view, whether from conviction or as a survival strategy. The iron strength of Witnesses, in contrast, and their ability to turn belief into action, whatever the cost, became the heart of a serious resistance and challenge to the Nazis.

Is Peace Possible?

We often struggle, particularly in teaching the young, between the ideal of peaceful non-violence and a world where aggression is seen as the inevitable and only response to conflict. The story of the Witnesses and their stance for non-violence forces me to reconsider the received orthodoxy that peace-keeping can only be achieved by arms.

I have been privileged, through my research, to meet a number of Witness survivors of the concentration camps. I admire their courage, their humanity and their faith. This most unlikely set of heroes consider themselves as having done what any Witness would do, and indeed is called on to do all over the world since the end of the Second World War – that is, to put their beliefs into action, whatever the cost. The Witnesses speak of the call to 'stand firm'. Whatever our beliefs, if we preach or teach non-violence and peace, may we have the courage to do the same.

Christine E. King is Vice-Chancellor and Chief Executive of Staffordshire University in England. She is a Professor of History and her research interests are medieval and modern pilgrimage and the history of religion, especially the non-Jewish victims of the Nazis.

Hédi Fried

discusses neo-Nazism as the same old philosophy of hatred and the need to defend democracy.

Could anybody be interested in what an old survivor has to say about the Holocaust? Hasn't everything been said? What is the Holocaust? Hundreds of pieces of evidence, endless research and still there is no consensus.

Each survivor tells an individual story. These vary from country to country, from person to person. Details can be depicted differently even by two people who experienced the same event. Memory can play tricks; what you remember is tinted by the emotions you had at the time. However, the bloodstained thread of the Holocaust is the same in the evidence of every survivor, reproduced alike by every one: how the persecutions of the Jews began, though in different years in the different countries, the application of the Nuremberg Laws, the yellow star, the ghetto confinement and the cattle cars to the death camps. There, after selections, gas chambers and crematoria awaited the majority of the arrivals.

"Each survivor tells an individual story. These vary from country to country, from person to person."

Originally from Hungary, I myself have described these stages in my book, *The Road to Auschwitz*, explaining how the Hungarian Jews were to be exterminated at the 11th hour of the war, with extensive help from the Hungarian gendarmes. I described the way in which we were herded together and how, immediately after the Germans entered Hungary on 19 March 1944, we were ordered to wear the yellow star. Four weeks later, we were taken to the ghetto, and after a further four weeks, on 15 May 1944, we were squeezed into cattle cars and transported to Auschwitz. There, the men were separated from the women, the elderly and children, and my 44-year-old mother was sent 'to the left', i.e. to the gas chambers. Glancing in that direction, we could see chimneys spreading heavy black smoke and flaming up occasionally.

The United States Holocaust Memorial Museum (USHMM), on its website, defines the Holocaust as "the systematic, bureaucratic, state-sponsored

Questions

1. What do historians have to say about the Holocaust? How do they evaluate the evidence for Nazi crimes against the Jewish people – and other peoples – in Nazi-occupied Europe during World War II?

2. Why do some people deny the Holocaust?

3. What are some forms of Holocaust denial? How can we deal with Holocaust denial in our churches, mosques, schools and universities?

persecution and murder of approximately six million Jews by the Nazi regime and its collaborators." The USHMM also points out that because of their perceived 'racial inferiority', Roma (Gypsies), the disabled, and some of the Slavic peoples (Poles, Russians, and others) were also targeted. Other groups were persecuted on political, ideological and behavioural grounds, among them Communists, Socialists, Jehovah's Witnesses, and homosexuals.

On its website, Yad Vashem adds that the Holocaust is defined "as the sum total of all anti-Jewish actions carried out by the Nazi-regime between 1933-1945, from stripping the German Jews of their legal and economic status in the 1930s," to segregating and starving Jews in the various occupied countries. The Holocaust was "the murder of close to six million Jews in Europe".

The historian Michael Marrus stresses the totality of the event when he writes that:

> Unlike the case with any other group, and unlike the massacres before or since, every single one of the millions of targeted Jews was to be murdered. Eradication was to be total. In principle, no Jew was to escape. In this important respect, the Nazis' assault upon Jewry differed from the campaign against other peoples and groups, Gypsies, Jehovah's Witnesses, homosexuals, Poles, Ukrainians and so on. Assaults on these people could indeed be murderous; their victims number in the million, and their ashes mingle with those of the Jews in Auschwitz and many other camps across Europe. But Nazi ideology did not require their total disappearance. In this respect the fate of the Jews was unique.

Why was the Jew an object of hate for Hitler? Why did he choose the Jews as his special target for extermination? How would the world look today if he had succeeded in his plan to exterminate all the Jews of Europe? Would he have stopped there? Or would he have found other "*Unmenschen*," people not worthy of life, to eliminate completely? These questions are difficult to answer, but are worth considering.

Another question to ponder:

Why do some people deny the Holocaust? There is clear evidence available about the Holocaust, besides that given by the survivors. Further proof can be found in the confessions given at various trials by high-ranking Nazis, including the trial of Adolf Eichmann in Jerusalem in the 1960s.

After 1945, when the truth about the death camps emerged, a shocked world cried out with one voice: "**Never again**". At the same time, nobody was willing to talk about the cruelties of the Nazis, hoping that forgetting would prevent repetition of such events. Young people grew up without any knowledge of the Holocaust. Thus, those wanting to revive Nazi ideology had an easy task. To make it more attractive, the element of killing was screened out; and by denying the extermination, the Neo-Nazi movement could once again easily be built up.

Today, this faction exists again in some countries. Neo-Nazi ideology is the same old philosophy of hate and we must give heed to these developments. Wherever Nazi ideology is spread – as well as all other ideologies which involve the idea of genocide, such as Communism and radical Islamic fundamentalism – democracy is in danger. (Hitler wanted to come to power in a democratic way, only to abolish democracy.) It is our responsibility to coming generations to defend democracy and we appeal to Your Holiness to help us in this endeavour. To this end, it is imperative to carry out extensive teaching about the Holocaust and to silence all Holocaust deniers.

Your Holiness, as one of the world's real leaders, you are in a unique position. We ask you to share your thoughts with all of us about how you, and we, can contribute to a greater global awareness of the danger of such ideologies. We need you to help us to transmit knowledge about the Holocaust to the world at large, and we need you to silence Holocaust deniers in your Roman Catholic Church community. Justice demands it. Truth requires it.

For Further Reading

Yehuda Bauer. *Rethinking the Holocaust.* Yale University Press, 2001.

David Cesarani. *Eichmann: His Life and Crimes.* Vintage, 2005.

Deborah Lipstadt. *Denying the Holocaust: The Growing Assault on Truth and Memory.* Penguin, 1994.

Hédi Fried was born in Sighet, Romania. She was deported to Auschwitz in 1944 and to various labour camps, and was liberated in Bergen-Belsen. She was taken to Sweden by the Red Cross in July 1945, where she eventually married and had three children; her husband died in 1962. In 1980, Hédi obtained a Degree in Psychology and Pedagogy and since 1984 has been Director of Café 84, a Psychosocial Centre for Survivors. She is the author of several books, including in English, *The Road to Auschwitz.* She lectures regularly in universities and educational institutes and acts as an advisor to the Swedish Government.

Mimi Schwartz

describes the small human acts of decency that could make a difference.

Small stories of decency often get lost in the larger Holocaust narrative, as I discovered in a tiny village north of Haifa in Israel, founded by a group of 29 Jewish families who fled my father's German village together in 1938. It was there, in a Memorial Room to honour the 89 village Jews killed in Nazi concentration camps, that I saw the Torah that had been rescued on *Kristallnacht* in 1938 – not by Jews, but by their Catholic neighbours. (Only three Protestant families lived in the village in those days.)

I can still hear an old man in a blue kibbutz cap telling me, "*Ja*, Nazi orders or no, the neighbours decided to save what they could for the Jews. They buried the Torah outside the Jewish cemetery, deep in the woods, and after all the craziness ended, they sent it to us here. And we have it still."

I was surprised. I grew up in post-war America on Hollywood movies of evil Germans killing Jews and didn't think of other Germans who might rescue anything Jewish in those days. True, my father had told me that in his village of 1,200, 60 kilometres south of Stuttgart, "Everyone – Christian and Jew – got along very well when I was a boy," but that was 40 years before Hitler. This Torah rescue was in the middle of the Third Reich. I wondered who did it and why?

That story led me on a twelve-year quest on three continents: into the living rooms and kitchens of the village Jews who fled, and now live in Israel and America, and to their former Christian neighbours, still in the village today. The result is my memoir, *Good Neighbors, Bad Times*, about the struggles of people who tried to do what they could without risking too much – and how everyone remembers their shared past, now lost.

I wasn't interested in the enthusiastic Nazis and the rabid antisemites. We know a lot about them, but what about people who weren't very brave or evil, but nor were they indifferent? How did they negotiate those times – and what can their struggles tell us, as neighbours, today?

Questions

1. Why do small stories of decency not get told – and do we need to hear them?

2. Do you agree with the author that small acts of decency are a form of resistance and that if enough people engage in them, the extremists could be stopped?

3. Would you have risked doing small acts of decency? What would you do now if your neighbours became enemies of the state through no fault of their own?

I would have liked to find out that half the village took part in rescuing Jews, but that didn't happen. What I heard were more small stories of decency that were imbedded in the memories of families who had known each other for centuries until the deportations in 1941-42. Those I heard several times from different people include:

- The shoemaker kept fixing Jewish shoes and shared his ration cards.
- The barber cut Jewish hair under the sign "No Jews Allowed Here."
- The farmer's daughter cleaned house, washed and brought food to her old Jewish neighbour.
- The barber's daughter lent her good raincoat.
- The shopkeeper gave food over the back fence at night.
- The bus driver kept driving the Jews, one even to Switzerland.
- A farmer had power of attorney over Jewish fields. He gave them back after the war.
- The three nuns kept helping the Jews until the nuns were transferred to another village.
- The beloved mayor kept helping the Jews until he was transferred.
- The priest spoke out against what was happening to the Jews in a sermon. He was reprimanded.
- The head of Hitler Youth lit the Shabbat candles for the Jewish youth group that met in the same building on Friday nights.
- Someone let the Jewish schoolteacher file an official complaint about the vandals in the Jewish cemetery.
- The Jews kept drinking beer in the *Gasthaus* even though it was forbidden.
- The Christians paid back debts to Jews even though Nazi law said they didn't have to.
- A farmer's wife said at the farmers' meeting, "Law or no law, I will not force Jews to work for me on their Sabbath."
- Someone hid the plaque of the Jewish war dead from World War I in the archives.
- At least ten neighbours helped a half-Jewish family survive for five years. The rest let them be.
- Carpenters fixed the Jewish windows after *Kristallnacht* and were sent to the Front a week later "as punishment", people said. None came back.

Small acts of defiance. Nothing anyone bragged about. But I, for one, would like to be able to make a mark beside every one, announcing, "I would have done that!" And more, yes... maybe – if I knew others would join me, not betray me. But how would I know? For decency is often such a solitary act; it's evil that draws a noisy crowd.

For Further Reading

Eva Fogelman. *Conscience & Courage: Rescuers of Jews during the Holocaust*. Anchor, 1995.

Eva Gossman. *Good Beyond Evil*. Vallentine-Mitchell, 2002.

Victor Klemperer. *I Will Bear Witness 1942-1945: A Diary of the Nazi Years*. Modern Library, 2001.

Fred Uhlman. *Reunion*. Vintage Classics, 2006.

"Small acts of defiance. Nothing anyone bragged about."

In Israel, you will certainly go to Yad Vashem and honour those who risked their lives to save Jews. None of the people of my father's village will be listed there – for their rescues are too small for public recognition. However, there are public stories about this little German village because since 1973, it has been building a bridge of reconciliation with the little Israeli village that it spawned. Last year, an exhibition called *Ort der Zuflucht und Verheissung* (Place of Refuge and Promise) opened in what was the synagogue and is now the Protestant Church. The exhibition tells the story, in photographs, oral histories and archival records, of how this group of village Jews started again in Eretz Israel and of the effort to reconnect a bridge of goodwill that was destroyed 70 years before. The opening of the exhibit was held on the exact date, 10 February, when the group left Germany for Haifa together. Over 5,000 Germans from southwest Germany went to see the exhibit in the four weeks it was there. From there, it went to the village in Israel where thousands also came. And then on to Jerusalem and Berlin and Stuttgart.

The story of the Torah is part of the exhibit. You can see its photograph, the soiled edges; there is even a knife slash, but it is open for all to see. I hope that all who do will learn, as I did, that if enough of us practise decency – say 80 per cent, not 15 per cent – we can stop the extremists who don't, wherever we live.

Mimi Schwartz has published five books, most recently *Good Neighbors, Bad Times – Echoes of My Father's German Village* (2008); *Thoughts from a Queen-Sized Bed* (2006); and *Writing True, the Art and Craft of Creative Nonfiction* (2006, with Sondra Perl). Dr Schwartz is Professor Emerita of Richard Stockton College of New Jersey, USA.

Manfred Deselaers

asks where was G-d and where were the Christians?

With great thankfulness we remember your visit to Auschwitz in May 2006. Even more important than the words you said were the signs: your silent walk through the Auschwitz camp, your silent prayer in front of the death-wall, your quiet encounter face-to-face with the survivors, your quiet blessing of the Centre for Dialogue and Prayer and of the Carmelite Sisters, the silent prayer in Birkenau in front of the memorial, the prayer together with other Christians and with Jews. A rainbow showed up.

In January this year, the Chief Rabbi of Poland, Michael Schudrich, said at a meeting with the Archbishop of Warsaw: "The most important rainbow was when Benedict XVI visited Auschwitz. It came when G-d saw that His children are together." You yourself remembered: "The rainbow was, as it were, a response: Yes, I exist, and the words of the promise, of the Covenant which I spoke after the flood, are still valid today."

It is about hope after Auschwitz.

When we look at what happened at Auschwitz, our hearts are deeply wounded still today. It is important not to fall into despair. We need Faith after Auschwitz. G-d created a good world where the power of evil is not equal with G-d; every human being has a divine dignity; the History of Salvation did not end in Auschwitz, because He is faithful, even if we are not. The credibility of such a testimony is important for the whole world.

The real testimony of faith cannot be anything other than a testimony of love. The victims looking at us awaken our conscience. G-d looks to us through their faces.

Much more than the question "Where was G-d?", the question "Where were we?" moves me. I am a German Catholic priest living in Oswiecim (Auschwitz) near the former concentration camps. I believe that G-d did not forget about His people and I believe that the message of the Cross is

Questions

1. What are the foundations of our hope "after Auschwitz"?

2. What is the relationship between hope and examination of conscience?

3. What connects responsibility after Auschwitz with responsibility for Israel and the people in the Holy Land?

just about that. But if so, where were the German Christians? (I do not write in the name of Polish Christians who often were among the victims.) And what about the Christian tradition of contempt for the Jews? At Auschwitz these questions run very deep.

To forget the victims means to forget G-d calling us. It is the examination of conscience that cleanses our faith. This is a matter of relationship. Auschwitz began with the destruction of relationships. Healing begins by crying about the wounded and destroyed relationships. This is the only way to regain trust.

The memory of Auschwitz is a constant challenge for the examination of conscience, for healing encounters and for the testimony of faith.

We are not called to change the past. We should not forget or lie about it; we should listen to its truth and learn from it. We are called to be responsible for the future.

Today we are called into the 'Holy Land'. This is also about hope. This wounded land is a challenge no less less than the memory of Auschwitz.

This is much more than only a question of support for the Christian communities and the Christian holy places. We need to understand what the State of Israel means – after Auschwitz – to the Jewish people, in the History of Salvation and for Christian-Jewish relations. And we need to ask what this means for the Palestinians and their place in G-d's plans.

Again we will find G-d only in face-to-face encounter, from where He speaks to our conscience and calls for our answer. Do we again leave them all alone, leave Him alone?

If we believe in the faithfulness of G-d, if we believe that His love will have the last word, a lived testimony of faith, hope and love in the Promised Land is most necessary for the credibility of the Church. This is crucial on the way to peace and has an impact on the whole world.

These few thoughts I want to offer in deep solidarity on the occasion of Your Holiness's visit to Israel.

For Further Reading

M. Deselaers, ed. *Dialog u progu Auschwitz* (Dialogue at the edge of Auschwitz). Cracow, 2003.

M. Deselaers, L. Lysien, J. Nowak, eds. *God and Auschwitz*. Cracow, 2008.

Emil Fackenheim. *To Mend the World: Foundations of Future Jewish Thought*. Bloomington: Indiana University Press, 1994.

Manfred Deselaers is a Catholic priest from Germany, living since 1990 in Oswiecim (Auschwitz), Poland. He lectures on "*Theology after Auschwitz*" at the Pontifical Academy of Theology in Cracow. He is responsible for the Programme Department at the Centre for Dialogue and Prayer in Oswiecim and is a member of the International Auschwitz Council. Dr Deselaers is the author and editor of several books, including "*The Way of the Cross: Meditation in Auschwitz*", 2001; "*Edith Stein: Message of the Cross and Auschwitz*", 2002; and "*Dialog u progu Auschwitz*" ("Dialogue at the Threshold of Auschwitz").

Myrna Goldenberg

explores conscience, complicity, 2,580 brave priests and 'raining death on earth'.

In her journal, Holocaust victim Hélène Berr recorded her anger, resentment and embarrassment when she was forced to comply with the edict that required Jews to wear a yellow star. Even the familiar streets of Paris, she thought, became hostile. On her way home from the Sorbonne one evening in 1944, she felt particularly conspicuous and frightened. Comfort and reassurance came from a stranger:

> ...walking down avenue de la Bourdonnais,... I suddenly became aware that a man was approaching me... He offered me his hand and said, loudly: 'A French Catholic shakes your hand...' I said thank you, and as I walked on, I realized what had happened... that was a decent thing to do.[1]

"The few who defied Hitler are conspicuous because they were few."

As an assimilated Jew in Catholic France, she had Christian and Jewish friends and expressed concern for Catholic friends who "no longer have the freedom to follow their conscience, they do what their priests tell them to do..."[2] A twenty-one-year-old university student who was deported and sent to Auschwitz and Bergen-Belsen, where she died from starvation and typhus, Hélène recognized the power of Vatican leadership. She expected Catholics to value the teachings of Jesus as universal and applicable to the wider community that encompasses us all. She let herself imagine a protest by Catholics and other Christians, led by Church fathers who would refuse to remain "impotent bystander(s) to the most flagrant violations of Christ's Law." She was incredulous that the Church was all but silent.

Hélène did not know about the 2,580 priests[3] interned in Dachau for their refusal to follow Nazi policy, or about the priests and nuns who

Questions

1. What is the responsibility of the Church in the face of extreme violence, particularly mass murder?

2. What role can the Church play in resolving conflicts that result from religious and racial disputes?

3. How can the Church exercise its moral authority to move humanity closer to the principles of those faiths that value life as 'the spark of the divine' in each of us?

4. What will the Church do to engage in dialogues with other religions in joint efforts to 'mend the world' or *tikkun olam*?

sheltered or otherwise aided Jews. She had no way of knowing about Father Bruno, the Belgian monk who hid my friend Flora Singer and her sisters.[4] Neither could she know about Catholic laity, such as the devout owners of a cleaning business who, in 1943, in their own words, "helped because they [were] religious."[5] These Catholics followed their conscience rather than the complicit priests whom they could neither trust nor respect. From Hélène's perspective, limited as it was, the vast majority of Christians were bystanders, or worse. And the vast majority were, in fact, bystanders, and too many were perpetrators. The few who defied Hitler are conspicuous because they *were* few. In contrast, public leadership from the Vatican was noticeable in its absence. Would that there had been hordes of followers of Father Bernard Lichtenberg who, in the heart of Nazism, condemned the Nazis and antisemitism from the pulpit and offered prayers on behalf of the Jews. For his moral courage, he was arrested, abused, and he ultimately died on his way to Dachau.

Much has changed since the Holocaust. Beginning in 1959 with the Second Vatican Council, the Church embraced ecumenism when it faced the dark history of its relationship with the Jewish people. *Nostra Aetate* acknowledged the Church's active complicity over the centuries in spreading anti-Judaism and, in the last century, in helping to condition Europe to accept Hitler's extreme antisemitism. A new page in the relationship between Jews and Catholics was opened. The Second Vatican Council renounced the centuries-held charge of deicide which accused all Jews – past, present and yet unborn – of responsibility for the death of Jesus. In 1980, Pope John Paul II established diplomatic ties with the State of Israel and, disavowing supercessionism and antisemitism in strong terms, he recognized Judaism as a covenantal religion. Again, in 1998, *We Remember: A Reflection on the Shoah* affirmed the Holocaust as "a major fact of the history of this [20th] century, a fact which still concerns us today". With respect to the Holocaust, the Vatican defined repentance as a "binding commitment". It is ironic that, in the 21st century, Holocaust denial continues to concern us. I am reiterating the recent history of Catholic-Jewish dialogue to underscore the milestones that have demonstrated our mutual understanding and respect. What are we to infer from the reinstatement of Bishop Williamson? Are we to infer that the ties between Catholics and Jews are less sturdy now than we had imagined?

Today, after the Holocaust and genocide in Rwanda, where the Church was again silent, the Vatican must be the unambiguous force that inspires Christian clergy and lay persons to act morally and publicly. Your Holiness cannot remain timid nor stay neutral in a world that is characterized more by war and suffering than by justice and mercy. Neither can the Church merely deny the deniers and restate its position against Holocaust denial and antisemitism. Such a statement, though comfortable, borders on indifference. Reinstating Bishop Williamson, even in diminished status, was tantamount to legitimizing Holocaust denial within the Church itself and invites these same attitudes among those clergy and laity who are susceptible to antisemitism. It betrays Catholic-Jewish dialogue that has been a healing force for the past 40 years. Christian and Jewish communities await concrete actions that repudiate the opinions of Williamson and his followers. Moreover, inaction condones the extreme fundamentalism that now grips much of the world, a fundamentalism that disputes science, rewards prejudice and sanctions violence in the name of God.

The Church has made too much progress in humanitarian efforts to now turn a blind eye to any form of extremism. Not only Christians but Jews as well expect that continued Vatican support of programmes that foster tolerance as a first step to compassion for the Other will lead to increased mutual appreciation and esteem. Through joint projects with Christians, Muslims and Jews, the Church can help alleviate poverty and illness and nurture programmes that advance education above the basic level of literacy. While no one institution can obliterate intolerance and ignorance, no religious institution in the free world can ignore these inequities. Religious leaders, particularly of your unique stature, influence both free and oppressed peoples, and the Vatican has a responsibility to all people who look to religious leaders for guidance and sustenance.

Hélène Berr's condemnation of her own era, "It is raining Death on earth,"[6] must not continue to be the description of the 21st century. As the source of morality for millions, the Holy See is obligated to act vigorously – to act against the obscenities of bigotry and hatred and, in our troubled world, against bystandership. No leader, spiritual or political, can claim to support morality without a public and sincere commitment to justice and truth. Peter's successors are not exempt from action. It is not enough to denounce bias. The Vatican is morally bound to exercise its mandate to act in consonance with Christ's teachings.

Notes

1. Hélène Berr, *The Journals of Hélène Berr*, trans. David Bellos, (New York: Weinstein Books, 2008), p. 81.
2. Ibid. p. 160.
3. Konnilyn Feig, *Hitler's Death Camps: The Sanity of Madness*, (New York: Holmes & Meier, 1981), p. 59.
4. Flora Singer, *I Was But a Child*, (Jerusalem: Yad Vashem, 2007). Flora was among the thousands the Pope blessed in Washington, DC, 2008. When he received a copy of her memoir and learned that she had suffered two strokes, his secretary wrote to thank her and to let her know that she would be included in his prayers.
5. Ilse Rewald, "Berliners Who Helped Us to Survive the Hitler Dictatorship," trans. Hanna Silver, pamphlet, German Resistance Memorial Centre, Berlin, 1990. n.p.
6. Op.cit. p. 195.

For Further Reading

T. Bayfield, S. Brichto and E. Fisher, eds. *He Kissed Him and They Wept: Towards a Theology of Jewish-Catholic Partnership*. London: SCM Press, 2001.

Michael Phayer. *Pius XII, the Holocaust, and the Cold War*. Bloomington, IN: Indiana University Press, 2007.

Susan Zuccotti. *Under His Very Windows: The Vatican and the Holocaust in Italy*. New Haven: Yale University Press, 2000.

Myrna Goldenberg is Professor Emerita, Montgomery College, MD, and was Ida E. King Distinguished Visiting Scholar, The Richard Stockton College of NJ, 2005-2006. Dr Goldenberg founded and directed the Paul Peck Humanities Institute, Washington DC. She is the co-editor of *Experience and Expression: Women, the Nazis, and the Holocaust*, and *Testimony, Tensions, and Tikkun: Teaching the Holocaust in Colleges and Universities*.

President Mahmoud Abbas. The Pope also visits the Palestinian Authority. Relations with the Palestinian population are critical to the future peace of the region.
Courtesy of World Economic Forum.

Relationships

Alan L. Berger

writes on hesbon nefesh*, an open window and 'The Plague' that never dies.*

There is a tale circulating that Pope John XXIII, when asked by a visitor to the Vatican the meaning of *aggiornamento*, did not respond verbally. Rather, he went to the window, opened it and let in fresh air. In the wake of the *Shoah*, this response was both welcome and necessary. The fresh air symbolized the Church's *hesbon nefesh*, reckoning of the soul, which marked two new beginnings: one was the Church entering the modern world, and the second was the Church's self-critique of its negative theology of the Jewish people. These new beginnings made possible an authentic Jewish-Christian dialogue based on mutual respect. The purpose of my letter is to urge you to keep Pope John XXIII's window open. I believe that we share the hope symbolized by his courageous action. Closing the window would lead to a resumption of the bad old theological days.

"The post-Vatican II world simply cannot tolerate religious intolerance."

On the eve of your visit to the State of Israel, it is timely to enquire how we can, together, pursue the dialogue, still in its infancy, which replaced 1,900 years of Christian theological triumphalism and the teaching of contempt for Judaism. An important first step is the admission that the era of cognitive monopoly, when one tradition makes claims to exclusive theological truth, has ended. The post-Vatican II world simply cannot tolerate religious intolerance. *Nostra Aetate* recognizes a plurality of truth claims. Its subsequent implementing documents reinforce and extend the Church's commitment to, and understanding of, the special theological relationship between Christianity and Judaism – Jesus and the apostles were Jewish, as was Mary – a relationship unparalleled in the history of religions, as well as a source of both inspiration and dreadful ambiguity.

Moreover, as the contemporary dialogue moves from infancy towards maturity, there is a growing recognition that accepting differences, no less than agreements, is a way of deepening mutual respect and furthering self-understanding of one's own tradition. These differences define us no less than do our commonalities, serving in fact as a solid basis of continuous dialogue despite the inevitable "bumps in the road". There can, however, be no difference between us on the matter of combating antisemitism. Pope John Paul II rightly called Jew-hatred a sin against the Holy Spirit. Early in your papacy, you visited the synagogue in Cologne, Germany, where you emphatically rejected antisemitism. Three years later, when addressing Jewish leaders in France, you elaborated your stance on antisemitism, claiming that Jew-hatred "can never be theologically justified".

Currently, there are two crises confronting the Church: one is internal and the second is external, although both share the same source. Your decision to lift the excommunication of Bishop Richard Williamson, a known antisemite who denies the existence of gas chambers and who radically minimizes the number of Jewish dead in the Holocaust, has rightly brought worldwide protest from both ecclesiastical and governmental officials. This response is heartening and supports the contention that it is immoral to stand idly by when evil is being perpetrated. If this attitude had been widespread during the time of the Holocaust, both Judaism and Christianity would have benefitted. I refrain from commenting on this dimension of the crisis, except to say that I respect your claim to have been unaware of Williamson's odious views.

The present crisis in Jewish-Catholic dialogue, however, demands comment. The dialogue of the past 40-plus years cannot, and should not, escape the ominous hovering presence of the *Shoah*. Had there been a clear and unambiguous response from the wartime pope to National Socialism and its extermination of the Jewish people, the Vatican would not have abdicated its moral leadership during the unparalleled time of theological testing. Antisemitism is the oldest social and theological pathology. It reappears, in various guises, throughout time. Albert Camus wrote of this situation in his wartime allegorical novel *The Plague*. Disease-carrying rats exact a heavy toll, nearly wiping out a town. Then they disappear underground. The populace celebrates the end of the plague. But the physician, Dr Rieux, knows that "the plague bacillus [Jew-hatred] never dies or disappears for good." The rats merely await their time of return. For good – healthy Jewish-Christian dialogue – to triumph over evil – the theology of supercession – the rats should have been totally eradicated in the first place.[1]

The nature of the Vatican's response to the current manifestation of Jew-hatred will, moreover, go a long way in helping determine exactly what beliefs and values our two great faith communities share. Furthermore, in my view, the future health of the dialogue will in no small measure be determined by this response. In this matter, I am heartened by your condemnation of antisemitism. Our two faith communities share much, including a concern

Questions

1. What makes the relationship between Judaism and Christianity distinct?

2. What is the contribution of *Nostra Aetate* to Jewish-Christian dialogue?

3. Pope Benedict XVI's lifting of the excommunication of Bishop Richard Williamson caused a crisis both for the Church and for Jewish-Christian relations. Why?

4. What opportunity for growth can emerge from these crises?

5. What can Pope Benedict do to ally himself with Popes John XXIII and John Paul II?

for fraternal reading of the Bible, engagement with social justice issues, ecological matters and a commitment to memory. However, the edifice of our shared values must be continuously strengthened, not merely by pronouncements but by deeds. The rats bearing the plague of antisemitism will, if unchecked, gnaw away at the foundation of inter-faith trust that is slowly, and even painfully, being established after the *Shoah*.

Every crisis is also an opportunity for growth. The Ba'al Shem Tov, founder of Hasidism, attested that evil [in this case antisemitism and Holocaust trivialization] can serve as the footstool of good. All depends on the intention of those responding to it. Pope John Paul II, in his Introductory Letter to *We Remember: A Reflection on the Shoah*, rightly termed the Holocaust "an indelible stain on the history of the century that is coming to a close". You have endorsed and accepted this statement, as well as the document's two-fold call: that Catholics "renew their awareness of the Hebrew roots of their faith," and that the Catholic Church should heed the lessons and legacies of the Holocaust. Moreover, you concurred with Pope John Paul II's wise 1994 stance: "We would risk causing the victims of the most atrocious deaths to die again if we do not have an ardent desire for justice, if we do not commit ourselves to ensure that evil does not prevail over good as it did for millions of children of the Jewish people... Humanity cannot permit all that to happen again." The Catholic Church, and all Christianity, must not in either word or deed kill the victims of the Holocaust a second time.

These statements express a firm resolve to seek a new relationship with the Jewish people and a future free of anti-Judaism among Christians and anti-Christian sentiment among Jews. But it is crucial to recall the fundamental asymmetry – both demographic and theological – between Judaism and Christianity. Jews number some 14 million throughout the world, while there are approximately 1.1 billion Christians. Furthermore, Judaism is theologically complete without Christianity. The reverse cannot be maintained. Historically, when Christianity denied or cut itself off from its Jewish roots, disaster ensued, with the Church becoming theologically compromised and the Jews physically imperilled. Mutual respect should replace animosity. It is worth noting here that Mr Gordon Brown, the British Prime Minister, became the first world leader to sign the London Declaration on combating antisemitism. His exemplary act should be emulated by leaders of all governments.

Your journey to Israel provides an unparalleled opportunity for you to state unequivocally Christianity's bond with Judaism. By proclaiming the Church's unambiguous stance that it is theologically impossible to be a Christian and an antisemite, you will have advanced the progress of interfaith dialogue, underscored the integrity of the Church and reaffirmed the fact that the light of God's love shines equally on both Jews and Christians. Your pilgrimage to the Holy Land should make clear that Pope John XXIII's window should remain wide open in Jerusalem. This "signal from

For Further Reading

Judith H. Banki and John T. Pawlikowski, eds. *Ethics in the Shadow of the Holocaust: Christian and Jewish Perspectives*. Chicago: Sheed & Ward, 2001.

Alan L. Berger & David Patterson. *Jewish-Christian Dialogue: Drawing Honey from the Rock*. Minneapolis: Paragon House, 2008.

James Carroll. *Constantine's Sword: The Church and the Jews*. Boston: Houghton Mifflin, 2001.

Irving Greenberg. *For the Sake of Heaven and Earth: The New Encounter Between Judaism and Christianity. Philadelphia*: Jewish Publication Society, 2004.

Franklin H. Littell. *The Crucifixion of the Jews*. Atlanta: Mercer University Press, 2000.

"Every crisis is also an opportunity for growth."

the top" of the Catholic Church would transmit a simple and fundamental truth: no obstacle – and there will be obstacles – which lies ahead on the path of interfaith dialogue is insurmountable.[2]

Notes

1. Father Thomas F. Stransky, reflecting on this passage at the occasion of the 20th anniversary of *Nostra Aetate*, wrote: "Indeed, twenty years ago I learned from Camus that with the promulgation of *Nostra Aetate*, Catholics, indeed all Christians, should go ahead, but be more vigilant than ever." His observation bears great contemporary relevance. Stransky, "Holy Diplomacy: Making the Impossible Possible," in *Unanswered Questions:Theological Views of Jewish-Catholic Relations*, edited by Roger Brooks (Notre Dame: The University of Notre Dame Press, 1995), p. 68.
2. An additional signal that would attest to the Vatican's sincere abhorrence of antisemitism and Holocaust denial is to declare that those Christians, women and men, who saved Jewish lives at great peril to their own are the ones who truly followed the teachings of Jesus. Moreover, the Church should offer to financially assist rescuers, many of whom are in dire straits and who have suffered at the hands of false Christians for their life-saving actions.

Alan L. Berger holds the Raddock Family Eminent Scholar Chair of Holocaust Studies at Florida Atlantic University, where he also directs the Center for the Study of Values and Violence After Auschwitz. Among his recent books are *Jewish-Christian Dialogue: Drawing Honey from the Rock* and *Encyclopedia of Jewish American Literature* [co-editor].

John T. Pawlikowski

reflects on steps backwards, the Jews and Christ, distinctive paths and the need for theological clarity.

You entered the papacy with some track record with respect to Catholic-Jewish relations. This is especially true in terms of the theological understanding of Christianity's relationship with Judaism. Several times at the outset of your time as Pope, you reiterated your intention to follow in the footsteps of your predecessor, Pope John Paul II, who contributed so much to the implementation of chapter four of the Second Vatican Council Declaration *Nostra Aetate*, which fundamentally reoriented the Church's relationship to the Jewish People. I must confess, however, to some disappointment that you have not followed up with any development of the ideas you put forth prior to coming to the papacy. And your creation of a new Good Friday prayer for the Tridentine liturgy, while removing the worst features of the previous prayer in this form of the liturgy, nonetheless represents a step backward theologically from the far more constructive prayer composed for the 1970 Missal in light of *Nostra Aetate*. And your more recent actions relative to the Society of St Pius X have sown the seeds of further deterioration of the vision of Vatican II regarding Jews and Judaism. My hope remains that in light of these two controversial actions you will see fit to present a comprehensive statement on the theological bonds between Judaism and Christianity rooted in the vision of *Nostra Aetate*.

"My hope remains that... you will see fit to present a comprehensive statement on the theological bonds between Judaism and Christianity rooted in the vision of Nostra Aetate*."*

I am aware of the controversy you created in October 1987 in an interview in the Italian Catholic paper *Il Sabato*. Speaking to the paper's interviewer, you argued that Church teaching must always reflect the "theological line" that Judaism finds its fulfilment in Christianity. While you rightly stressed Catholicism's ties to the faith of Abraham, your statement did not seem to allow for any continuing positive role for Judaism after Christ.[1] As you will recall, this interview generated considerable controversy in Jewish circles, and rightly so because it seemed to leave Judaism without any genuine, continuing role in the process of salvation.

At the end of the 1990s and in early 2000, you did offer some succinct perspectives whereby you seemed to be working on a theological approach to the Church's relationship with Judaism that went beyond the simple "fulfilment" line of thought that you proposed in 1987. In two articles, one book and in the laudatory introduction you wrote for the 2001 Pontifical Biblical Commission's 200-plus page monograph on "The Jewish People and their Sacred Scriptures in the Christian Bible,"[2] you began to recognize that, as you put it in your official note from the Congregation on Doctrine on the book by the late Fr. Jacques Dupuis, S.J. on religious pluralism, the relationship between Christianity and Judaism requires "an altogether singular explanation". The articles to which I refer were "The Heritage of Abraham: The Gift of Christmas," which was published in the 29 December 2000 edition of *L'Osservatore Romano* and a Spring 1998 essay in *Communio* entitled "Interreligious Dialogue and Jewish-Christian Relations." The latter piece was eventually incorporated into a full-length book (though in a somewhat different translation), *Many Religions – One Covenant: Israel, The Church and the World.*[3]

In the two major articles, you seem to propose an understanding of the Christian-Jewish relationship as one in which the two faith communities move along distinctive, but not separated paths (hence your insistence on a single covenantal perspective) towards an eschatological culmination. Though you insist on one covenant in the end, pre-eschatologically there exist two separate paths. You appear to affirm that the Jewish community advances to final salvation through continuing obedience to its revealed covenantal tradition. In the end, you do say that from a Christian theological viewpoint, Christ will confirm that Jewish covenantal path. Thus Christ remains central in your outlook to ultimate Jewish salvation.

As far as I can see, you have never pursued these questions any further. This is certainly the case during your papacy. I can find no evidence of Pope Benedict quoting Cardinal Ratzinger, if I may put it that way, on the issue of the theological link between Judaism and Christianity. I would hope that you might consider resuming the reflections you began a decade or so ago. You need to clarify a number of questions associated with your previous views. They include whether Jews need to acknowledge Christ specifically to attain full salvation at the end of their pre-eschatological journey. In the Pontifical Biblical Commission's document which you strongly endorsed, it is said that when the Jewish Messiah appears at the end of time he shall have the same traits which Christians have already seen in Christ. The question remains unanswered whether Jews can express these Messianic traits in language and symbols central to their own tradition or must they finally adopt expressly Christological language? Another question in light of your support

Questions

1. How can Judaism and Christianity mutually enrich each other as religious traditions?

2. Is Jesus a bond or a barrier to enhanced Jewish-Christian solidarity?

3. Does the new understanding of a very gradual separation between the Church and the Jewish community affect the understanding of the theological relationship between them?

4. Do the teachings of St Paul enhance or undercut a positive connection between Jews and Christians?

of a distinctive pre-eschatological path for Jews is whether any proselytizing of Jews remains obligatory during this period. Your apparent endorsement of Cardinal Walter Kasper's eschatological interpretation of your new Tridentine Good Friday prayer might well indicate that you join with Cardinal Kasper in arguing against the need for any such proselytizing. But you definitely need to clarify your position in this regard.

I should also mention that your "two distinctive, but not distinct" paths perspective is further enhanced by your explicit support in your Introduction to the Pontifical Biblical Commission's document statement that Jewish messianic hopes are not in vain. While this is rather oblique language, it would seem to argue for the existence of an authentic, parallel interpretation of biblical messianic texts within Judaism as the basis of their distinctive path towards the eschatological era. You need to expound on your endorsement of this statement in terms of a more comprehensive presentation of your theology of the Christian-Jewish relationship.

Finally, I would make reference to your dialogue with the writings of the well-known Jewish scholar Jacob Neusner in your book *Jesus of Nazareth: From the Baptism in the Jordan to the Transfiguration*.[4] Though written during your papacy, you make it clear that you are speaking in this volume as a theologian rather than as Pope. You clearly encourage a critical encounter with this work. In that spirit, I would argue that what is missing on your part is any integration of the scholarship connected with the ongoing "Parting of the Ways" discussion in contemporary biblical scholarship. That scholarship, though hardly at the point of consensus, on many points is in the process of a major transformation of our understanding of the origins of Christianity and its relationship with the Judaism of Jesus' day. More and more, we see that the early Christian movement remained deeply entrenched in the Jewish community for almost a century beyond Jesus' death and even beyond that in certain regions. This new scholarship has profound implications for how we now might conceive the theological relationship between the Church and the Jewish People. It also impacts our understanding of the Apostle Paul's views on this relationship, something that I unfortunately find missing in any of the writings you have offered the Christian community in this Pauline Jubilee Year.

It is my firm hope that you will find the time to address the theological relationship between Judaism and Christianity far more comprehensively than you have to date. I also hope that in so doing, you would build upon the "theological kernels" you presented while at the Vatican's doctrinal commission.

For Further Reading

Mary Boys. *Has God Only One Blessing?* New York/Mahweh: Paulist Press, 2000.

Edward Kessler and Melanie J. Wright, eds., *Themes in Jewish-Christian Relations*. Cambridge, UK: Orchard Academic, 2005.

Matt Jackson-McCabe, ed., *Jewish Christianity Reconsidered*. Minneapolis: Fortress Press, 2007.

Cardinal Joseph Ratzinger. *Many Religions – One Covenant*. San Francisco: Ignatius Press, 2000.

Notes

1. Cf. Ari L. Goldman, "Cardinal's Remarks on Jews Questioned," *New York Times*, 18 November 1987, 10; "Dialogue with Jews must reflect Catholic theology, says official," *National Catholic Reporter*, 30 October 1987.
2. Pontifical Biblical Commission, "The Jewish People and their Sacred Scripture in the Christian Bible," (Vatican City: Libreria Edifice Vaticana, 2002). For a discussion of this document, including an essay by myself, cf. the special issue of *The Bible Today*, May/June 2003.
3. Cardinal Joseph Ratzinger, *Many Religions – One Covenant* (San Francisco: Ignatius Press, 2000).
4. Joseph Ratzinger/Pope Benedict XVI, *Jesus of Nazareth: From the Baptism in the Jordan to the Transfiguration* (New York/London: Doubleday, 2007).

John T. Pawlikowski, OSM, a priest of the Servite Order, is Professor of Social Ethics and Director of the Catholic-Jewish Studies Program at Catholic Theological Union in Chicago. Dr Pawlikowski has authored/edited some 15 books in the area of Christian-Jewish Relations. He served for six years as President of the International Council of Christians and Jews and continues as a member of its Executive Council. Fr. Pawlikowski is also a founding member of the US Holocaust Memorial Council, having been appointed by President Jimmy Carter in 1980. He currently serves as the Chairperson of the Council's Subcommittee on Church Relations.

Audrey Doetzel

is concerned about the Good Friday prayer and the ambivalence lurking below the surface of Catholic theology when it comes to Jews and Judaism.

Today is Ash Wednesday. This holy day is a vivid reminder that this year on Good Friday, some faithful in our ecclesial community will again be praying a *Pro Conversione Judaeorum* prayer.[1] This prayer evokes what I heard in church as a child: that the perfidious Jews may have the veil removed from their hearts, that this blind people may be delivered from their darkness by acknowledging Jesus Christ and so not be excluded from God's mercy.[2] Meanwhile, the rest of us will be praying for these "people you first made your own... that they may continue to grow in the love of [God's] name and in faithfulness to his covenant".[3]

A strangely familiar ambivalence arises within me as I am taken back to my childhood when my nascent conscience spontaneously queried, "How is it that the priest's words so starkly contrast with the care and respect with which my father speaks of and relates to the Jewish family in our town?"[4]

I later learned that some European women in the religious community to which I now belong – the Sisters of Our Lady of Sion – experienced a similar, very troubling ambivalence during the Nazi era when they were praying for the conversion of the Jews in keeping with their 1874 Constitution, which expressed their "particular aim" as "the sanctification of the Children of Israel". At the same time, they were witnessing the catastrophic effects of centuries of Christian theological supercessionism and teaching of contempt. They had become all too familiar with fellow Catholics piously participating in the Good Friday service and then energetically engaging in pogroms and random violence which turned particularly aggressive on that *Good* and holy day. This led the Sisters to serious soul-searching about the mission of Sion as expressed in the Order's Constitution, compelling them

"Now, with... two very different Good Friday liturgical prayers for the Jews, are we not declaring to the world a deep ambivalence in our theology vis-à-vis Jews and Judaism?"

to embark on a process of revising their officially approved *Way of Life*.[5]

Your Holiness, on 6 May 1984 the Holy See approved and blessed our new Sion Constitution. The opening words of this ecclesial document now read: "They are Israelites, and to them belong the sonship, the glory, the covenants, the giving of the law, the worship and the promises." (Rom 9:4). Its Inspiration section tells us: "The divisions, the agony of so many people, and the tragedies of our time reveal that the messianic promises are far from being realized in the world. This challenges our faith and calls forth our response. With the whole Church *and with the Jewish people*[6] we hope, pray and work for the day when all will know the Lord and 'justice and peace will embrace'" (Ps 85:10; cf. Is 11:9).

Our new *Way of Life* now expresses a mission "with" Jews, no longer a mission "to" Jews.[7] This is fully consistent with the Church's teaching in *Nostra Aetate*, §4, and in the many ecclesial documents which have spelled out further its spirit and vision.[8] We, the Sisters of Sion, now realize that while we were praying for the conversion of 'the other,' we were the ones in need of conversion and transformation. The same holds true for the Church as the vision of Vatican Council II and the trajectory of the development of its teachings dramatically convey.

Holy Father, your Good Friday prayer of 6 February 2008, intended for use in the Tridentine Rite, does not follow this trajectory. It is a stark aberration. Many have tried to express this to you, including Cardinal Tarcisio Bertone who, right at the outset, proposed that the Tridentine Rite simply use the Latin translation of the normative Roman Rite prayer which we use today. In an effort to help heal the rupture of the mutual trust between Catholics and Jews which has developed over the past several decades, Cardinal Walter Kasper expressed an eschatological understanding of your prayer.[9]

In your rejection of Cardinal Bertone's proposal, were you expressing some disagreement with what our normative Good Friday prayer expresses? If so, why not 'lay this on the table' for open dialogue, especially with the many seriously committed Roman Catholics who, having engaged for several decades in dialogue with Jews and in Christian-Jewish scholarship, have come to grasp Judaism's profound religious depth? Our Church, aware that the *praxis* of its faithful frequently precedes and helps shape its formalized *doxa*, has a long tradition of listening to the *sensus fidelium*. This *sensus fidelium* today, following Vatican Council II, has implicitly rejected the proselytization of Jews, a rejection consistent with the developing trajectory of Vatican II teachings.

Your Holiness, in your work with the Pontifical Biblical Commission (PBC), you have listened so well to the *sensus fidelium* of the biblical scholars. Of particular note is the Commission's 2001 document, *The Jewish People and their Sacred Scriptures in the Christian Bible*. In the Preface to this document, your words, as Cardinal Joseph Ratzinger, appear in sharp contrast to the spirit of the words in your 2008 Good Friday Prayer. In the

Questions

1. In his effort to heal real and potential divisions in our Church, is the Holy Father allowing internal Church matters to interfere with the theological teaching of the Church about Jews and Judaism? In your judgment, how do you think these two priorities could be effectively weighed and dealt with?

2. Do you think the majority of people in our pews and in our elementary and high school classrooms are able to grasp the theological nuances of the two approved Good Friday prayers? If so, how might you express its essence more simply for use in sermons and catechesis?

3. Do you think Pope Benedict's 2008 Good Friday prayer may leave Roman Catholic Christians on a 'slippery' slope leading to a narrowed Christian self-understanding vis-à-vis Jews and Judaism?

4. What message do you think the 2008 Good Friday prayer holds for the increasing number of messianic Jewish movements and the Christian organizations overtly advocating the "ingrafting" of Jews to the Church?

Preface you acknowledge that, "in good conscience... the biblical commission could not ignore the contemporary context, where the shock of the *Shoah* has put the whole question under a new light." But was it not this same contemporary context that directed the shaping of *Nostra Aetate*, §4, and the 1970 Good Friday prayer which, in the words of Hans Hermann Henrix, "implements in worship the Second Vatican Council's acknowledgment of Israel's dignity in the history of salvation and in theology"?[10]

Is it not through our liturgy, the primary collective praxis of our belief, that we commit to, and declare publicly to the world, our ecclesial identity? Does not our communal liturgical action express, through symbol, ritual and cult, how we know God and the world?[11] Now, with these two very different Good Friday liturgical prayers for the Jews, are we not declaring to the world a deep ambivalence in our theology vis-à-vis Jews and Judaism?

Your Holiness, as we begin the 2009 holy season of Lent, my prayer, along with the prayer of many concerned Roman Catholics, is that this ambivalence lurking below the surface of our theology regarding Jews and Judaism be brought out into the open and explicitly addressed, so that internal Catholic dialogue is not closed off at this critical point in our history. May we as Catholics continue to counter the increasing antisemitism which the world is witnessing today with the oft-repeated message of Pope John Paul II: "God's covenant with the Jewish people has never been revoked."[12] And may we increasingly understand this message to mean, as Cardinal Walter Kasper has expressed, that "the faithful response of the Jewish people to God's irrevocable covenant, is salvific for them, because God is faithful to his promises."[13]

For Further Reading

Mary C. Boys. "Does the Catholic Church Have a Mission 'with' Jews or 'to' Jews?", *Studies in Christian-Jewish Relations*, Volume 3, 2008, http://escholarship.bc.edu/scjr/vol3

Mary C. Boys. *Has God Only One Blessing? Judaism as a Source of Christian Self-Understanding.* New York: Paulist Press, 2000.

Mary C. Boys ed. *Seeing Judaism Anew: Christianity's Sacred Obligation.* New York: Rowman & Littlefield Publishers, Inc., 2005.

Audrey Doetzel. "Branches of That Good Olive Tree: 21st-Century Liturgical Challenges and Possibilities," in *Studies in Christian-Jewish Relations*, Volume 1, Issue 1, 2005-2006, http://escholarship.bc.edu/scjr/vol1/iss1

Hans Hermann Henrix. "The Controversy Surrounding the 2008 Good Friday Prayer in Europe: The Discussion and its Theological Implications," in *Studies in Christian-Jewish Relations*, Volume 3, 2008, http://escholarship.bc.edu/scjr/vol3/

Notes

1. In the *Motu Proprio Summorum Pontificium* of 7 July 2007, Pope Benedict XVI gave greater latitude for the celebration of the Latin Tridentine Rite. The Tridentine Mass is a common name for the form of the Roman Rite Mass contained in the typical editions of the Roman Missal that were published from 1570 to 1962. On 6 February 2008, Pope Benedict XVI presented a new Good Friday Prayer for the Jews to be used in the Tridentine Rite. Though Pope Benedict's Good Friday Prayer for the Jews does not contain the word *conversion*, he has apparently retained the Latin heading from the Missal of 1962: *Pro Conversione Judaeorum*.
2. An English translation of the full text of Pope Benedict XVI's 6 February 2008 Good Friday Prayer for the Jews: "Let us pray also for the Jews. That our Lord and God may enlighten their hearts, that they may acknowledge Jesus Christ as the saviour of all men. Almighty ever living God, who wills that all men would be saved and come to the knowledge of the truth, graciously grant that all Israel may be saved when the fullness of nations enters into your Church. Through Christ our Lord. Amen."
3. An English translation of the full text of the (normative) 1970 Good Friday Prayer for the Jews: "Let us pray for the Jewish people, the first to hear the word of God, that they may continue to grow in the love of his name and in faithfulness to his covenant. Almighty and eternal God, long ago you gave your promise to Abraham and his posterity. Listen to your Church as we pray that the people you first made your own may arrive at the fullness of redemption. We ask this through Christ our Lord. Amen."

4. My father had emigrated from Russia to mid-western Canada at the age of 19, in view of the darkness looming on the Eastern European horizon. He and his family were descendants from the German emigration to Russia under Catherine the Great. He lived and studied in the Saratov area near the Volga River. Though I unfortunately did not have an opportunity to discuss this at length with my father before he died, I am sure he knew members of the Jewish community in the Saratov region, knew of the 1853 blood libel conviction of three Jews in Saratov, the late 1890s' czarist policy of pauperization of the Jews, and the pogroms throughout Russia during the 1890s and early 1900s – especially the pogroms in the Saratov region.
5. For an extensive study of the evolution of Sion's change in self-understanding, see Mary C. Boys, "The Sisters of Sion: From a Conversionist Stance to a Dialogical Way of Life," *Journal of Ecumenical Studies* 31/1-2 (1994): 27-48. See also Ch. 1, "Sion's Story" in Mary C. Boys, *Has God Only One Blessing? Judaism as a Source of Christian Self-Understanding* (New York: Paulist Press, 2000).
6. Italics added for emphasis.
7. This distinction is addressed at greater length in Mary C. Boys, "Does the Catholic Church have a Mission 'with' Jews or 'to' Jews?" in *Studies in Christian-Jewish Relations*, Vol. 3 (2008) http://escholarship.bc.edu/scjr/vol3
8. See especially the following documents, all available at http://www.bc.edu/research/cjl/cjrelations/resources/documents/catholic.html
By the Commission on Religious Relations with the Jews: (1998) *We Remember: A Reflection on the Shoah;* (1985) Notes on the Correct Way to Present Jews and Judaism in Preaching and Catechesis in the Roman Catholic Church; (1974) Guidelines and Suggestions for Implementing the Conciliar Declaration *Nostra Aetate*,§4; By the Pontifical Biblical Commission: (2001) The Jewish People and their Sacred Scriptures in the Christian Bible; (1993) The Interpretation of the Bible in the Church; By the United States Conference of Catholic Bishops: (2001) Catholic Teaching on the *Shoah*: Implementing the Holy See's We Remember; (1988) God's Mercy Endures Forever: Guidelines on the Presentation of Jews and Judaism in Catholic Preaching; (1988) Criteria for Evaluation of Dramatizations of the Passion; *Notable Documents by European Catholic Bishops Conferences; Selected Letters and Addresses by Pope John Paul II (1979-2005).*
9. Cardinal Walter Kasper, President of the Commission for Religious Relations with the Jews, writing in *L'Osservatore Romano*, April 2008 stated: "Prayer for the coming of God's kingdom and for the fulfilment of the mystery of salvation... respects the complete inscrutability of the hidden God. So with this prayer the Church does not take direct charge of the fulfilment of the unfathomable mystery. She just cannot do that. Rather, she leaves the when and the how wholly in God's hands. God alone can initiate the Kingdom of God in which all Israel is saved, and eschatological peace is granted to the world."
10. See Hans Hermann Henrix, "The Controversy Surrounding the 2008 Good Friday Prayer in Europe: The Discussion and its Theological Implications," in *Studies in Christian-Jewish Relations*, Volume 3, 2008, http://escholarship.bc.edu/scjr/vol3/
11. See Audrey Doetzel, "Branches of that Good Olive Tree: 21st-Century Liturgical Challenges and Possibilities," in *Studies in Christian-Jewish Relations*, Volume 1, Issue 1 (2005-2006), p. 129, http://escholarship.bc.edu/scjr/vol1/iss1
12. Though expressed on numerous occasions by Pope John Paul II, it is usually referenced to his address to Jewish leaders in Mainz on 17 November 1980.
13. Address on *Dominus Iesus* delivered by Cardinal Walter Kasper at the 17th meeting of the International Catholic-Jewish Liaison Committee, New York, 1 May 2001, http://www.bc.edu/research/cjl/meta-elements/texts/cjrelations/resources/articles/kasper_dominus_iesus.htm

Audrey Doetzel, a Sister of Our Lady of Sion, is Associate Director of the Center for Christian-Jewish Learning at Boston College. She is managing editor of the scholarly peer-reviewed ejournal, *Studies in Christian-Jewish Relations*. Following leadership as Provincial of the Canada-USA Sion province, Dr Doetzel was for ten years the coordinator/director of Christian-Jewish Relation and Encounter, the province's Jewish-Christian and interreligious ministry.

Kevin P. Spicer

recognises the impact of painful Christian action towards the Jews and the link between antisemitism and the Holocaust.

I write to you with a heavy heart. Since my ordination in 1992, I have been involved in Jewish-Catholic dialogue. As an academic and priest studying, analysing and reflecting upon German history and the Holocaust, this would seem natural. Generally, I have been pleased to follow the developments between the Holy See and Jews, especially when Pope John Paul II made his historic visit to Israel and asked Jews worldwide for forgiveness for the mistreatment of Jews by Catholics over the centuries. Similarly, when you were elected to the Chair of Peter, I had great hopes for your papacy in this regard. As a native German who grew up under National Socialist rule and was involuntarily inducted into the Hitler Youth as a teenager, you more than anyone, I believed, would follow in the steps of your predecessor and continue to work for reconciliation and understanding between Catholics and Jews. Still living in this hope and believing in your good will, I have been shaken by recent events taking place in your pontificate. For example, in a *motu proprio* declaration issued in 2007, you, Holy Father, reauthorized the use of the 1962 Missal of John XXIII, which includes the Good Friday service that contains a prayer for the conversion of Jews. After an outcry from many sectors, both within and outside of the Church, you published in February 2008 a reformulation of this same prayer that currently reads:

> Let us also pray for the Jews. May the Lord our God illuminate their hearts so that they may recognize Jesus Christ as saviour of all men. Let us pray. Almighty and everlasting God, you who want all men to be saved and to gain knowledge of the Truth, kindly allow that, as the fullness of peoples enter into your Church, all of Israel may be saved. Through Christ our Lord.

"While it is important that you acknowledged the horrific nature of the Shoah, *you did so by denying the historical underlayer of its Catholic-Christian societal roots."*

"Nevertheless, the Vatican has regularly denied the Christian basis for the Holocaust, played out in thousands of European communities over the centuries, however much we today want to claim that such antisemitism was based on a misinterpretation of our theology."

This surprised me as this reformulation contains explicit language (i.e., "May the Lord our God illuminate their hearts") that may be construed as promoting missionary or proselytizing efforts to convert Jews. Such prayers also seem to negate the first covenant concluded between God the Father and Abraham, which remains salvific for Jews.

Even more troubling is the most recent action of lifting the excommunication of four bishops of the Pius X Society. Not only do these four bishops deny the basic teachings of Vatican II, including its declaration *Nostra Aetate*, but one of them, Richard Williamson, denies the Holocaust. Although on 4 February 2009 the Vatican Secretariat of State clarified the theological reasons for this step and made it positively clear that the Catholic Church condemns Holocaust denial, I still find it troubling that the Holy See has once again engaged in an action that is deeply offensive to Jews. Such repeated actions bring unprecedented distress for so many people and serve to open painful memories and barely healed wounds. I can offer a specific example from my own ministry at Stonehill College. Upon learning that you had lifted the excommunication of Bishop Williamson, a colleague and friend of mine, so distraught over the action and the bishop's Holocaust denial, returned to his family's painful past and recalled publicly in an open letter the family members he had lost during the Holocaust, in an effort to assure people here that the Holocaust had actually happened. It dismays me as a Catholic to think that such an action of our Holy Father had caused such pain. Nevertheless, these actions are just a few of several that have brought increasing difficulty in Jewish-Catholic relations.

Soon after your election as pope, you spoke on Friday 19 August 2005 at the Cologne synagogue. In the midst of offering hopeful words concerning the Cologne Jewish community, you, Holy Father, stated that, "in the twentieth century, in the darkest period of German and European history, an insane racist ideology, born of neo-paganism, gave rise to the attempt, planned and systematically carried out by the regime, to exterminate European Jewry. The result has passed into history as the *Shoah*." While it is important that you acknowledged the horrific nature of the *Shoah*, you did so by denying the historical underlayer of its Catholic-Christian societal roots. National Socialist racist ideology was not solely "born of neo-paganism," but as Father John Pawlikowski, a leading expert in Catholic-Jewish relations, has stated, "While the Holocaust had many parents, it could not have been realized without the indispensable seedbed of Christian antisemitism." Nevertheless, the Vatican has regularly denied the Christian basis for the Holocaust, played out in thousands of European communities over the centuries, however much we today want to claim that such antisemitism was based on a misinterpretation of our theology.

For example, even in March 1998, during Pope John Paul II's pontificate, the Vatican's Commission for Religious Relations with the Jews issued the

Questions

1. What is problematic about referring to National Socialist ideology solely as neo-pagan?

2. What issues arise from the Pope's 2007 *motu proprio* in regard to the Tridentine Good Friday liturgy?

3. What role did Christian antisemitism play in the origins of the Holocaust?

document, *We Remember*, that contained similar language concerning the origins of the Holocaust. In this document one reads: "The *Shoah* was the work of a thoroughly modern neo-pagan regime. Its anti-Semitism had its roots outside of Christianity and, in pursuing its aims, it did not hesitate to oppose the Church and persecute her members also." Sadly, such a statement denies the incalculable influence Christian practice had on societal antisemitism, especially virulent in Europe, upon which the Nazis built their annihilative antisemitism. I have addressed this issue in my own work on German and Austrian Catholic priests who embraced National Socialism when I wrote: "Historically, the Catholic Church tolerated discrimination against Jews who allegedly betrayed the basic tenets of their own revealed faith by becoming obsessed with money and material goods. In turn, the Church believed that these same unfaithful Jews, especially through the influence of the Enlightenment and modernity, had attacked and undermined Christianity and its moral and religious teaching through their 'pernicious influence' on business, the press, art, theater, film, and politics. Though the Church rejected the National Socialist racist form of antisemitism that preached 'a struggle against the Jewish race' and made blood the sole determining factor of Jewish identity, it nevertheless, almost since its foundation, continued to promote a religious-based antisemitism, often referred to as anti-Judaism, by blaming Jews for Jesus' crucifixion. Regardless of the theological logic underlying antisemitism, the negative portrayal of Jews facilitated discrimination and persecution. Even when Catholics tried to distance themselves from antisemitism or at least demonstrate moral sympathy toward Jews, it was very difficult for them to show any theological sympathy. This lack of theological sympathy led Catholics to a reductive appraisal of Jews as persistent non-believers, too alien and obstinate for the Church's leaders to include in the gospel mandate to 'love thy neighbor.' The Catholic imagination had only to clothe these liturgical and homiletic perceptions into common and everyday antisemitic language. Consequently, [some Catholics during the Nazi period] attempted to institutionalize antisemitism as a Christian mandate as well as a patriotic one. In retrospect, [such individuals] were only attempting to rehearse earlier and more elemental antisemitic texts in the Catholic and Christian tradition, which were centuries old. From this referential perspective, much of the antisemitism in the Catholic Church was perceived as being partially in agreement with the spirit of Nazi racial teaching and National Socialism's eventual antisemitic legislation. For the ordinary Catholic then, the lines between these various forms of antisemitism – racial, theological, economic, and cultural – became not only indistinguishable but mutually reinforcing."

It is my sincere hope that Your Holiness will truly reflect upon the recent difficult events in Catholic-Jewish relations and diligently work to strengthen the bonds that already exist (albeit tentative at times) between

For Further Reading

Otto Dov Kulka and Paul R. Mendes-Flohr, eds. *Judaism and Christianity under the Impact of National Socialism.* Jerusalem: The Historical Society of Israel and the Zalman Shazar Center for Jewish History, 1987.

Kevin P. Spicer, C.S.C. *Hitler's Priests: Catholic Clergy and National Socialism.* DeKalb, IL: Northern Illinois University Press in association with the United States Holocaust Memorial Museum, 2008.

Kevin P. Spicer, C.S.C., ed. *Antisemitism, Christian Ambivalence, and the Holocaust.* Bloomington, IN: Indiana University Press in association with the United States Holocaust Memorial Museum, 2007.

Kevin P. Spicer, C.S.C. *Resisting the Third Reich: The Catholic Clergy in Hitler's Berlin.* DeKalb, IL: Northern Illinois University Press, 2004.

Richard Steigmann-Gall. *The Holy Reich. Nazi Conceptions of Christianity.* Cambridge: Cambridge University Press, 2003.

our two traditions. By fully recognizing our Church's painful past actions toward Jews (especially in Europe) and the direct tie this past bears – whether implicitly or explicitly – on the origins of National Socialist ideology and the Holocaust, you, Holy Father, have the ability to usher a new Catholic-Jewish dialogue into a new era and deeper level of mutual understanding and respect.

Kevin P. Spicer, CSC, is Associate Professor of History at Stonehill College, Easton, Massachusetts. He is the author of *Hitler's Priests: Catholic Clergy and National Socialism* (North Illinois University Press, 2008) and *Resisting the Third Reich: The Catholic Clergy in Hitler's Berlin* (North Illinois University Press, 2004) and editor of *Antisemitism, Christian Ambivalence, and the Holocaust* (Indiana University Press, 2007). Dr Spicer is a member of the Church Relations Committee of the Center for Advanced Holocaust Studies, United States Holocaust Memorial Museum.

Eugene J. Fisher

deals with the 'tsunami sweeping the landscape of dialogue'.

I was, after a hectic, family-filled 2008 Christmas season, relaxed and ready to sit down to offer some hopefully useful suggestions to Pope Benedict XVI on furthering Catholic-Jewish relations when, in the apt phrasing of Fr. John Donahue, SJ, an unseasonable tsunami swept across the landscape of the dialogue, leaving all of us involved in disarray and with a renewed sense of the vulnerability and fragility of the relationship, even in its fifth decade since the Second Vatican Council. The storm was, of course, that caused by the Pope's lifting of the excommunication of four bishops of the Society of St Pius X (SSPX) in an understandable effort to reach out to heal the only formal schism stemming from the Council. For some weeks at this writing, equally understandably, we in the dialogue, Catholics no less than Jews, have been intensely focused on it, to the exclusion of virtually everything else.

Not only was one of the bishops, Williamson of England, a hard-core, Holocaust-denying antisemite, but one of the half-dozen major difficulties the Society had with the Council that precipitated their move into schism was precisely their uneasiness over its teachings on Jews and Judaism, along with related core teachings such as those on religious liberty, ecumenism and other world religions. We were all, as it were, thrust back to the basics, arguing, in essence, that the same rules of adherence to the official teachings of the Magisterium, especially as enunciated in an ecumenical council of the Church, should apply to all its members, SSPX no less than the rest of us. To allow them to simply waive acknowledgement of the Magisterium's authority, not as a matter of interpretation of the Council but of rejection of its authority altogether, seemed then, and seems now, to be a recipe for long-range catastrophe, an unravelling of that which binds us together in communion in the one Catholic Church.

We all, therefore, welcomed the clear statement of the Holy See to

"... the Dogmatic Constitution on the Church, Lumen Gentium, *no. 16... affirms that there is a special relationship between the Church and God's People, the Jews, which the Church has with no other world religion."*

Williamson that he must abandon his Holocaust denial and related views (as of this writing he has yet to do so), and to the Society that it will have to formally acknowledge the teaching authority of the Second Vatican Council, as a whole and not choosing some teachings while rejecting those it does not like. In an article I published in the British journal, *The Tablet*,[1] I emphasized the importance of the Society doing this (for its own sake if it wishes to be truly a part of the Church, as well as for the future of Catholic-Jewish relations) and spelled out what, I believe, the document they would be asked to sign would look like, at least in its section on the Council's teaching on the Jews. While the full text of this suggestion to the Holy See can be found in *The Tablet*, a brief summary of its four key parts is in order here, since such a specific and detailed Vatican document, I believe, must be presented for signature to the Society before the Catholic-Jewish dialogue can once again take up its deeper work of probing the beliefs and values we share, so that the Catholic Church and the Jewish People can together witness to them to the world and work together to make our common vision for humanity a reality. These are:

First, the Dogmatic Constitution on the Church, *Lumen Gentium*, no. 16. This affirms that there is a special relationship between the Church and God's People, the Jews, which the Church has with no other world religion. Citing Romans 9:4-5, the Council stated that the Jews "on account of their fathers, remain [note present tense] most dear to God, for God does not repent of the gifts He makes nor of the calls He issues (cf. Romans 11: 28-29)."

Second, the Conciliar Declaration, *Nostra Aetate*, no. 4, which interprets and elaborates upon the Dogmatic Constitution. It rejects fully any notion of collective guilt of Jews "then or now" for the death of Jesus. Here it is in continuity with the *Roman Catechism* of the Council of Trent which notes that our guilt as Christians is "enormous" in comparison to that of the Jews, since, citing Jesus' last words, what the Jews did they did in ignorance, while we Christians "professing to know him" crucify him with our sins, for which he died (Article IV). Likewise, *Nostra Aetate* emphasizes that it was not by accident but by divine plan that Jesus, Mary and the apostles were Jews, and officially condemns antisemitism, which Pope John Paul II was to call "sinful".

Third, the Society, as must the rest of us, must acknowledge the authority of subsequent official documents of the Holy See implementing and elaborating upon the Council's universally binding teachings. Among these are the statements of the Holy See's Commission for Religious Relations with the Jews, specifically the 1974 *Guidelines and Suggestions for Implementing Nostra Aetate, no. 4*; the 1985 *Notes on the Correct Way to Present the Jews and Judaism in Catholic Teaching and Preaching*; and the 1998 *We Remember: A Catholic Reflection on the Shoah*. Included here should also be the 2002 statement of the Pontifical Biblical Commission

Questions

1. In what ways does the common understanding of humanity as created in the image and likeness of God make the theology and moral values of Judaism and Christianity similar to each other and distinct from other understandings of the nature of humanity?

2. In what ways does the common understanding of the destiny of humanity (coming/return of the Messiah inauguring a resurrection from the dead, a final judgement and the Reign of God/*Malchuth Shamayim*) make the theology and moral values of Judaism and Christianity similar to each other and distinct from other understandings of the nature and destiny of humanity?

3. What theological and moral teachings are central to the official Church documents?

4. How do the statements of the US Conference of Catholic Bishops flesh out the teachings of question 3 above?

(which reported it to the head of the Congregation for the Doctrine of the Faith, Cardinal Joseph Ratzinger, who wrote a strongly affirmative introduction for its publication), *The Jews and Their Scriptures in the Catholic Bible*.

Fourth, in whatever country the Society is, there will likely be official statements of its Catholic Bishops' Conference interpreting and implementing the universal Church teaching for the local Church. In the United States, for example, the US Conference of Catholic Bishops, over the years, has promulgated such official documents as its 1967 *Guidelines for Catholic-Jewish Relations* (updated in 1987, with a third update now pending); *Criteria for the Evaluation of Dramatizations of the Passion* (1988); *God's Mercy Endures Forever: Guidelines on the Presentation of Jews and Judaism in Catholic Preaching* (1988); and *Catholic Teaching on the Shoah: Implementing the Holy See's We Remember* (2001). In 2004, the US Conference of Catholic Bishops published an excellent collection of official Catholic documents pertinent to understanding Christ's Passion, *The Bible, the Jews and the Death of Jesus*.

The above advice, of course, touches on a number of key Catholic and Jewish beliefs and certainly shared values, such as the value of remembering for the sake of the future with regard to the *Shoah*. I would argue that the values we share vastly outnumber the very few in which we have significant differences, because we share the same faith in the One God, the God of Israel, and in his revealed word in the Hebrew Scripture, which define and delimit our moral values and their implications for our understanding of good and evil. (Note that the serpent spoke truth to Eve when he said that eating of the fruit of the forbidden tree would give our forebears the knowledge of good and evil!)

Indeed, so close is our sharing of beliefs and values that it is inaccurate to say that Catholic-Jewish dialogue is "interfaith". Christians know no other faith than the faith of Abraham and Sarah. By definition. It can be called "interreligious," since we are bound separately, if interconnectedly, to our own communities of faith, though to the same God. We hold in common the vision of Genesis in which each human is the image and likeness of God in the world, with the awesome responsibility of living up to that mandate and mission. We hold in common our sense of the destiny of humanity, that we are called by God to witness together to and to prepare the way for the Reign of God, the *Malchuth Shamayim*. We are called, equally, by the Holiness Code of Leviticus and Jesus' Sermon on the Mount to strive to create the just society in preparation for the coming (or return) of the Messiah and God's Reign, showing compassion and mercy to the least and most needful among us.

During the Millennial Year, I participated in a major Jewish-Catholic symposium in London, co-sponsored by the World Union for Progressive Judaism and the Holy See's Commission for Religious Relations with the Jews. The papers and discussions were published in T. Bayfield, S. Brichto

For Further Reading

Irvin J. Borowsky, ed. *Defining New Christian/Jewish Dialogue.* New York: Crossroad, 2004.

Anthony J. Cernera, ed. *Examining Nostra Aetate after 40 Years: Catholic-Jewish Relations in Our Time.* Fairfield, CT: Sacred Heart University Press, 2007.

Neville Lamdan and Alberto Melloni, eds. *Nostra Aetate: Origins, Promulgation, Impact on Jewish-Catholic Relations.* Berlin: LIT Verlag Dr. W. Hopf, 2007.

and E. Fisher, editors, *He Kissed Him and They Wept: Towards a Theology of Jewish-Catholic Partnership.*[2] Topics included our two traditions' understandings of Covenant, Election and Scripture; how we can, together, respond to modernity and provide leadership for "postmodernity" in the 21st century; and Government and Society. Rabbi Sidney Brichto, of blessed memory, and myself discussed "The Values We Bring to (Our) Partnership for the Glory of God, the Good of Humanity and the Future of the Planet."[3] Had the above-mentioned surprise tsunami not occurred, this essay would have been devoted to summarizing some of the very rich insights that emerged in that dialogue, which illustrated well both the breadth and depth of what Catholics and Jews share and the values and goals we are jointly challenged to meet. Suffice it to say, however, that I highly recommend the volume from the Millennium Conference to the Pope as he considers what direction he would like to take for the remainder of his pontificate in Catholic-Jewish relations.

Notes

1. "Now It's Up to Them," 14 February 2009, p. 10.
2. London: SCM Press, 2001.
3. Op.cit., pp. 218-251.

Eugene Fisher was director of Catholic-Jewish relations for the National Conference of Catholic Bishops from 1977 to 2007. He was also a Consultor to the Vatican Commission for Religious Relations with the Jews and a member of the International Vatican-Jewish Liaison Committee, representing the Holy See. Dr Fisher has published over 20 books and 300 articles, among them *Faith Without Prejudice: Rebuilding Christian Attitudes Toward Judaism* (1977, 1993), *Seminary Education and Christian-Jewish Relations* (1983, 1988), *He Kissed Him and They Wept: Towards a Theology of Jewish Catholic Partnership* (with Tony Bayfield & Sidney Brichto, 2001).

Clemens N. Nathan

writes on the ambiguity of rehabilitating Luther, ignoring the facts and inadvertently alienating the Jews again.

We look with joy to your visit to Israel, knowing that you have a high regard for reconciliation and peace among all of us. Your visits to the synagogues have been very much appreciated.

I personally feel an affinity towards you because of your career at Tübingen. My late uncle was a surgeon in Hamburg and fled to the United States during the Hitler period, but after the war he was invited by Tübingen to come back as a distinguished foreign doctor to show his brilliant skills in surgery to the students in Tübingen. Most of his original types of operations were videoed in colour and are available, I believe, for medical students at your former university. My uncle believed in forgiveness, and after the Second World War he brought young doctors over from Germany to show them what democracy meant and how tolerance was possible. The Albert Einstein College of Medicine, where he was Professor of Surgery, had students of all races, creeds and nationalities. They all worked harmoniously together, and each respected the other's traditions. Would it not be wonderful if such a thing could exist elsewhere?

I am conscious of your wish for reconciliation with all kinds of faiths and traditions, and therefore I am reluctant to highlight a decision which would be deeply hurtful to the world Jewish community. Your intention to rehabilitate the sixteenth-century Protestant theologian, Martin Luther, driven by the desire to reconcile two divided sections of the Christian Church, runs the risk of alienating the world's Jewry even more. Whilst you are correct in your historical judgement that Martin Luther did not intend to split the Church, only to rid it of corruption, the difficulty in praising one part of Luther's mission is that it ignores some other deplorable aspects of his beliefs. If it may be time for a more positive view of Luther for the sake of the Protestant Church, it must not allow historians and theologians the opportunity to ignore the negative side of Luther.

"In our modern world, it is surely possible to remain committed to sharing beliefs and values between traditions without having to whitewash the past."

Questions

1. Is Martin Luther so tainted by antisemitism that we cannot rescue anything worthwhile from the rest of his thought?

2. Is there any significant difference between modern Nazi antisemitism and Luther's sixteenth-century antisemitism?

3. How could the Pope affirm Luther's theology, whilst distancing himself from the antisemitic feeling of his writings?

4. Should the papacy be affirming, even canonizing, people from non-Christian traditions in an attempt to increase communication between different faiths and communities?

Of course no figure from the past is perfect – all have some beliefs and actions which we might both condemn and condone. However, I believe the attitude of Luther towards Jews far outweighs any positive lesson we may choose to take from him, and it is an imbalance that the Christian Church has ignored for over 400 years – and for which we paid an inexcusably heavy price during World War II.

I understand that some of your own academic work took you into Luther's world and thought, and we admire your significant contribution to scholarship. However, I have always felt the hatred of Martin Luther towards our Jewish community. Luther's advice to the princes regarding how to deal with Jews was the beginning of much hatred towards Jews. It is beyond doubt that this became deeply entrenched in Germany, culminating in the popularity of Adolf Hitler and his gangsters. They exploited this education among the general population. How can one possibly not look at this?

I know that Martin Luther may have many other qualities – for example, you recently praised him because of his desire to rid the Church of corruption, and you spoke positively of his understanding of justification in an attempt to narrow the gap between Catholicism and Lutheranism. But surely, for those of us who are the elder brothers of your Church, to totally rehabilitate Luther would be an insult that is beyond our comprehension. Many of Luther's works exhibit an antisemitism which, although of course not Nazism, is nevertheless virulent in its hatred of Jews. Furthermore, whilst we may be told that Luther used strong, angry language when writing about many subjects, and that there are differences between his antisemitism and modern Nazi antisemitism, none of these 'excuses' are strong enough to mitigate what he actually wrote and preached. The groundwork for German antisemitism was there in Luther's writings.

In *The Jews and their Lies* he wrote,

> Therefore be on your guard against the Jews, knowing that wherever they have their synagogues, nothing is found but a den of devils in which sheer self-glory, conceit, lies, blasphemy and defaming of God and men are practiced most maliciously and veheming his eyes on them.[1]

Luther played heavily on the text of the gospels that has Jesus call the Jews a "brood of vipers". He did not call them Abraham's children, but a "brood of vipers" [Matt. 3:7]. Oh, that was too insulting for the noble blood and race of Israel, and they declared, "He has a demon" [Matt 11:18]. Our Lord also calls them a "brood of vipers"; furthermore in John 8 [39, 44] he states: "If you were Abraham's children ye would do what Abraham did... You are of your father the devil." It was intolerable to them to hear that they were not Abraham's but the devil's children; nor can they bear to hear this today.

These texts were seized upon by the Nazis and, whether opportunist or not, the widespread message of Luther through the Church that followed him was one of antisemitism. Hitler's Education Minister, Bernhard Rust, was one of many Nazis who applauded Luther:

> Since Martin Luther closed his eyes, no such son of our people has appeared again. It has been decided that we shall be the first to witness his reappearance... I think the time is past when one may not say the names of Hitler and Luther in the same breath. They belong together; they are of the same old stamp.[2]

There are of course caveats to be made, qualifications here and there, and exceptions to be pointed out. However, the general academic consensus, from historians, theologians and sociologists, is that Luther's views on Jews played a large part in the success of antisemitism at the start of the twentieth century in central Europe.

So my question to you, your Eminence, is this: Why do you wish to take the rehabilitation of Luther further? I applaud your commitment to reconciliation, to sharing beliefs and values between different traditions – it is something to which I have committed my life in many different avenues. However, to try to achieve this by ignoring the facts of history runs the risk of driving even deeper divisions elsewhere.

In our modern world, it is surely possible to remain committed to sharing beliefs and values between traditions without having to whitewash the past. In my own work with organisations that are committed to such principles (Consultative Council of Jewish Organisations, United Nations, Three Faiths Forum, Woolf Institute), these organisations also welcome people from all traditions. Our only way to move forward is not to ignore the past, but to learn from the past and then work harder. To rehabilitate Luther would not help in sharing beliefs and values; it would only damage this process. A much more positive path would be to examine Luther closely, to praise the good and condemn the bad, to admit that the great figures of the past are coloured with a mixture of both positive and negative, to share this learning, and then to work hard to educate today's students as to how to appraise Luther, his work and his influence.

Notes

1. *The Jews and their Lies,* Martin Luther's works (Philadelphia: Fortress Press, 1971), vol. 47, p. 268ff.
2. "Volkischer Beobachter," 25 August 1933, cited in Richard Steigmann-Gall, *The Holy Reich: Conceptions of Christianity* (Cambridge: CUP, 2003), pp. 136-7.

For Further Reading

Lucy Dawidowicz. *The War against the Jews, 1933-1945.* Bantam, 1986.

Martin Luther. *"On the Jews and their Lies,"* in *Luther's Works*, Philadelphia: Fortress Press, 1971.

Robert Michael. "Luther, Luther Scholars, and the Jews," *Encounter* 46:4. Autumn 1985.

Heiko Obberman. *Luther: Man Between God and the Devil.* Image Books, 1989.

Clemens N. Nathan is Joint Chairman of the Consultative Council of Jewish Organisations (CCJO) and as such is active at the United Nations, mainly in Geneva and New York. He is a Board Member of the Conference on Jewish Material Claims, the Memorial Foundation for Jewish Culture and the Three Faiths Forum, and Director of the Sephardi Centre, London. He is Vice-President of the Anglo-Jewish Association (President 1983-1989). He was the First Chairman (1998-2003) and is a present Board Member of the Centre for Jewish-Christian Relations, Cambridge.

Yohanna Katanacho

reflects on Hagar: A Victim of Injustice.

Sarah and Hagar on the façade of Strasbourg Cathedral.
© Thomas Kratz

No doubt, the biblical figure called Hagar is controversial.[1] First, several Jewish interpreters who interpret Genesis 16 and 21 are either indifferent to Hagar or side with Sarah against her.[2] On the other hand, several African-American interpreters are sympathetic with Hagar, giving her a lot of attention.[3] Second, artists participate in increasing the discord related to Hagar. For example, in front of the Cathedral of Strasbourg stand the thirteenth-century sculptures of Sarah and Hagar. Many Christians throughout the centuries saw Sarah as the victorious queen who holds the cross and cup, while Hagar is the defeated woman holding the tablets of the law. The former is the mother church while the latter represents Judaism.[4] This perception corresponds with Paul's arguments in Galatians 4: 21-31.

Contrary to this depiction, in the seventeenth century Rembrandt "creates the beautiful, stately, and pregnant Hagar next to the bent over old crone, Sarah."[5] Third, several liberation theologians/feminists tend to focus on Hagar's oppression in an androcentric patriarchal culture while several conservative Christians see Hagar as a mistake that brought trouble and reflected unbelief.[6] Fourth, several prominent Arabic translations of the Bible differ with King James Bible, New International Version, as well as Revised Standard Version in translating Gen 16: 6.[7] Unlike the pertinent English translations, Arabic translations describe Sarah's action against Hagar as oppressive and humiliating.[8]

Admittedly, these controversies reflect conflicting opinions that are shaped by different presuppositions and social locations. But they also point out the richness of the Hagar figure that continues to provoke the imagination of different peoples from different backgrounds. We hope to add to this rich spectrum of interpretations by reading the Hagar story from a Palestinian Christian perspective, hoping to see in Hagar a source of hope for both Jewish as well as Palestinian victims of injustice. Hagar represented both Judaism and oppressed Christians among different interpreters. In fact, Hagar is not only a part of the Christian, Muslim and Jewish heritage, but is also a source of hope and inspiration for all of us. This essay will first describe Hagar's difficulty, then it will point out her transformation in the midst of her ordeal.

Hagar's Difficulty

Genesis 16 starts in the Holy Land and ends in it. In the first part (vv 1-6), we see the rise and fall of Sarah's maid. The first four verses delineate the elevation of Hagar in the following way: she is a maid with a known name (v 1); she has the potential of producing children (v 2); she is Abram's wife (v 3); she is a pregnant wife (v4). Hagar's status has been transformed from Sarah's maid into Abram's pregnant wife. However, her joy did not last, for Sarah alters her success into misery. Sarah insists that Hagar is her maid (v 5) and Abram responds by returning Hagar to his barren wife, describing her as Sarah's maid (Gen 16: 6). However, this time she is not the maid that Sarah endorses but the one whom Sarah dethrones. The barren wife seems to be asking Abram for justice (v 5) but it is more likely that she is pursuing revenge. As soon as Abram releases Hagar into her hands, she oppresses her to the extent that made Hagar run away (v 6) and made the angel of the Lord describe Hagar's life before escaping as affliction or misery (Gen 16: 11). Obviously, Sarah's action convinced Hagar that it was better to risk her life and the life of her pre-born baby in the wilderness than to stay with her oppressive mistress.

"In the last century, the European Church oppressed the Jews in the Holocaust and in this century some Israeli Jews are enforcing oppressive military measures against Palestinians."

Seeing Hagar from this perspective, oppressed Jews as well as Palestinian Christians can empathize with Hagar in their struggle against Sarah, whether the latter represents the Church or the first matriarch of the Jewish people. In the last century, the European Church oppressed the Jews in the Holocaust and in this century some Israeli Jews are enforcing oppressive military measures against Palestinians. Both Jewish victims of the Holocaust and Palestinian Christians struggle with a group who claim divine rights based on their propinquity to Abram and Sarah. Interestingly, Hagar was in the Promised Land with the family that would be the means of blessing the whole world, but she was miserable because of Sarah's sinful behaviour and Abram's indifference. Sarah's oppressive actions might be seen not only in the Holocaust but also in the Palestinian-Israeli conflict. Just like Hagar, some are dethroned, oppressed and considered inferior.[9] These difficulties have contributed to increasing Palestinian immigration. The numbers of Palestinian Christians, in particular, are dwindling very fast. Similar to Hagar, many victims of the Holocaust and Palestinian Christians decided to escape. The former escaped from Europe, but the latter are leaving the Holy Land. The Church rightly recognized the pain of the victims of the Holocaust and their right to live secure and in dignity. Now the Church is also expected to comfort

Questions

1. What is the role of the Roman Catholic Church in advocating justice, peace and security among Palestinians and Israelis?

2. What are the implications of affirming the wrong done against the Jewish victims of the Holocaust without pointing out the oppressive Israeli military measures executed against Palestinians?

3. How can the Roman Catholic Church empower the Palestinian Church in its efforts to be the light of Christ as well as the bridge of peace and reconciliation between two nations and three religions in the Holy Land?

the Palestinian victims in their pain and to participate in lifting every form of injustice against them.

Hagar's Transformation

After Hagar escapes from the Holy Land, the angel of the Lord meets her and speaks to her four times (Gen 16: 8, 9, 10, 11). Hagar is instructed to face her difficulties differently. Instead of escaping from the Holy Land and the harsh holy family, she should choose to go back. The angel of the Lord says to her, "Go back to your mistress and submit to her" (Gen 16: 9). This is not an endorsement of Sarah's oppression but an encouragement to transform our situations by changing our expectations and strategy. Hagar is instructed to adopt the same strategy as advocated in the Sermon on the Mount i.e. the oppressed one is challenging the oppressive system in non-violent ways. The victim of injustice is becoming the messenger of God. The oppressed one is responding to violence by opening the channels of dialogue. Hagar is called to resist evil with good. She is called to bless the barren Sarah whose seed is supposed to bless the whole world. Sarah might reject Hagar but cannot reject her testimony that points to a just God.

Indeed, Hagar is called to obey God and be a blessing. The blessing that is entrusted into the hands of Hagar can be summarized in two divine attributes: the God who hears and the God who sees. First, the angel of the Lord informs Hagar that her child shall be called Ishmael (yishmāʿ-ʾēl), which means God hears. Ishmael is the answer to Hagar's affliction (Gen 16: 11). He shall be a living sermon that reminds Hagar of her value in the eyes of God. In Genesis 16, God chooses to speak not to Abram or Sarah but to the "inferior" Hagar, for no one can monopolize God. Every time Hagar and Abram call the name Ishmael, they will affirm that God hears the cry of the oppressed ones. God heard Hagar's aspirations for freedom by giving her Ishmael, who shall be a free nomad who is not bound by slavery.[10] Through the birth of Ishmael and his numerous seed Hagar will be transformed from a slave into a matriarch. Hagar's self-understanding is no longer defined by how Sarah views her, but by the promises of God. Similar to Hagar, victims of injustice can affirm that God hears their cries.[11]

The second attribute is the God who sees. Seeing is a clear concern in Genesis 16.[12] When Hagar was in the Promised Land (Gen 16: 1-6), her eyes were focused on Sarah. She compared herself to Sarah. On the other hand, Sarah's eyes were on Hagar. She made her the object of humiliation. However, God helped Hagar to stop looking at herself or at Sarah. Instead, the object of Hagar's eyes is ʾēl-Roʾî, i.e. the God who sees or provides. Hagar's experience of God qualified her to be God's messenger. Hagar goes back to Abram and Sarah, telling them about ʾēl-Roʾî and the angel of the Lord. Consequently, Abram names his first-born son Ishmael (Gen 16: 15). Many years later, the angel of the Lord appears to Abram, who remembers the lessons that he has learned from Hagar. He tells his son Isaac that God will provide (yir'eh) the sacrifice (Gen 22: 8). When God does provide it, Abram calls him: Yahweh who provides (yhwh yir'eh), using a divine epithet that is so similar to the one that Hagar used.

Stated differently, victims of injustice must turn their eyes from focusing on the difficulties they encounter to the God in whom they believe. Like Hagar, they can be transformed and become a blessing even to their oppressors. This does not mean endorsing oppression, but it is fighting evil with good. It is also affirming that the election of Abram and Sarah does not justify the oppression of Hagar. The Church needs to demonstrate the love of Christ towards the Jews. Concomitantly, Israeli Jews must love their Palestinian neighbour and vice versa. In light of this understanding, I urge the Catholic Church and Israeli Jews to consider not only the Hagar of the Holocaust, but also the Hagar among Palestinian Christians who need to stop their demographic haemorrhage and be empowered as they strive to be the light of Christ and the yeast of his love in a country that is marked by darkness and hatred. Help us to work on mending the painful wounds of Jews, Christians and Muslims by fighting all forms of injustice and by recognizing not only the injustices of the Holocaust but also the need of oppressed Palestinians for a just peace.

Notes

1. This essay is based on an earlier article that I have published: Yohanna Katanacho, "Hagar from a Palestinian Arab Evangelical Perspective," *Roundtable* (2008), 55-59.
2. Sarah is the wife of Abram. Her name was changed from Sarai to Sarah. This essay will use the name Sarah unless it is a direct quotation from primary or secondary sources. It will also use the name Abram even though it was later changed to Abraham.
3. Wilma Bailey and Renita Weems are two African-American representatives of this trend while Susan Niditch, Aviva Zornberg and Tikva Frymer-Kensky are Jewish interpreters. Wilma Bailey, "Hagar: A Model of an Anabaptist Feminist?" *The Mennonite Quarterly Review* 68 (April 1994), 219-228; Renita Weems, *Just A Sister Away: A Womanist Vision of Women's Relationships in the Bible* (San Diego: LuraMedia, 1988); Susan Niditch, "Genesis," in *The Women's Bible Commentary*, ed. Carol Newsom and Sharon Ringe (Louisville: Westminster/John Knox, 1992); Avivah Zornberg, *Genesis: The Beginning of Desire* (Philadelphia: The Jewish Publication Society, 1995); Tikva Frymer-Kensky, *In the Wake of the Goddesses* (New York: Fawcett Columbine, 1992). For further information, see Wilma Bailey, "Black and Jewish Women Consider Hagar," *Encounter* 63 (2002), 37-44.
4. Irene Pabst, *The Interpretations of the Sarah-Hagar Stories in Rabbinic and Patristic Literature*, available from http://www.lectio.unibe.ch/03_1/pabst.pdf.
5. Kathleen O'Connor, "Abraham's Unholy Family: Mirror, Witness, Summons," *Journal for Preachers* 21 (1997), 26-34 (26).
6. See for example Trible's feminist depiction or the typical evangelical conservative approach found in Hamilton or Campbell. Phyllis Trible, "The Other Woman: A Literary and Theological Study of the Hagar Story," in *Understanding the Word: Essays in Honor of Bernhard W. Anderson*, ed. James Butler et al., JSOTSup 37, ed. David J. A. Clines and Philip R. Davies (Sheffield: JSOT Press, 1985), 238; Victor Hamilton, *Handbook on the Pentateuch* (Grand Rapids: Baker Book House, 1982), pp. 96-101; George Campbell, "Rushing Ahead of God: An Exposition of Genesis 16: 1-16," *Bibliotheca Sacra* 163 (2006): 276-291.

For Further Reading

Alex Awad. *Palestinian Memories: The Story of a Palestinian Mother and Her People.* Bethlehem: Bethlehem Bible College, 2008.

Elias Chacour and David Hazard. *Blood Brothers.* Grand Rapids: Chosen Books, 2003.

Yohanna Katanacho. "Christ Is the Owner of Haaretz," *Christian Scholar's Review* 34 (2005): 425-441.

Yohanna Katanacho is a Palestinian Christian from Jerusalem. He completed his MA at Wheaton College and his Master of Divinity and Ph.D. in the Old Testament at Trinity International University. He has published several books and articles in English and Arabic. He is currently serving as the Academic Dean of Bethlehem Bible College and Galilee Bible College.

7. Some of the Arabic translations are: *Van Dyck Bible* (Cairo: Bible Society, 1999); *El-Kitab el Muqadas* (Lebanon: Bible Society, 1995); Brian Walton, *Biblia Sacra Polyglotta: Tomus Primus* (Austria: Akademische Druck, 1963). It is worth noting that in Genesis 16 the living Bible is closer to the Arabic versions.
8. The Hebrew word 'ānâ in Gen. 16: 6 denotes oppression, violence, as well as physical and psychological torture. The pertinent verb occurs 80 times in the Hebrew Bible and has a range of negative meanings that reflects a strong oppressive nature. For further details, see Avraham Even-Soshan, *Konkordantsyah Hadeshah le-Torah, Nevi'im, u-Khetuvim* (Jerusalem: Kiryat Sefer, 1982), pp. 901-902; Paul Wegner, "ענה," *NIDOTTE* 3:449-452.
9. For further details, see Gary Burge, *Whose Land? Whose Promise?: What Christians Are Not Being Told about Israel and the Palestinians* (Cleveland: Pilgrim Press, 2003).
10. Shimon Bar-Efrat, *Narrative Art in the Bible*, JSOTSup 70, ed. David J. A. Clines and Philip R. Davies, Bible and Literature series 17, ed. David M. Gunn (Sheffield: Almond Press, 1989), p. 207.
11. The connection between Hagar and Palestinians might also be strengthened if we consider that Muslim tradition sees Hagar as the mother of Ishmael, who is the father of arabized Arabs. Although this connection cannot adequately be established biologically or etiologically, the association between Arabs and Ishmael cannot also be completely dismissed.
12. In the Hebrew text of Gen 16: 1-6, we notice that the verb "see" is mentioned twice and the word "eye" is mentioned three times. Further, in the wilderness, or in Gen 16: 7-14, the verb "see" or one of its related forms is repeated four times.

Michael Berenbaum

urges Roman Catholics to deepen their response to the Shoah and continue to engage the modern world as critics and conscience.

Permit me to begin with a few words about my background that informs the content of this letter.

I am a graduate of Jewish parochial schools and was raised in the Orthodox tradition and ordained a rabbi by the time I was 23. My world was infused with Judaism without much exposure to other religious traditions. Then I went to graduate school, where my closest friend and deepest intellectual colleague was a Roman Catholic nun, a member of the Religious Sisters of Mercy.

Lawrence Cunningham, currently a Professor of Theology at the University of Notre Dame (USA), was my teacher. He sat on my doctoral committee and his work shaped my own. I began my academic career at Wesleyan University in Middletown, Connecticut (USA), teaching in the Religion Department and serving as University Jewish Chaplain along with my Roman Catholic colleague, Father Charles Gonzalez, S.J., who later became the Rector of the Georgetown University Jesuit community in Washington, DC. He was – and remains – a revered colleague and cherished friend. We have spoken deeply about matters of faith, friend to friend, believer to believer.

I later had the privilege to teach in the Department of Theology at Georgetown University for 15 years, where I taught Modern Jewish Thought, the Holocaust and an occasional course in Rabbinic Judaism. My colleagues were often Jesuits and my students were overwhelmingly Roman Catholic, proud and successful graduates of its parochial schools – as I had been of Jewish parochial schools – who understood religious faith and often explored their own in dialogue with the Jewish texts they were studying and the Jewish historical experience they were encountering, many for the very first time.

I also served as Project Director of the United States Holocaust Memorial Museum in Washington, DC, overseeing the creation of its permanent

"... I am a friend and an admirer of the Roman Catholic Church, and an even better friend and admirer of the men and women it has produced to serve the Church and God."

exhibition and working closely with Roman Catholic leaders, both within the National Conference of Catholic Bishops (NCCB) and from the academic community, as well as with Roman Catholic educators who were teaching about the Holocaust. Professionally, I have presented papers and responded to papers at the Catholic Theological Society of America (CTSA) and attended their annual conferences. These are all experiences I prize.

I mention all of this because I want you to grasp the point that I am a friend and an admirer of the Roman Catholic Church, and an even better friend and admirer of the men and women it has produced to serve the Church and God. Many of the men and women with whom I have worked and interacted over the years were shaped by the religious atmosphere and the interreligious respect and cooperation ushered in by *Nostra Aetate*, that seminal document of Vatican II on The Relation of the Church to Non-Christian Religions, proclaimed by His Holiness Pope Paul VI on 28 October 1965.

As you undoubtedly know, but will learn again from the contents of this book, many of my colleagues and friends, and I myself, belong to a generation that has been formed by that Vatican II proclamation and by the many contacts and documents, dialogues and discussions, articles and books that have ensued ever since.

For Jews of my post-World War II generation, the most important interreligious story of the past half century has been the dramatic improvement in Jewish-Catholic relations and the mutual respect and cooperation between and among Roman Catholic and Jewish clerics, Roman Catholic and Jewish scholars, as well as between and among Roman Catholic and Jewish laypeople. The progress has been so enormous that we fear that the younger generation has taken it for granted and that other priorities will so move the Church that it will not see the need to foster those relations.

We also fear that a new generation is arising that has not been shaped by the events of the *Shoah* and precisely because of the distance that we have travelled will not appreciate the journey we have taken under the papacy of Popes John XXIII, Paul VI, John Paul I and John Paul II.

Fear often leads to suspicion, and it does not take much to arouse Jewish suspicions, especially among colleagues who have not had the sustained and intense contact with Roman Catholic leadership – both scholarly and diocesan – as I and many of my colleagues have had.

As a Jew who prays daily in Hebrew and who attends religious services in synagogues throughout the world, I well understand the importance of the Latin Mass and the desire of a new generation to return to this authentic liturgy. Even the most liberal and least Orthodox of Jewish denominations have returned to the Hebrew, the Holy Tongue for prayer, understanding full well that while prayer in one's native language provides accessibility, it is often at the loss of mystery. In addition, the debasement of languages in our

Questions

1. How have Roman Catholic Christians been shaped by the documents of Vatican II?

2. What effect did Vatican II have on how Jews began to relate to Christians, particularly Roman Catholic Christians?

3. Why do Jews still tend to be suspicious of Christians, even after all the "official" statements, documents and meetings related to Christian-Jewish relations?

day makes it ever more difficult to pray in them. Furthermore, a universal Church must provide prayers accessible to parishioners wherever they travel in our global universe. Thus, I have admired the return to tradition and the attempt to reach out to your more devout, more traditional believers, but I believe that you can understand our historic sensitivity to the prayer for the conversion of Jews.

Conversion today is the option of free men and women, seeking to understand God and tradition and to find an institution that makes God's presence manifest in a tradition that is meaningful and accessible. Historically, this was not the case for millennia. For believing Jews, our faith and our deeds sustain us; our lives reflect our all-too-human attempt to fulfil God's will as best we understand it, and we chose to remain faithful to the teachings of our tradition. Even for non-believers, the request for conversion is perceived as an insult, a sense that one is inadequate as a person before God and before our fellows. Furthermore, when Christians – both Roman Catholic and Protestant Christians – try to convert us, we Jews feel our faith and our tradition are disrespected by those seeking to convert us.

With regard to the *Shoah*, the primary focus of my own academic research, your statements against Holocaust denial and for remembrance have been admirable and unequivocal. I suspect that we both regret the recent circumstances that made it imperative for you to speak so forcefully. I know that we would have celebrated such statements if they had seemed more like noble leadership and less like damage control. Surely, your staff should have been more sensitive to the full record of these Lefevbrist bishops whom you seek to reconcile with the Church. Your statement condemning antisemitism is also most respected, especially at a time when we have seen its increase on the European continent and within the Islamic world.

In my work, I have written that the Roman Catholic Church is perhaps the most important example of what Emil Fackenheim described as *tikkun*, the repair of the rupture rent by the Holocaust. The religious imperative to mend the world is clear not just in relation to the past – perhaps not even primarily to the past – but to the future. We live in a world where when brokenness is recognized, mending, *tikkun*, is possible; but where the recognition is absent, there can be no healing.

We share a love for tradition and a veneration of religious intensity, piety and intellectual rigour. What I have so admired in the Church under the leadership of Popes John XXIII, Paul VI and John Paul II was the way it used the tools of tradition to emphasize, transmit and reinforce religious teachings that did not allow the intensity and piety of religious traditionalism to degenerate into the kind of fanaticism that did not respect other religious traditions. Out of the depths of our own faith, and because of the depth of our own faith, we must emphasize the religious heritage common to all humanity: all are God's creation; all are entitled to fundamental human

"For believing Jews, our faith and our deeds sustain us..."

For Further Reading

Michael Berenbaum, ed. *Not Your Father's Antisemitism: Hatred of the Jews in the 21st Century*. St Paul, MN: Paragon House, 2008.

Mary C. Boys. *Jewish-Christian Dialogue: One Woman's Experience*. New York: Paulist Press, 1997.

Richard L. Rubenstein & John K. Roth, eds. *Approaches to Auschwitz: The Holocaust and its Legacy*. 2nd ed. Louisville. KY: Westminster John Knox Press, 2003.

dignity and respect. I am certain that you share my alarm at the climate of contemporary religious life in which people are killing each other because of religious difference, where religious faith is not tempered by the acknowledgement of the other – even the one with whom we vehemently disagree – as created in the image of God and therefore entitled to respect and veneration.

The Church is at a crossroads. A new generation is arising that takes the contemporary climate of Jewish-Catholic relations as a given, that reads it back into history as if it were always so. That new generation was born long after the Holocaust and has not learned its implication for interreligious tolerance, and for the potential of intolerance to lead men and women of religious faith to act out of a misperception of that faith to destroy the other.

You are perhaps the last to hold your exalted office who has been shaped by the events of the *Shoah* and, therefore, it is important for you to ensure that its legacy endures in the Church long after your leadership.

Roman Catholicism is more noble, more Godly because of how it has responded to the *Shoah* and I urge you to deepen its response to this formative event. Roman Catholicism is more admirable because it has accepted the religious pluralism of the modern world and because it has engaged with the modern world as both critic and conscience, while not rejecting that which can be Godly in our world. I urge you to continue that as well.

I join with my fellow Jews in welcoming you to Israel. Now that the issue of Vatican recognition of Israel is out of the way, the Church is able to come to grips with the two major forms that Jewish life has taken since the time of Jesus of Nazareth: Rabbinic Judaism and the State of Israel. I am certain that you will understand from your brief visit that Israel is diverse and democratic, still struggling for acceptance among its neighbours and for a sense of how to understand its role as a Jewish state and a state for all its citizens. You will meet Jews of diverse opinion and of different relationships to their tradition and their past. You will meet those who are suspicious and fearful of the Church and those who are open to its message and to your presence. All of us hope that the direction charted in the past few decades will chart the future direction of Jewish-Catholic relations.

Baruch Haba, Blessed be the one who comes. Shalom – hello, welcome, peace.

Michael Berenbaum is Professor of Jewish Studies and Director of the Sigi Ziering Institute: Exploring the Ethical and Religious Implications of the Holocaust. He was Executive Editor of the *Encyclopaedia Judaica*, Second Edition [22 volumes, 16 million words] which won the Dartmouth Award of the American Library Association as the Outstanding Reference Work of 2006. Dr Berenbaum is the author and editor of 18 books and was Project Director overseeing the creation of the United States Holocaust Memorial Museum and later director of its Research Institute.

Grotto of the Nativity in Bethlehem. Israel is the promised land of the Jews, the cradle of Christianity and has sites holy to Muslims. It can divide us or bring us together. The challenges are very real.

Israel

Jane Clements

is concerned about understanding Israel as crucial to Christian-Jewish unity.

Recently I had a slightly unnerving experience. I was persuaded to appear on a Teheran-based TV station to discuss, as I thought, freedom of speech versus religious sensibilities. Once the live programme began, however, I found that the questions soon turned to the relationship between the Vatican, Israel and Jews in general. Since I am an Anglican, much of this is not exactly my sphere of expertise, but I did my best. At this point, I began to think seriously about the reasons why an Iranian English-language programme should wish to spend half an hour on this somewhat specialised subject.

Christian-Jewish relations are facing, I believe, their greatest challenge since the Second Vatican Council when, in the terrible aftermath of the *Shoah* and as we sought to find some way forward in our relationship with God's first covenant people, the modest declarations of *Nostra Aetate* came like a Sinai moment. The directive was clear, even if the details had yet to be made apparent: Christians were to turn aside from previous attitudes and enter into a new relationship with those they had formerly vilified.

In the decades of dialogue which have followed, Jews and Christians have been able to focus together on what unites us. We have learned to live amicably and respectfully together – for the most part. Certainly, a great deal still divides us, not just theologically, but in matters of approach and perception. We still 'get it wrong', failing to understand or allow for each other, even with all the goodwill and opportunities for interaction over the years. But the spectre of racist antisemitism has largely departed the Church. A survey carried out by the Council of Christians and Jews in 2008 among Christians in England found that all those questioned thoroughly repudiated any tendencies which could be identified as antisemitic. There was also a resistance to 'anti-Judaism' – the tendency to portray 'Synagoga' as the blinded and

"Christian-Jewish relations are facing... their greatest challenge since the Second Vatican Council when, in the terrible aftermath of the Shoah *and as we sought to find some way forward in our relationship with God's first covenant people, the modest declarations of* Nostra Aetate *came like a Sinai moment."*

"For Jews, the land of Israel, however its borders are defined (but always including Jerusalem), is at once precious and fragile."

crushed adversary of the triumphant 'Ecclesia'. Such approaches are due in no small measure to the clear stance of the Roman Catholic Church on Christian-Jewish relations in recent decades.

As we have drawn closer, our areas of disagreement have been thrown into stark relief. Ironically, we have learnt to work creatively with our greatest point of difference, Jesus Christ. However, the one topic which threatens to derail all our best efforts is that of how we approach and relate to the State of Israel.

When we visit our Arab brothers and sisters in communities both within Israel and in the Palestinian territories, we feel called upon to stand alongside them, to acknowledge above all the divine requirement according to the prophet Micah – to do justice, to love mercy and to walk humbly with our God. We have no such imperative on which we can all so easily agree when it comes to the State of Israel. For Jews, the land of Israel, however its borders are defined (but always including Jerusalem), is at once precious and fragile. It is precious for any number of reasons – a bolt-hole, a place where one can rejoice in normality and the geographical focus, liturgically, historically and eschatologically. Its fragility derives from the real fear – rational or otherwise – that all the weapons in the international arsenal cannot guarantee its existence from the forces which seek to destroy it.

Christian approaches are far more complex. For many Christians, the biblical covenant has ceded the land to the Jewish people in perpetuity. But, as a whole, we still grapple with the issue of covenant. Is there one covenant, now removed from the Jews and passed to the Church? Or are there two covenants – one for the Jews and one for the Gentiles? Or is a 'covenant relationship' available to both Jews and Christians in the context of eternal promises? Your own work on this[1] demonstrates that creative theological thought can provide a sound basis for teaching. And what of prophecy? Is the land to be given to the descendants of Jacob because it is promised to him in the Scripture? Writers such as Colin Chapman[2] argue that the covenant achieved its fulfilment in Jesus and therefore Jews, who have largely failed to accept Him, have forfeited their part in the covenant promises. Post-modernism has at least given us a healthy suspicion of the meta-narrative and encouraged us to think about how truths relate to each individual experience. But while most theologians grapple with these issues 'for the sake of heaven', as Jews would say, some do so to provide weapons to attack Jewish understanding of identity and tradition.

Scholarship which sheds light on biblical history and, in particular, the peoples of the land prior to the exile, can underline the fact that modern Jewry is essentially different socially and ethnographically from the people of David's minor 'kingdom'. Michael Prior,[3] for example, describes historic Jewish identity as a social or even literary construct, with no real basis in objective historical fact. This is a widely accepted academic view and, on the face of it, non-controversial. Unfortunately, it can also be wielded as a tool

Questions

1. How can we seek to be both truly pro-Palestinian and pro-Israeli, in the pattern of Christ?

2. How do we understand the nature of covenant? Is our understanding inclusive?

3. Can people in seemingly intractable conflict in one part of the world learn from others in another part of the world who have sorted out their conflict?

of dispossession. Modern Palestinians, it is argued, living in the land for generations, are the genetic descendants of the Patriarchs and therefore are the true inheritors of this promise, if ever a promise there was. Those of us who have struggled long and hard to encourage Christians to accept the concept of 'Jesus the Jew' can find it discouraging to be faced with 'Jesus the Palestinian'. On the face of it, Jesus is, of course, universal, incarnated alongside those in need or suffering oppression. On the other hand, the use of the term specifically to negate the Jewishness of Jesus is not acceptable.

Our own tradition encourages the 'spiritualisation' of Jerusalem; the people of God are the Church, even if we have learnt to say that in some other special way, the Jews are, too. We find it difficult to understand a link to geography as visceral as it is spiritual, like the old Australian aboriginal beliefs in the Dreamtime. As we struggle to discover approaches we can agree on as Christians, all this is made more complex by unease – or worse by the actions and policies of successive Israeli Governments.

It is a modern truism that legitimate criticism of the actions of the Israeli Government does not, in itself, constitute antisemitism. In practice, however, such criticism of Israel can be grasped by those with antisemitic tendencies to bolster their prejudice. Furthermore, racist thugs will use such a climate of antipathy as a 'reason' for their violence. It is acknowledged that attacks on Jews in the Diaspora, as a response to actions of the Israeli Government, are terribly unjust. However, this can be made more complex by a sense of natural solidarity that most Jews feel with Israel as a concept. The age-old question about whether Jewishness is religious or racial in essence – or both, or neither – is used to debate the legitimacy of the State of Israel as a 'Jewish state'. The anomalous nature of what it means to be Jewish defines identity, irrespective of belief or practice, at the core of one's being, and we must acknowledge that it also centres on issues of tradition and heritage. As Christians, we must be wary of all attacks which seek to deny the identity, heritage or 'specialness' of Jews, both 'for the sake of heaven' and for the consequences to our understanding of Christianity.

The relationship between Jews and Christians is an immensely complex one. While Judaism can be practised, often more easily, in the absence of Christianity, the same is not true in reverse. Our scripture and liturgy are embedded in Hebrew scripture and Jewish practice; we need to know how to read our difficult texts so that they perpetuate a 'right relationship' with Jews rather than the centuries of anti-Judaism which *Nostra Aetate* was designed to overcome. I believe it is time to admit that the description of Judaism as Christianity's 'older sibling' seems a little patronising today; we must go further and recognise that our relationship includes a duty to seek the common good.

The Christian world has become sadly polarised; it seems that one must either be 'pro-Palestinian' or 'pro-Israeli'. In this, one hears the echo of St

For Further Reading

Walter Brueggeman. *The Land: Place as Gift, Promise and Challenge in Biblical Faith*. Minneapolis: Fortress Press, 2002.

Elias Chacour. *Faith Beyond Despair: Building Hope in the Holy Land*. London: Canterbury Press, 2002.

Helen Fry, ed. 'Israel' in *Christian-Jewish Dialogue: A Reader*. Exeter: Exeter University Press, 1996.

David Stevens. *The Land of Unlikeness: Explorations into Reconciliation*. Dublin: The Columba Press, 2004.

Paul berating us from the opening verses of I Corinthians to be "united in the same mind and the same judgement" lest we say: "Is Christ divided?" To stand in solidarity with suffering Palestinians and to uphold their rights and dignity does not mean that we should seek to belittle or demonise Israel. Neither should we compound the sense of victimisation and paralysing fear felt both by Israelis and Diaspora Jews, but rather work to encourage Israel's ethical and honoured standing in the international community.

This will inevitably involve being critical of Israel as the need arises, and as joint inheritors of the biblical concepts of righteousness and justice. But it is also incumbent on us to take a more pro-active role in addressing the crisis. The Sermon on the Mount gives us a clear directive to be active peacemakers, to seek the moral and physical well-being of both Jews and Palestinians. Glen Stassen, in calling us to our duty, writes:

> God was angry with us for our disobedience and enmity, so God took a grace-based transforming initiative and came to us in Christ and made peace. This is an imperative, a command. It is not, 'if you think the one you are angry at is good enough, deserving enough, open-minded enough, then do this'; it is a command from Jesus.[4]

We should note that in coming to us in Christ, God was not blind to our faults, but rather sought to address them in complete unity with humanity. This is, I believe, our pattern for our dealings with both Israelis and Palestinians. The Iranian TV programme reminded me that the world watches how we respond as Christians to the issue of Israel, sometimes more than any other. I encourage you as you continue to seek God's will and labour to effect a real change for peace. Such a path demands wisdom, courage and the ability to hold opposing positions in tension; the legacy of *Nostra Aetate* shows that it can be done where the Vatican takes a lead. In the words of Rabbi Hillel,

> If I am not for myself, then who will be for me? And if I am only for myself, then what am I? And if not now, when?[5]

Jane Clements is the Founder and Director of FODIP (The Forum for Discussion of Israel and Palestine), having worked for many years in Christian-Jewish relations. She has a Ph.D in Holocaust Education from the University of London and is a Trustee of the UK's Holocaust Memorial Day Trust. An Anglican Christian, Jane serves on the Archbishop of Canterbury's Commission to the Chief Rabbinate of Israel.

Notes

1. Joseph Cardinal Ratzinger, *Many Religions, One Covenant: Israel, the Church and the World*, (San Francisco: Ignatius Press, 1999).
2. Colin Chapman, *Whose Promised Land?* (Oxford: Lion Publishing, 2002).
3. Michael Prior CM, ed., *Western Scholarship and the History of Palestine*, (London: Melisende, 1998).
4. Glen Stassen, "Jesus and the Just Peacemaking Theory," in Brown and Penner, eds., *Christian Perspectives on the Israeli-Palestinian Conflict*, (Schwarzenfeld, Germany: Neufeld Verlag, 2008), p. 205.
5. Pirkei Avot 1:14.

Richard L. Rubenstein

discusses deicide, Judas, exile and return, and the problem of proportionality.

In addressing this letter to you, I would like to express myself from the perspective of the continuing threats to the very existence of Judaism and the Jewish people.

I was born in the United States in 1924. My parents were assimilated American Jews. As I grew up, I received neither religious instruction nor access to the rituals of Judaism. I first became aware of the rise of Hitler and the Third Reich no later than the spring of 1936. In spite of my parents' deficit of religious commitment, I was strongly influenced by events in Europe and at age 16 decided to study for the rabbinate. That decision and a later decision to pursue advanced studies at Harvard in Christian theology and the history of religion was partly due to my growing conviction that religion is, as my teacher at Harvard, Paul Johannes Tillich, observed, the ground of culture. I did not take Tillich's observation to mean that the Western world's predominant religion was responsible for the rise of National Socialism. Nevertheless, I did not regard it as a mere coincidence that the Jew, the villain par excellence of National Socialism, was also the perennial villain in the Christian religious universe, at least before Vatican II.

"...I did not regard it as a mere coincidence that the Jew, the villain par excellence of National Socialism, was also the perennial villain in the Christian religious universe, at least before Vatican II."

Having learned to take religion very seriously, I was frightened by two related accusations, one explicit, the other implicit, which, when activated, have proven capable of utterly poisoning Jewish-Christian relations and endangering the very existence of the Jewish people within Christendom. They are (a) the deicide accusation and (b) the identification of Jews with Judas, the disciple who betrays his Master for money with a deceitful kiss. For many Christians, the deicide accusation explicitly depicts all Jews who are faithful to their own tradition as the basest of criminals, for what crime could be more diabolical than the murder of God? Insofar as Jews have been identified with Judas, it has been difficult, if not impossible, for Christians to trust them, especially in times of social, political and economic stress. No matter how trustworthy Jews may appear, the kiss of Judas can cast a dark and terrible shadow of suspicion over them. Moreover, the Judas identification also rendered credible both the *Dolchstoß in den Rücken* legend and *The Protocols of the Elders of Zion* as "proof" that Germany did not lose World War I but was "betrayed" by its Jews, the vast majority of whom were loyal to the *Kaiserreich*.[1] We know the terrible price all of Europe's Jews were to pay for this alleged betrayal.

I am, of course, aware of the fact that Pope Paul VI's Proclamation of *Nostra Aetate*, the Declaration on the Relation of the Church with Non-Christian Religions of the Second Vatican Council, has done much to mitigate the severity of those terrible accusations and to improve Jewish-Catholic relations. Regrettably, the mitigation came after the *Shoah*, during which the deicide accusation was employed by some priests and members of the hierarchy to justify the Nazi deportation of the Jews from their country of birth.[2]

I received my first inkling of the full horror of the *Shoah* in the fall of 1944. One of Western civilization's most advanced nations had created a new and unique institution, the bureaucratically-managed, quasi-industrial facility for the processing of live human beings into corpses and ashes.[3] I was 20 years old at the time and fully understood the fate that would have awaited me had my great-grandfather and grandparents not understood the fate that Europe had in store for us. Your Holiness, I say Europe advisedly, for the deed was not done by National Socialist Germany alone. From that moment on, my life was permanently changed. No matter what doubts I might have had concerning my inherited religious tradition, I was more than ever determined to pursue a religious vocation.

When the war ended in May 1945, all of Europe had become a charnel house for the Jewish survivors. Unwelcome in the countries of their birth, an estimated 250,000 found shelter under miserable conditions in Displaced Persons camps in Germany, Austria and Italy. Their number was augmented by Eastern European survivors who, when they attempted to return to their homes, often found that they were returning to pogroms.

For many Jews, the *Shoah* and the subsequent return of the survivors to Palestine exemplified a fundamental theme in Jewish religious experience, exile (*galuth*) and return. Certainly, the *Shoah* demonstrated the most extreme perils of *galuth*; return to Palestine represented fulfilment of the dream of the end to exile. Unfortunately, return from exile could only be achieved by a war that involved a new exile, the flight of hundreds of thousands of Arabs from the land in which their ancestors had been domiciled for centuries. Not without reason, the Arabs called their defeat in 1948 *al-Naqba*, the catastrophe.

Regrettably, it is a terrible fact of human existence that civilizations tend to be built on war. In the era of St Augustine and St Ambrose, for example,

Questions

1. Why do some people still believe that *The Protocols of the Elders of Zion* is true? Is it sheer hatred? Ignorance? Or stubbornness?

2. How important is the State of Israel for Jews worldwide? Why?

3. Who was Fr. Samir Khalil Samir? What role, if any, has he played in Jewish-Christian relations?

North Africa, Rome and Milan were part of one Christian world. With the seventh-century Umayyad conquest of North Africa, that world was split asunder by the success of Islamic arms. One also thinks of the *reconquista*, without which Christian civilization would never have been reconstituted in Spain.

Israel's War of Independence was different. In 1942, in anticipation of Rommel's victory in North Africa, the *Reichssicherheitshauptamt* set up *Einsatzkommando Ägypten* in Athens whose mission was to follow Rommel into Palestine and exterminate Palestine's Jews.[4] The operation had the full support of Haj Amin al-Husseini, the former Mufti of Jerusalem and the most important religious and political leader of Palestine's Arabs at the time. The Mufti spent the war years in Berlin, where he used his contacts with National Socialist leaders, such as Joachim von Ribbentrop and Heinrich Himmler, to keep Europe's Jews bottled up in Europe in the full knowledge of the fate that awaited them.[5] When the war was over, he received a hero's welcome in Egypt. Both that country and Syria became havens for some of the most notorious perpetrators of the Holocaust who were determined to continue their extermination project in the Middle East. Unwanted in Europe and in the world of Islam, Jewish survival depended upon military victory against the Arabs. Unfortunately, all too often that war of survival has been depicted by leading Catholic spokespersons such as Fr. Samir Khalil Samir, S.J., as "*une impardonnable injustice contre la population palestinienne...*"[6]

Undeniably, Palestine's defeated Arabs had real grievances, but the leaders of the Arab world offered Palestine's Jews only expulsion or extermination. The fate of the defeated Arabs was cruel, but was it as cruel as the exodus of more than 12 million ethnic Germans from Eastern Europe in the aftermath of World War II? Six decades after the end of that war, many of the great-grandchildren of the Arab refugees of 1948 continue to languish in UNRWA-supported camps. By contrast, in spite of the hardships they endured, the *Volksdeutsch* have successfully integrated into Germany and have helped to make Germany Europe's most productive economy.

The difference between the two refugee groups is largely cultural. Most of the Germans abandoned dreams of conquest and return assured of the support of their fellow Germans, who were determined that their refugees would not endlessly remain dependent on international charity. By contrast, the Palestinians were largely unwelcome in the larger Arab world that saw advantage in keeping them penned up in camps, where they could nourish their resentment and dream of ultimately destroying Israel and exterminating its inhabitants.

Exterminate the Israelis? Your Holiness, please understand that after Hitler every responsible Jew believes that those who promise to destroy them fully intend to keep that promise if they can. And all too many Muslim leaders have publicly made that promise for responsible Jews to dismiss it as hyperbole.

"...please understand that after Hitler every responsible Jew believes that those who promise to destroy them fully intend to keep that promise if they can."

What does a people owe its adversaries when they include a critical mass that openly seeks its destruction? That question has confronted Israelis in every one of its conflicts from 1948 to the twenty-first century conflicts with Hizbollah, Hamas and Iran. The Holy See has offered its response: Israel's response must be "proportional," but what does proportionality consist of in the face of a declared intention to annihilate?[7] Or is it the counsel of the Holy See that Israel must ignore the threats of extermination in its responses?

Nevertheless, I cannot think of the encounter between the Israelis and Palestinians as other than tragic. I fear that both peoples are condemned to live next to each other in an Hobbesian state of nature. Although the Israelis have no annihilationist intentions vis-à-vis the Palestinians, all too many annihilationist threats have been made by politicians, preachers, journalists and other Muslim leaders for the Israelis to possess the luxury of ever trusting them.

Under the circumstances, it would appear that one of the most painful aspects of the relations between the Holy See and Judaism today has been the persistent tendency of important spokespersons and institutions of the Church, such as *L'Osservatore Romano*, to regard the Arabs as the victims and the Israelis as the oppressors in every conflict between the two sides. Even when representatives of the Holy See make a perfunctory attempt to suggest that both sides are somewhat at fault, the greater fault is invariably found to rest with the Israelis. Moreover, the Church would, if it could, impose greater moral burdens on Israel than on any other people. The Holy See has consistently lent its great moral authority to bolster Arab claims of a Palestinian "right of return" to the homeland from which they either departed or were expelled as a result of the Arab-Israeli wars since 1948. If accepted, such a "right" would "spell doom for the Jewish state, even more so when considering that no reciprocity for millions of Jewish refugees from the region could ever be seriously proposed".[8] The Vatican suggests no comparable "right" for the tens of millions of Europeans who have been compelled to leave their homelands due to the wars of the twentieth century. Presumably, the Church understands the chaos that would ensue from such repatriations, but would impose that catastrophic obligation solely on the Jews.[9]

The same tendency to depict Israel as the aggressor was evident in the recent remarks of Cardinal Renato Martino. When the Israelis finally decided to attempt to put an end to the rockets Hamas persisted in firing at its land and its people, Cardinal Martino declared, "*Guardiamo le condizioni di Gaza: assomiglia sempre più ad un grande campo di concentramento.*"[10] Cardinal Martino is an extraordinarily skilled diplomat who knows exactly how to choose his words. Unfortunately, the Cardinal's words seem to echo the canard so frequently expressed by sympathizers of the Palestinian cause that Israelis are like Nazis in their treatment of the Palestinians.

In effect, the Church, through institutions like *L'Osservatore Romano*, has taken sides in the propaganda war that is being waged against Israel. Such a war can have devastating consequences.

For Further Reading

Andrew Bostom, ed. *The Legacy of Islamic Anti-Semitism: From Sacred Texts to Solemn History*. Amherst, NY: Prometheus Books, 2008.

Raymond Ibrahim, ed. *The Al Qaeda Reader*. New York: Doubleday Broadway Books, 2007.

Bat Ye'or. *Eurabia: The Euro-Arab Axis*. Cranbury, NJ: Associated University Presses, 2005.

In conclusion, I would like to express the modest hope that the Holy See will be fair and objective with respect to the complex issues that underlie the conflict between Israel and the Palestinians and, truth to tell, much of the Muslim world.

Notes

1. In October1916, the German High Command ordered a *Judenzählung* to demonstrate that Jews were less patriotic than what at the time were considered their "fellow Germans". The findings demonstrated the opposite. Approximately 80 per cent of the Jews in the German army served in the front-lines. Over 100,000 Jews served out of a total German-Jewish population of 550,000; 12,000 died in battle; 30,000 were decorated for bravery. See Jacob Rosenthal, *"Die Ehre des jüdischen Soldaten": Die Judenzählung im Ersten Weltkrieg und ihre Folgen* (Frankfurt/Main: Campus Verlag, 2007), pp. 63-89; see also Deutsches Historisches Museum, "Die Judenzählung von 1916," http://www.dhm.de/lemo/html/wk1/innenpolitik/judenzaehlung/index.html, accessed 30 September 2008.
2. For example, between 26 March and 30 June 1942, 52,000 Slovakian Jews were deported to Poland. As the deportations continued, the bishops of Slovakia issued a pastoral letter describing the Jews as an accursed people for having failed to recognize the Redeemer and for "having prepared a terrible and ignominious death for him on the cross". The letter concluded, "The Church cannot be opposed, therefore, if the state with legal regulation hinders the influence of the Jews." The date of the letter was 26 April 1942, *Actes et Documents du Saint Siège Relatifs à la Seconde Guerre Mondiale* (ADSS), vol. 8, no. 519.
3. I discuss the bureaucratic management of the *Shoah* in my book, *The Cunning of History* (New York: Harper and Row, 1975).
4. See Klaus-Michael Mallmann and Martin Cüppers, "'Elimination of the Jewish National Home in Palestine': The Einsatzkommando of the Panzer Army Africa, 1942," (Jerusalem: Yad Vashem Studies, XXXXV, 2007), p. 14: http://www1.yadvashem.org/about_holocaust/studies/vol35/Mallmann-Cuppers2.pdf; see also Mallman and Cüppers, *Halbmond und Hakenkreuz. Das Dritte Reich, die Araber und Palästina* (Darmstadt: Wissenschaftliche Buchgesellschaft, 2006), Volume 8 of the Publications of the Ludwigsburg Research Institute of the University of Stuttgart.
5. A representative sample of the Mufti's speeches and writings during World War II can be found in Gerhard Höpp, ed., *Mufti-Papiere. Briefe, Memoranden, Reden und Aufrufe Amîn al-Hussainis aus dem Exil, 1940-1945* (Berlin: Klaus Schwarz Verlag, 2001); for an Israeli biography of the Mufti, see Zvi Elpeleg, *The Grand Mufti : Haj Amin al-Hussaini, Founder of the Palestinian National Movement*, trans. David Harvey, ed. Shmuel Himelstein (Portland, OR: Frank Cass, 1993); for a biography by a Muslim scholar, see Philip Mattar, *The Mufti of Jerusalem: Al-Hajj Amin Al-Husayni and the Palestinian National Movement* (New York: Columbia University Press, 1988.
6. Samir Khalil Samir, S.J., "De la guerre inutile à la paix définitive au Moyen-Orient," *www.chiesa.espressonline.it*, 22 August 2006, http://chiesa.espresso.repubblica.it/articolo/78504.
7. Pietro de Marco, "'Proportionality' and the clashes of civilizations. A commentary on the third Lebanese war," http://chiesa.espresso.repubblica.it/articolo/78561?eng=y
8. Vittorio E. Parsi, "The Vatican and Israel: Policy Ordered More to Balance than Impartiality," October-December 2003 edition of "Diritto e Libertà, http://chiesa.espresso.repubblica.it/articolo/6991?eng=y
9. Ibid.
10. "ISRAELE/ Card. Martino: raccogliamo i frutti dell'egoismo. L'unica speranza è il dialogo," *Ilsussidiario.net*, 7 January 2009, http://www.ilsussidiario.net/articolo.aspx?articolo=10714 /

Richard L. Rubenstein has devoted his career to the study of contemporary religious thought, the Holocaust and genocide. He is the author of *After Auschwitz* and *The Cunning of History*. His most recent book, *La Perfidie de l'Histoire*, deals largely with the impact of Islam on contemporary Europe. He is currently completing *Jihad and Genocide*, a study of radical Islam. He received his rabbinic ordination from the Jewish Theological Seminary of America, the STM and Ph.D from Harvard.

David N. Myers

calls for sensitivity and understanding, and first steps to moral leadership in the region.

I write this letter in the wake of the recent controversy surrounding Richard Williamson, whom you have invited back into the Church along with three colleagues from the Society of St Pius X. It is heartening to see that you have heeded the calls of many groups and individuals and called on Mr Williamson to take further steps to renounce his odious views on the Jews and the Holocaust. While it is hardly the prerogative of Jews to tell the Catholic Church whom to include in its midst, the reinstatement of Mr Williamson without such a retraction would send an ominous signal to many of us that the age of ecumenical understanding inaugurated 45 years ago has come to an end. The Second Vatican Council marked an important new chapter in the long and vexed history of relations between Catholics and Jews – and the results have been tangible. Following the *Nostra Aetate* Declaration, Catholic-Jewish dialogue gained significant new momentum. Not just Catholics, but Jews too rethought long-held positions about the other, as the *Dabru Emet* statement of 2002 demonstrated. (It is incumbent upon me to mention in this context the diligent labours of that indefatigable champion of Catholic-Jewish dialogue, the late Rabbi Dr Michael Signer.) Historical scholarship challenged old assumptions of an unwavering theological enmity rooted in Jesus' own time. Educational curricula in both Jewish and Catholic institutions moved beyond stale stereotypes. And a new sensitivity to the tragedy of the *Shoah*, so profoundly evinced by Pope John Paul II, allowed Jews to regard Catholics with new trust.

"It is heartening to see that you have heeded the calls of many groups and individuals and called on Mr Williamson to take further steps to renounce his odious views on the Jews and the Holocaust."

Let us not allow, Your Eminence, the reservoir of good will built up in the wake of the Second Vatican Council to evaporate. I labour under no illusions that the main task of the Church you lead is to forge constructive relations with Jews. It is to tend to the flock of Catholic faithful. And that is certainly understandable. But to the extent that you imagine the Church as "catholic" – in the original Greek sense of "universal" – then a wider view of the world would seem warranted. And such a wider view would recognize that there are millions – indeed, billions – of people of faith who are not Catholic, but deeply believe in the God of Abraham. Such a wider view would also encourage an enhanced awareness both of the unique relationship between Jews and Christians and of the grave wounds incurred by Jews on their long historical journey.

Perhaps, at the end of the day, you share the view of the renowned American Orthodox rabbi, Joseph B. Soloveitchik, who opposed Jewish participation in theologically-based interfaith dialogue in advance of Vatican II. R. Soloveitchik maintained that since each religious tradition believed that "its system of dogmas, doctrines and values is best fitted for the attainment of the ultimate good," the grounds for earnest and productive exchange were quite limited. In other words, the exclusive truth claims of Judaism and Christianity preclude meaningful dialogue.

This is an intuitive and logical position; I am often drawn to it, and I suspect you are as well. But it belies a much more complicated reality on the ground – and after all, it is on the ground where we, who have not yet ascended to celestial heights, still dwell. Truth may well be singular and absolute. Its apprehension, though, is as variable as the rich mosaic of the human condition. As Rabbi Ishmael famously stated, "*dibra Torah kilshon bene adam*" – the Torah speaks in the language of humanity. And, of course, the Talmud reminds us, in thinking of the competing views of the ancient sages Hillel and Shammai, that "*elu ve-elu divre Elohim hayim*" (BT Eruvin 13) – both the view of Hillel and the view of Shammai are the words of a living God.

You are a highly skilled theologian who has thought long and hard about truth, faith and interpretation. This is not the place to resolve major epistemological questions regarding the multiple ways in which human beings understand the Divine. But I do wonder whether it is possible to open your heart and mind more to the variety of human experiences. Rather than initiating a dangerous descent into an abyss of relativism, that opening might well bestow upon you a new measure of moral integrity and authority. Is it not by understanding and identifying with the Other – instead of revelling in our distinctiveness and virtue – that we realize our capacity for morality?

I believe that this kind of openness, leading to moral integrity, is especially needed in one region of our troubled globe that is of keen interest to both of us: the Holy Land. Understandably, you are concerned about the fate of the shrinking Christian minority in the region, as we all should be. But that concern should not prevent you from aspiring to moral leadership in the larger conflict. That leadership must rest on a recognition of the multiple narratives and, dare I say, truths of the Israeli and Palestinian experiences.

Questions

1. What responsibility should the Church feel toward the Jews?

2. Can the Church be open to the multiple experiences, even truths, of the human condition?

3. What should be the goal of interfaith dialogue?

4. Have we reached the end of the Vatican II age?

5. What role can – and should – the Church play in the conflict between Israelis and Palestinians?

A first step toward assuming the mantle of moral leadership would be to continue to develop and give public voice to empathy for the historical experience of the Jews, particularly in modern times. Who if not you, a German-born man who came of age in the midst of the Nazi scourge, can fail to see the searing scar of Auschwitz on the Jewish body and the human soul? (It is the seeming absence of such empathy in the case of Richard Williamson that pains so many Jews.) The Holocaust is not the sole grounds of legitimation of the Jewish quest for self-determination. But it certainly revealed the compelling logic of the Jews' striving for a land of their own. I hope and trust that you and the Church you lead will come to appreciate more fully the desperate yearning – and survival instinct – at work in the Jews' return to their homeland.

Such a recognition is a necessary, but not sufficient, condition for assuming real moral leadership. The essential second step requires a degree of empathy for, and understanding of, the Palestinians as well. To a great extent, the narrative arcs of the Jews and Arabs in the Holy Land move in opposite directions: from exile to homeland in the former case, and from homeland to exile in the latter. Moreover, the great joy of the Jews at the creation of the State of Israel in 1948 coincided with the bitter tears of the Palestinians stemming from the Catastrophe, or *Nakba*, that befell them. We Jews must move far beyond our sense of self-virtue to acknowledge the pain of the Palestinians, and our own role – in the midst of a bitter political and military conflict – in causing it.

All fair-minded people – those who follow the words of our shared Scripture, "Justice, justice, you shall pursue" (Deuteronomy 16:20) – must recognize the pain of the Palestinians. I would hope that you do so not by engaging in a zero sum game, as so many Israeli and Palestinians do – that is, by affirming their own pain to the exclusion of the other's. You can assume the mantle of moral leadership by acknowledging the virtue and justice of both sides, while also attending to the lingering injustice that abounds. Your statement calling for negotiation in the midst of the Gaza war of January 2009 points in the direction of such leadership. But a more sustained, empathic and proactive vision is needed. For, indeed, to see the divine spark inhering in Jews and Arabs, Israelis and Palestinians alike, is a moral and catholic imperative.

I began this letter by writing about Richard Williamson, and I conclude by writing about Israelis and Palestinians. The common thread linking them is the need for sensitivity to, and understanding of, the experiences of others. May you continue to seek out such sensitivity and understanding in your important work on behalf of the Catholic faith.

For Further Reading

Dabru Emet, http://www.jcrelations.net/en/?item=1014

Zvi Kolitz. *Yosl Rakover Talks to God*. Vintage, 2001.

Antonio Muñoz Molina. *Sepharad*. Harvest Books, 2008.

Sari Nusseibeh. *Once Upon a Country: A Palestinian Life*. Halban. 2007.

Amos Oz. *A Tale of Love and Darkness*. Vintage, 2005.

David N. Myers is Professor of Jewish History and Director of the Center for Jewish Studies at UCLA in Los Angeles, CA. His books include *Re-inventing the Jewish Past* (Oxford, 1995); *Resisting History: The Crisis of Historicism in German-Jewish Thought* (Princeton, 2003); and *Between Jew and Arab: The Lost Voice of Simon Rawidowicz* (Brandeis, 2008).

Marc Ellis

asks the Pope to speak with 'Jews of Conscience' and not just the Jewish establishment.

When you travelled to Auschwitz a few years ago, I was writing a series of commentaries on life and commitment. Since your visit coincided with my writing, I wrote about your visit, marvelling at your own journey as a German to the highest office in the Roman Catholic Church. As a Jew, I also noted how far the Church has come in its own history. Where once Jews were reviled, now we are accorded our due respect.

At Auschwitz, you carried yourself with dignity and your message resounded: Never again could such behaviour be tolerated or even imagined. The dignity of all persons needs to be respected; Christians – but any person with a religious sensibility – should lead others in the way of compassion and justice. An obvious point, perhaps, but one in which the Church and many Christians have too often been lacking historically. As human beings and as communities, we still struggle with these questions and limitations. You spoke about that during your time at Auschwitz. Many in the world were listening to you. I was among them.

"... you will be travelling where Palestinians lived before the creation of the State of Israel and where more than a million Palestinians who are citizens of Israel still live."

Now you are travelling to Israel – and I suspect to Palestine as well. Though your itinerary hasn't been published as yet and I am writing to you in advance, I assume that you will travel in Palestinian areas. I assume that because even if you don't go to the West Bank or Gaza – if you just travel in Israel proper – you will be travelling where Palestinians lived before the creation of the State of Israel and where more than a million Palestinians who are citizens of Israel still live. So there is no way you can travel to Israel without travelling to Palestine. This is the same for me. When I, as a Jew, travel to Israel, I also travel to Palestine – or what is left of it.

Beside the more than 700,000 Palestinians who were driven out of Palestine in the creation of the State of Israel, the Palestinians who live within

"Many Jews who carry this message of justice and conscience have left the mainstream Jewish community or have been driven out."

Israel, though citizens, suffer discrimination and sometimes recrimination. There are some Israelis, represented in the Knesset itself, who seek to drive these remaining Palestinians out of Israel so that only Jews will remain. I am sure that you are also aware of the increasing Israeli settlements in the West Bank, many of them ringing a constantly expanding Jerusalem. Some believe, as do I, that those settlements, along with the Wall being built in the West Bank, represent a further cleansing of the Palestinian population from the State of Israel. You may be aware that President Carter has called the system developing in the West Bank "apartheid". Some Israeli historians and commentators assert that in the very creation of the State of Israel there was a crime. They refer to the expulsion of Palestinians in 1947-1948 as "ethnic cleansing".

As with many nation-states, the State of Israel carries a hope and possibility and a heavy historical burden of crimes and complicity. As leader of the Catholic Church, you know intimately the difficulties of living within this complex of future hope and historical burden. Your very presence in Israel – and Palestine – exemplifies this. Especially when you visit Yad Vashem, I am sure you will feel this deeply as Pope and as a Christian. Would Jews have needed their own state without the history of antisemitism that was constitutive of Christianity for more than 1,500 years?

I am sure that others write letters to you about the history of Christian antisemitism, so I will continue on. In fact, I have no choice in moving on, since even as I am writing this letter, the Israeli bombardment and invasion of Gaza enters its third week. Though the invasion will be old news in the international community by the time you visit Israel – and Palestine – the effects of the war on Palestinians will be long-lasting. A new round of war may be looming on the horizon.

While what the Palestinians are suffering should arouse the conscience of people everywhere, I am writing to you as Jew who opposes this invasion and indeed almost all of Israel's policies toward Palestinians. As a Jew. While we can discuss the ethics of war in general, and even the particular provocations on both sides that led to this most recent invasion, my complaint runs deeper: Israel's actions are a violation of the Jewish ethical tradition; this is especially so in light of the Holocaust. In fact, I hope that you are aware that Yad Vashem itself is built on territory that many years ago was confiscated from Palestinians. Geographically, it is also quite close to Deir Yassin, a Palestinians' village that witnessed the massacre of Palestinians in 1948, an event which has come to symbolize the ethnic cleansing of Palestine that stands at the centre of what Palestinians call the *Nakba*, their catastrophe.

"Speak the truth of Christian antisemitism and the suffering of Palestinians. At Yad Vashem."

I am also a teacher of the Holocaust – at a Christian university – and as I write I am also beginning a new semester of teaching this course. It is an odd situation to be in: teaching the Holocaust while the bombing of defenceless civilians in Gaza continues at pace, often with the Holocaust used as a justification. Many Jews now invoke the issue of terrorism as a cover for this invasion, but at its core is a sense that others are out to destroy Jews and the Jewish homeland. As has happened before in history, the most recent example being the Holocaust.

So all of us stand within these historical contradictions, Jews included now, but you wouldn't know this from our Jewish leadership. For many of these leaders, some of whom meet with you at the Vatican and others you will meet in Israel, we as Jews are innocent. They also believe that the State of Israel, as a response to the Holocaust, is our redemption. However, there are other Jews who are not invited to the Vatican, or to meet with you in Israel. These Jews feel differently. Because of our history with Palestinians, these Jews believe that we as a people are now culpable in a suffering that has gone on far too long and needs to be redressed. While understanding the need for Jews to be empowered, these Jews desire an interdependent empowerment – with Palestinians. These Jews believe that Palestinians deserve to be free in their homeland, either in their own full and viable state on the West Bank and Gaza with East Jerusalem as its capital, or in one state with Israelis, where Jews and Palestinians are equal citizens, carrying the same privileges and obligations.

This future is very far off. Indeed it may not happen in the lifetime of Jews who have these views. Yet the damage done to the Jewish ethical tradition and the future of Judaism is already in evidence. And more. Many Jews who carry this message of justice and conscience have left the mainstream Jewish community or have been driven out. You don't see them, nor do your representatives who frequent the ongoing Jewish-Christian dialogue. In my view, this dialogue has become a deal – I have called it the "interfaith ecumenical deal" – where Jews speak about the historic sufferings of the Jewish people and demand Christian support for Israel and silence on its history and present policies toward Palestinians. If Christians speak forthrightly about the Palestinians, they are suspected of not taking the Holocaust seriously. They may even be labelled as modern-day antisemites.

I call the Jews who seek a deep engagement with the violence that has become an accepted part of Jewish life, Jews of Conscience. My sense is that Jews of Conscience are battling what you in the Vatican inherit, a Constantinian mentality that allows the religious ethical tradition to be utilized by state power. Today there is a triumphal Constantinian Judaism which argues for the State of Israel and its present policies within Israel and also in the United States, Israel's most faithful political ally. Though Jews of Conscience are mindful of our past suffering, and perhaps because of it, they cannot be silent in the face of injustices against Palestinians. By going against the norm, Jews of Conscience are in exile from Constantinian Judaism. And though many of these Jews lack an overt religiosity, they are practising Judaism in its deepest form, as a commitment to justice and against the idolatrous

Questions

1. Are you familiar with the history of Christian antisemitism and the statements Christian Churches, including the Roman Catholic Church, have developed? How do these statements discuss the Holocaust, the State of Israel and the Palestinians? Is sufficient attention paid to each? In light of recent developments, does there need to be new attention paid to the Palestinians?

2. When you read Church statements, are you also reading histories of the Israeli-Palestinian conflict? Are you reading both mainstream histories as well as the more critical histories written by some of the new Israeli historians?

3. Are you aware that the Jewish community is diverse? Do you seek out Jews of Conscience who have a different perspective from that of the established Jewish community?

practices of the state. It seems to me that Jews of Conscience are carrying the covenant into exile with them.

Where is this letter leading? I know that the Vatican has tried to balance its own history of antisemitism, its new, much more positive relationship with Jews and the ongoing conflict in the Middle East. As a friend of many Palestinian Christians, I know how important your voice is for them. Of course, the Muslim world, in its size and intensity, is also of interest and concern to the Church. So you, like all of us, live in a historical thicket when approaching the question of Israel and Palestine. But Jews also need a clear voice. If you summon up your own courage, facing the historical complicity of the Church in antisemitism and the Holocaust, while also stating that what Jews have done and are doing to the Palestinians is wrong, your voice may represent a breakthrough. At the very least, the truth of the situation would have been spoken by a moral spokesperson on the international stage.

Regardless of this evident complexity involved, and perhaps because of it, we desperately need a breakthrough. Palestinians need a breakthrough badly as the daily news reports out of Gaza testify. We Jews also need a way out, lest we solidify our Constantinianism as the Church did for so long. I know so many Christians who are struggling against that Constantinian heritage; they are trying to reclaim the heritage of the early Christians as the essence of the Christian witness. Jews of Conscience are entering the dark terrain of Constantinian Judaism. We need voices from all quarters to help us in our struggle. In a peculiar and ironic twist of history, your visit might help in this struggle. It might even move the interfaith ecumenical deal into a new geography of truth-telling and justice-seeking.

So meet with Jews of Conscience in Israel. At Yad Vashem. And, when you return to Rome, schedule meetings with Jews of Conscience at the Vatican. Speak the truth of Christian antisemitism and the suffering of Palestinians. At Yad Vashem. And if it isn't on your itinerary right now, after you read this letter, schedule a visit to Deir Yassin. It is so close to Yad Vashem you will feel the common suffering to be overcome and reconciled. Now. Before it is too late.

For Further Reading

Marc H. Ellis. *Judaism Does Not Equal Israel.* New York: The New Press, 2009.

Ilan Pappe, *The Ethnic Cleansing of Palestine.* London: Oneworld Publications, 2007.

Rafi Segal and Eyal Weizman, eds., *A Civilian Occupation: The Politics of Israeli Architecture.* London: Verso, 2003.

Marc H. Ellis is Professor of History, University Professor of Jewish Studies and Director of the Center for Jewish Studies at Baylor University, USA. Professor Ellis has lectured around the world and his writings have been translated into nine languages. He is the author and editor of more than 20 books including *Toward a Jewish Theology of Liberation*, now in its 3rd edition, and most recently *Judaism Does Not Equal Israel.*

Ruth Lautt

is concerned about double standards towards Israel's right to self-determination.

On this extraordinary occasion of the visit of His Holiness Pope Benedict XVI to Israel and the Holy Land, Catholics in the United States (and indeed all over the world) may wish to take the time to reflect on the significance of this event and the complex relationship between the Church, Jews and the Jewish state.

Pope Benedict's predecessor, Pope John Paul II, reminded us that before Jews and Christians could fulfil their biblical mandate to be a blessing to the world they must "... first be a blessing to one another."[1] Yet it is no secret that for most of our 2,000 years of shared salvation history, Christians have not been a blessing to Jews. Teachings of deicide and supercessionism led to Jewish isolation and discrimination against them.

"...it is no secret that for most of our 2,000 years of shared salvation history, Christians have not been a blessing to Jews."

In 1965, however, the Church inexorably repudiated antisemitism. *Nostra Aetate* transformed the Church's relationship with the Jewish people and ushered in a new era, characterized by respectful dialogue and mutual attempts at understanding. In spite of occasional disputes, this new relationship is thriving. However, a troubling new phenomenon has emerged that needs to be carefully examined.

While the Roman Catholic hierarchy has remained a principled and neutral voice when it comes to the conflict between Israel and its Arab neighbours, discussion of the Arab/Israeli conflict within some factions of our Church reveals that Israel is frequently subjected to a double standard. No other country seems subject to such endless scrutiny by some Catholic religious orders, NGOs, Catholic social justice groups and some of the Catholic media, which repeatedly place Israel under a critical ethical microscope and seem almost to lie in wait to pounce whenever they conclude that the Jewish state has strayed from a standard they apply to no other country and no other

Questions

1. In the history of relations between the Church and the modern state of Israel, what are the high points and the low points? Are we growing towards being a blessing to one another?

2. How can Catholics begin the important task of discerning our fairness (or lack thereof) when dealing with matters regarding the Jewish state?

3. Why is it important, as the Vatican Commission for Religious Relations understood, to distinguish between an understanding of the land of Israel and the State of Israel?

4. Do you agree that many people tend to hold Israel to a different standard than we hold other nations? In what ways? Why do we do that?

group of people. Tending to say very little about any culpability the Palestinians or Arab nations might have in the conflict, they blame the Israeli 'occupation' or the separation barrier, or whatever the alleged Israeli sin of the day is – always somehow the misdeeds of Israel are focused upon.

Recently, we have witnessed attacks on Israel's fundamental legitimacy, with accusations coming from some quarters that it is somehow inherently racist for the Jewish people to want the same right of political sovereignty and self-determination that we take for granted that other peoples are entitled to. Frequently, the very same people who hurl the accusation of inherent racism at Jewish nationalism extol other forms of nationalism as liberation movements and as heroic. What emerges is a clear double standard – the actions and the very existence of the Jewish state are not judged by the same standards applied to other nations.

How are Catholics to understand the nature of a Jewish state and how are they to interpret the actions of such a state? While *Nostra Aetate* offered no guidance as to the Church's understanding of a modern Jewish state, 20 years later the Church did grapple with this issue. In1985, the Vatican Commission for Religious Relations With The Jews distinguished between theological and political considerations, and noted that Christians should strive to understand the deep religious significance of the *land* of Israel to Jews and Judaism, while interpreting the existence of the *State* of Israel according to principles of international law.[2] Almost another 20 years later, in the *Joint Declaration* of the International Catholic-Jewish Liaison Committee (2004), the Church restated its commitment to rejecting antisemitism and specifically cited anti-Zionism as a more recent form of this bias.[3]

Having proclaimed that the State of Israel is to be judged by the same principles of law that other countries are judged by, and having warned of anti-Zionism as a manifestation of antisemitism, the Church must carefully discern first whether Israel is held to uniquely high legal and moral standards, and then routinely adjudged guilty of failing to meet them. If this is the case – and the frequency and vigour of criticism levelled at Israel by certain of the social justice and other factions of the Church suggests that it is – then the reason for this must be carefully and honestly discerned. Might this excessive criticism be reflective of a fundamental failure to fully embrace the principles declared more than 40 years ago in *Nostra Aetate*?

The danger inherent in holding one people (particularly a historically oppressed minority) to a different and higher standard than others are held to cannot be overstated: it is illustrated in an exhibit in Yad Vashem which recalls a massacre of Jews in a particular town early in the Nazi era. The Nazis rounded up a group of Jews. Then they invited their non-Jewish neighbours to shout and yell at the Jews about every misdeed or transgression, no matter how small, that they could recall each one ever committing. By focusing intensely on the (ordinary, human) sins – lies, grudges, failure to repay debts –

of one particular group of people, another group can be made to feel justified in setting them apart, finding them uniquely corrupt and allowing, or even abetting, their punishment and slaughter. Any people can be effectively demonized by applying a standard to them that is applied to no other. If this is, in effect, what is being done to the citizens of the Jewish state by some in our Church, a conscious and a diligent effort must be made to stop it.

My hope and prayer is that the Church celebrates the occasion of the Pope's visit to the Holy Land by recommitting to the noble objectives first stated more than 40 years ago in *Nostra Aetate* – rejection of antisemitism in all of its forms, including, to the extent that it exists, excessive criticism, scrutiny and bias against the Jewish state.

Notes

1. Pope John Paul II, on the 50th Anniversary of the Warsaw Ghetto Uprising.
2. *Notes on the Correct Way to Present the Jews and Judaism in Preaching and Catechesis in the Roman Catholic Church.*
3. "We draw encouragement from the fruits of our collective strivings which include the recognition of the unique and unbroken covenantal relationship between God and the Jewish People and the total rejection of anti-Semitism in all its forms, including anti-Zionism as a more recent manifestation of anti-Semitism."

For Further Reading

Darrell Jodock, ed. *Covenantal Conversations: Christians in Dialogue With Jews and Judaism.* Minneapolis: Fortress Press, 2008.

Dennis Ross. *A Missing Peace: The Inside Story of the Fight for Middle-East Peace.* New York: Farrar, Straus and Giroux, 2005.

Ruth Lautt, OP, is the founder and National Director of Christians for Fair Witness on the Middle East. An attorney, Sr. Ruth earned her law degree at New York University Law School and was a practising litigator prior to founding Fair Witness in 2005. She is a member of the Sisters of the Order of St Dominic, Amityville, New York, USA.

George Schwab

describes progress as a step-by-step process and the exercise of sovereignty over East Jerusalem as the core issue of peace.

"The exercise of sovereignty over East Jerusalem is the core issue around which the peace process in the Middle East revolves."

"Sovereignty in name, autonomy in fact". Few would deny that the 27-square mile territory inhabited by descendants of the three Abrahamic religions is the nexus that keeps peace in the Holy Land at bay. And fewer still would refute the notion that the authority that emanates from your unique position in the world would enable Your Holiness to play a seminal role in orchestrating a peace process that would lead to the resolution of what appears to be an intractable problem, namely, the governorship of East Jerusalem.

The National Committee on American Foreign Policy (NCAFP) materially contributed to resolving the conflict in Northern Ireland by patient, confidence-building measures that included "hand-holding", listening impartially to all sides, and providing public forums to enable opposing parties in the conflict to state their positions. Under your auspices, I am certain, a majority of moderate, peace-loving Israeli Jews and Arab Muslims and Christians, in the West Bank and elsewhere, would welcome a similar process.

In the case of Northern Ireland, for example, William J. Flynn, Chairman of the NCAFP, helped to obtain a 48-hour visa for Gerry Adams of Sinn Fein to enter the United States and participate in a National Committee-sponsored conference on Northern Ireland that was held in New York City in early 1994. This was later followed by visits to the National Committee by Loyalist and Unionist leaders, including the Reverend Dr Ian Paisley, head of the Democratic Unionist Party (DUP). The NCAFP was fortunate in that it did not take long to win the confidence of the IRA (Irish Republican Army) and Loyalist paramilitary groups. Subsequently, they translated their emerging sense of trust into respective ceasefire declarations.

Many ups and downs followed in the intricate peace process whose success finally enabled the National Committee to phase out its project on

Northern Ireland in 2008. In the words of Dr Henry Kissinger, the National Committee's former honorary chairman, "If it [peace] could happen in Ireland, with the history of Ireland and the distrust, I'd like to think it could happen anywhere."

I do not mean to suggest that this model can be adopted without modification, but it could be used as a frame of reference in East Jerusalem. With variations, the National Committee has used this paradigm in its projects on North Korea and on US-China-Taiwan relations. According to leaders of the US, China and Taiwan, the National Committee's work has materially helped to bring about stability in the Taiwan Strait, although there is still a long way to go to achieve final resolution of the conflict, and for the time being, China and Taiwan have set aside the thorny issue of sovereignty.

The exercise of sovereignty over East Jerusalem is the core issue around which the peace process in the Middle East revolves. According to international law experts, including Sir Elihu Lauterpacht, Israel is legally sovereign over East Jerusalem. That status, it is argued, stems from the British withdrawal from Palestine, which was followed by the rejection of the United Nations Organization's partition plan by Arab states and their invasion of the Holy Land. According to international law, those developments created a sovereignty vacuum that was not filled by Jordan's military occupation of East Jerusalem. It is further argued that because of Arab aggression and Israel's victory in the Six Day War, Israel acquired the right to fill the sovereignty vacuum as a measure of self-defence. Jordan's withdrawal from all its claims to the West Bank and East Jerusalem in 1988 further fortified Israel's position, even though Jordan did not recognize the validity of Israel's sovereignty over East Jerusalem.

In view of East Jerusalem's population of Arab Muslims and Christians and of Israeli Jews proffering their respective claims, and notwithstanding the legitimacy and legality of Israel's claim, the conciliatory solution to which the three would in all likelihood adhere is a self-governing or autonomous East Jerusalem. By focusing on that goal, the peace process would lead to the gradual development of local governmental institutions with all that this implies, including the creation of an effective police force that would enable Israel to gradually thin out and finally terminate its military presence in East Jerusalem.

Sovereignty and autonomy are not mutually exclusive, as we have learned from the example of Finland's sovereignty over the Åland Islands and Åland's autonomy. As Your Holiness surely knows, the League of Nations in June 1921 granted Finland sovereignty over the Åland Islands with the exception of two limitations: (1) "The local population should be offered international guarantees for the preservation of their Swedish language, culture and local customs; (2) Åland should be demilitarized and neutralized under an international agreement." In exceptional circumstances, that is, in the event of "civil unrest or acute threats to Åland's neutralization," Finland "may

Questions

1. How realistic is it to suggest that the Pope could be a mediator or a facilitator in helping the aggrieved parties in the Holy Land to reach some sort of accommodation with each other?

2. How can the Roman Catholic Church work with others to promote peace between Israel and Palestine?

3. What is the role of Track 2 diplomacy in helping to sort out or solve the many complicated issues affecting the Middle East peace process?

introduce and temporarily maintain an armed force in Ålandic territory for the purpose of upholding order." To date, the evolution of the status of the Åland Islands has been remarkably steady and peaceful.

As is always the case, the devil resides in the details. From long experience in negotiating with the Irish, the Chinese and Taiwanese, and even the North Koreans, I assure you, Your Holiness, that issues can be defused and progress can be achieved on a step-by-step basis, however frustrating negotiations may turn out to be. In your presence and under your auspices, the leaders of the Middle East, reflecting the interests of the people, can resolve the status of East Jerusalem and open the gates to peace, which has eluded politicians and diplomats for so many years.

For Further Reading

Christians and the Middle East: Discussion Guide. Washington, DC: Sojourners/Call to Renewal, 2007.

Fundamental Agreement between the Holy See and the State of Israel (1993), http://www.bc.edu/research/cjl/cjrelations/resources/documents/catholic.html

Walter Laqueur and Barry Rubin, eds. *The Israel-Arab Reader: A Documentary History of the Middle East Conflict.* 7th edition. New York: Penguin, 2008.

George Schwab received his Ph.D. from Columbia University in 1968. His teaching career began at Columbia and followed at The City University of New York, where he taught in both the undergraduate and graduate schools. In 1974, he was one of the co-founders, with the late Professor Hans J. Morgenthau, of the National Committee on American Foreign Policy. He has been its president since 1993. Professor Schwab is the author or editor of many books and essays.

Ayelet Shahak

reflects on Bat-Chen who dreamt of peace but was murdered in cold blood.

On the Purim Holiday in 1996, our lives were transformed. Our daughter, Bat-Chen, was born on the Jewish holiday of Purim and murdered on her 15th birthday as a result of a suicide bombing in Tel Aviv on 4 March 1996. Since then, our lives have never been the same. Holiday and birthday celebrations have turned into a day of memories and sadness. Instead of holiday cakes, friends bring food for memorial ceremonies.

This tragedy has transformed our lives forever. We have turned into peace activists and are trying to use words instead of bullets.

"This tragedy has transformed our lives forever. We have turned into peace activists and are trying to use words instead of bullets."

I am Ayelet Shahak, born and raised in Jerusalem. During the Six-Day War in 1967, I was a teenager. During the Yom Kippur War in 1973, my uncle, Colonel Yitchak Ben-Shoham, was killed fighting on the Golan Heights, where soldiers bravely sacrificed their lives in order to prevent the Syrians from conquering the northern part of Israel.

After the war and completion of high school, I began my army service in the Israeli Navy – where I met my husband, Tzvika Shahak. During the Yom Kippur War, Tzvika – who was an officer in the Navy – made brave and courageous decisions while in dangerous and hostile waters during ferocious navy battles on the southern front. He was awarded a medal of bravery.

We married in 1978 and I began working as a teacher after completing my studies. Our first child, Bat-Chen, was born in 1981. Yaela, our second daughter, was born in 1983 and our son, Ofri, was born in 1987.

In 1996, Bat-Chen was murdered on her 15th birthday. Only after her tragic death did we discover a treasure – Bat-Chen's diaries in which she left us her legacy. There were two central themes emphasized in her diaries:

- to be a poet: "For me, writing is wonderful and it makes me a happy person" (from her sixth-grade diary).

- to live in peace with our Arab neighbours: "Everyone has a dream. One person wants to be a millionaire and the other wants to be a writer. I have a dream for peace."

Bat-Chen's legacy for peace

Bat-Chen's concern for peace began at an early age. In third grade, when asked what she would like from God for the new year, she wrote: "My first wish is that my grandfather return from the dead and second, that there be no wars, and third, that we live in peace with all countries."

Right before Independence Day, in third grade, when asked what she would like to bestow on her country, she wrote:

It's a beautiful good country that has everything.
It has flowers and trees and butterflies... lots of them.
You can find almost everything you would want in this wonderful country.
But one thing is missing... and that is peace.
It is really missing and every day I get up and hear on the radio about the 'intifada'... I get a bad feeling in my heart, I ask my mother, 'When will there be peace?'
I am waiting for it every day and I call out, "Come on, peace... come on already!' but is hasn't come.

Bat-Chen, the day before her death, dressed in her "last Purim costume", her mother's wedding dress.

We, Bat-Chen's parents, were particularly amazed to read the following text which was written when Bat-Chen was only 12:

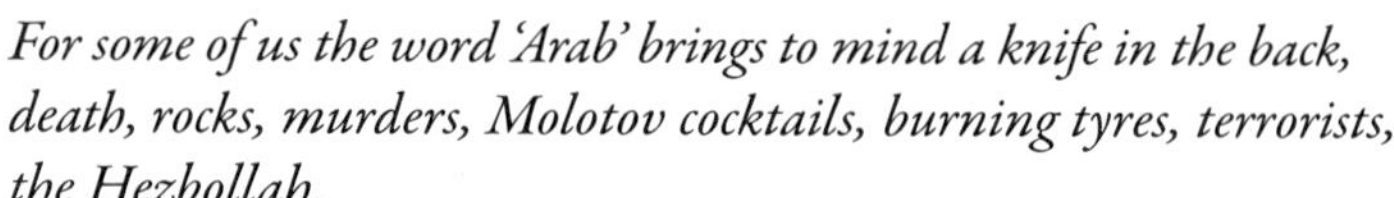

For some of us the word 'Arab' brings to mind a knife in the back, death, rocks, murders, Molotov cocktails, burning tyres, terrorists, the Hezbollah.
Some of us make a distinction: there are Arab murderers just as there are Jewish ones.
Every country has good and bad people and there are some who will say 'the Arabs are our good friends, they too have rights.'
There is a lot of unrest in our little country. There are three opinions about Arabs: the settlers and the 'radical right' hate the Arabs; the 'left' makes a distinction and the 'radical left' demands rights for the Arabs too!
It is very hard for me to make up my mind – which position to take. One moment I'm for the 'left' then suddenly the radio newsreader says, 'Jews have been murdered, the terrorists have been captured' and I say, 'It could have been one of my family.'
All this hatred has lasted over 2,000 years. We and the Arabs all live in fear.

I always say that there are good Arabs too; but I only hear about the murderers.
I want peace and believe that it will come in the end because peace is vital for the continuation of life...

During 8th Grade, in 1994, after the Peace Agreement with Jordan was signed, Bat-Chen decided to write a paper for school entitled, "War and Peace in my Family". She interviewed her maternal grandmother, who was invited by Prime Minister Yitzchak Rabin to attend the Peace Agreement Ceremony because she was born in Rabat Amon, Jordan. She also interviewed her father and emphasized details about the heroic battle which he led during the Yom Kippur War. She succeeded in capturing a vivid description of the times:

A Summary of War and Peace
There is not much left to say; We're in a halfway spot.
There isn't real peace in the Middle East,
Nor is there real war.
And for us, we're marching forward towards peace
Ready to understand the others; prepared to make changes
With one clear goal – to be rid of the hatred buried deep inside us for so long
And with the understanding that it's easy to make enemies
But that the wiser thing is to make friends.
We come as a people who know a lot about war but very little about peace.
From now on we'll begin to change that.

"... even though we have lost our precious daughter as a result of the Israeli-Palestinian conflict, we still believe in peace..."

That same year, Bat-Chen decided to participate in a pen-pal project with teenagers from the Israel-Arab village, Kafer Kassem. We found in one of her notebooks a draft letter to one of her friends:

Hello Nida. My hobbies include reading, writing, watching TV and horse-back riding. I was happy to receive your letter and sorry for sending this late. I look forward to our meeting. My birthday is on March 19. I support the peace process. I hate mathematics. I live in Tel-Mond.

When Bat-Chen was in 9th grade, on 4 November 1995, Prime Minister Rabin was assassinated. A week later, she wrote to his widow, Leah Rabin:

Three shots and it's all over –
Now one talks about him in the past tense.
Suddenly, the present becomes the past,

Questions

1. How would you suggest spreading Bat-Chen's message for peace and tolerance in your own community?

2. How would you encourage young people to begin keeping a diary and to help them realize and understand the advantages of doing so? As Bat-Chen wrote, "For me, writing is a wonderful thing."

3. Can you envision ways to make Jerusalem a true "City of Peace" for all people and religions?

And the past is only a memory.
We are standing, crying,
We want to believe it never happened,
That it is all a nightmare,
And when we wake up the next morning – it will not be so.
Instead, we wake up to a warped reality,
Where pain is laced with hate.
We cannot digest the enormity of this loss,
And we cannot comprehend its severity.
How can we understand such a tragedy,
In a civilization and not in the jungle?
Each one of us holds an opinion,
Yet, we do not have to agree.
We cannot turn the clock back,
But we can stop for today and remember...
It is like that first fallen domino,
That provokes a chain reaction.
We were beheaded, in every sense of the word,
And now it all crumbles.
As though he were the head, and we the body,
And when the head does not exist – the body dies!
It is impossible to build with parts that do not fit,
It is impossible to build with mismatched bricks.
It is an art to build a straight tower,
But a single kick can shatter it all.
And then,
Once can destroy a State!
I think we are all guilty for not showing how much we loved him...
... Maybe I am too naïve.
But I cannot understand,
How people take the law into their own hands!
How can we take the best gift ever given –
Life.
We are all one.
We share the same fate,
Old and young,
We stand grasping each other
And we cry...

In 1997, the Association for the Commemoration of Bat-Chen Shahak was established by Bat-Chen's parents, Ayelet and Tzvika. Its mission is based on Bat-Chen's legacy: to encourage literacy and to strengthen co-existence with our neighbours. The activities of the Association have grown and developed and include all age groups and cultural groups, as well as people from different religions. The Association organizes and facilitates learning seminars on diary-writing as a genre, writing competitions and workshops, support groups, meetings with wounded Palestinian children and families in Israeli hospitals, encounter groups with Jewish Israeli women and Arab Israeli women, along with meetings and presentations in the USA, England, Uzbekistan, Germany and Italy. The Association works closely with its Palestinian counterpart, Al Tariq. The activities have blossomed in response to current events, such as the recent hostilities in Gaza.

We are proud to say that the *Bat-Chen Diaries* have been published in Hebrew, English, Arabic, Dutch, Italian, German and Japanese.

In closing, even though we have lost our precious daughter as a result of the Israeli-Palestinian conflict, we still believe in peace and strive to actualize Bat-Chen's legacy through dialogue and building bridges to peace, understanding and co-existence.

For Further Reading

Bat-Chen Shahak, *The Bat-Chen Diaries*. Kar-Ben: Minneapolis, Minnesota, 2008.

David N. Myers. *Between Jew and Arab: The Lost Voice of Simon Rawidowicz.* Brandeis University Press, 2009.

Parents Circle – Families Forum: http://www.theparentscircle.com/

Ayelet Shahak, the mother of Bat-Chen, is a teacher and was born in Jerusalem. She and her husband, Tzvika, have made it their mission to pursue their daughter's hopes for peace. Mrs Shahak, along with her Palestinian partners, lectures in schools throughout Israel and in the West Bank.

Yousef Sahoury

invites Benedict XVI to Muqeibleh in Israel, to see the Catholic church built through the support of Jews, Muslims and Christians.

"... in our village of Muqeibleh, [we] have developed ways to coexist in mutual respect and admiration with Muslims and Jews, by searching for the common things between us and developing them so as to make them a light towards hope and a peaceful common life."

With heartfelt greeting, we welcome you, Your Holiness Pope Benedict XVI, the successor of St Peter and Vicar of Christ, to this land of peace, the birthplace of Jesus Christ.

Each man gets a share of his name. Your name in Arabic, "Benedict", means "Blessed". You are blessed; your steps are blessed, so is your visit to our land, our homes, our hearts and souls. We have been raised with the love of Jesus Christ who sacrificed Himself on the cross for the world, and through his death and resurrection, we shall be raised from the dead by the Saviour of humanity.

Your Holiness, you will arrive in the Holy Land, a land that was blessed and consecrated by all the prophets and apostles who have made it a land of love and brotherhood, the centre of the whole universe and the centre of humanity. I, Yousef Sahoury, am honoured to write this letter to Your Holiness because your arrival here in our midst will be such a historical day, for me and all Catholics, but also for the country and its inhabitants.

My family and I live in a village called Muqeibleh. It is located in the Ben Amer pasture in the State of Israel. It is a small village with a population of 3,500, among whom live 120 Christians. While we are small in number, make no mistake. Each one of us carries with us in our hearts and mind the message of Jesus Christ. Each one of us is a messenger of love among those who quarrel, and a messenger of justice among those in conflict with each other. Each one of us is the light that Jesus illuminates through the darkness of life with its many obstacles. We, modestly, consider ourselves the "protectors of the land" and we raise with our hands the cross of Jesus Christ. We watch over others in order to be effective "protectors" of this land.

Your Holiness, we, the "protectors of the land", live in peace and harmony with all others, despite all the tough circumstances and hardships that are imposed upon us. Gathered in this part of the world are the religions which believe in the One Eternal God, the Creator of the universe. Despite the minor differences among these religions, we, the "protectors of the land" in our village of Muqeibleh, have developed ways to coexist in mutual respect and admiration with Muslims and Jews, by searching for the common things between us and developing them so as to make them a light towards hope and a peaceful common life.

A few years ago, we were able to establish and build a beautiful Catholic church in our village. Our church has become a refuge for worshippers and a place of prayer. I want to tell you, and emphasize to you, that our church was built with the help of everyone – Jews, Muslims and Christians. The Regional Council gave us the land and supported us financially and morally. They offered us all the necessary facilities to help us achieve the noble goal of our project. We gratefully remember the generous helping hand extended to us by all our fellow citizens in the village. They did not hesitate to offer all the help we needed to build this beautiful church which has became the pride of all, Jews, Muslims and Christians alike.

In Israel, it is a well known fact that there is religious freedom among its citizens. We do not feel that either our Muslim or Jewish brothers prevent us from practising our religious traditions or stand in our way as Catholics. On the contrary, they offer every assistance we might need, just as they did during the building of the Transfiguration Church in our beloved village, Muqeibleh.

Your Holiness, the day our beautiful Church of the Transfiguration was dedicated was a marvellous sight. Those who attended and were in the audience included followers of all religions, Jews, Muslims and Christians. That celebration was like a festival of love, brotherhood and mutual respect among all three religions. This close relationship is not just related to events like a church dedication. On the contrary, it is a daily practice for us.

We Christians, Jews and Muslims are destined to live with each other. We are aware of, and we respect, the feelings of all our brothers and sisters of whatever religious tradition on their religious holidays. For example, on Yom Kippur, the Jews fast and refrain from every type of physical activity, including driving vehicles. In a show of respect to our Jewish brothers and sisters, we, too, refrain from travelling. Likewise, when our Muslim brothers and sisters fast during the month of Ramadan, all the Christians in our village of Muqeibleh refrain from eating or drinking in public places, as do the students in our schools. Also, on the Islamic holidays, we make mutual visits to offer greetings to each other, and on other religious occasions as well. At Christmas, Your Holiness, everyone is dressed in red. Streets and public places are filled with Christmas decorations, which makes it feel like it is a holiday for everyone. On New Year's Eve, parties are held everywhere. This symbolizes the intimate relations and brotherhood among the inhabitants of our village.

Questions

1. How has being Jewish/Christian/Muslim shaped your own attitude toward "serving God" in all aspects of your life?

2. What does your faith say about welcoming the stranger and attending to the needs of others?

3. How has being Jewish/Christian/Muslim shaped your own attitude toward the treatment of the hungry, the homeless, the poor, the sick or the imprisoned?

These are only some of the common examples of our living together. There are also other examples I could tell you about from our daily life at work, at school, in the office and so on.

Our main role as the "protectors of this land" is to be close to everyone, for it is Our Lord Jesus who taught us that love is the foundation of everything. We do not just talk about love; we also try to live our lives in love, by following in the footsteps and teachings of Our Lord Jesus.

Your Holiness, allow me, last but not least, to invite you to visit our humble village so you can bless us and all the houses in our village, and where you could see for yourself that this village of Muqeibleh is a model of good relations, mutual respect, harmony and coexistence. Perhaps our village could become a global symbol from which peace among the religions might emerge.

Dear Pope Benedict XVI, I wish you a long, healthy life so you can be a symbol of love and the light from whom we can derive the strength and inspiration to stay as the "protectors of this land," in the spirit of Jesus Christ, who loved all people and accepted all people. You are the Vicar of Christ on this earth, and so I promise we shall pray for you. We would be so happy to welcome you to our village of Muqeibleh, where we try to live together in peace and mutual respect with all our neighbours, Christian, Jewish and Muslim.

For Further Reading

Lawrence Boadt, CSP., and Kevin di Camillo, eds. *John Paul II: In the Holy Land: In His Own Words*. New York: Paulist Press, 2005.

Hans Kung. *Global Responsibility: In Search of a New World Ethic*. New York: Crossroad, 1991.

Pope Benedict XVI. *Christ Our Hope*. New York: Paulist Press, 2008.

Yousef Sahoury is an accountant by profession. He and his wife, who is a teacher in the village school, are the parents of four beautiful children. They live in Muqeibleh village, which is near Nazareth, in the Galilee in the north of Israel. Yousef and his family are part of the small Christian community in the village, where they live peaceably with Muslims and Jews. They are active members of the Catholic Church of the Transfiguration in the village.

Jerusalem is a city of many traditions. The Pope's visit to Israel provides a significant opportunity to forge a shared future – if that opportunity can be taken.

Suggestions

John K. Roth

calls for bold steps and a papal encyclical on the Church, Jews, Judaism and the Holocaust.

January 2009 events immensely complicated your plans to visit Israel the following May. My comments about those events and plans come from a particular perspective, for I am an American Protestant Christian, a philosopher, and a professor whose career has been devoted to Holocaust and genocide studies and to Christian-Jewish relations. Although our identities are different, we have much in common. Both of us are Christians, philosophers and persons who care deeply about the Holocaust and its reverberations for Christianity and Christian-Jewish relations in particular. We also share high expectations and hopes for the papal office and for the person who occupies it.

You feel profoundly the multiple and frequently conflicting responsibilities that your office confers upon you. I want you to do so, for even though I am not a Roman Catholic, I recognize that no Christian is more visible, more emblematic of the Christian tradition, than the person who is the pope at any given time. I want the pope to be the best Christian, the truest follower of Jesus that he can possibly be, because the world's judgment of Christianity hinges importantly on the pope's words, deeds and accountability.

"I want the pope to be the best Christian, the truest follower of Jesus that he can possibly be, because the world's judgment of Christianity hinges importantly on the pope's words, deeds and accountability."

As you know better than anyone, papal responsibility is never abstract or general, but always accepted or evaded in particular times, ways and places. In 2009, but by no means only then, papal credibility has much to do with Christian-Jewish relations. For centuries, and largely owing to Christian hostility toward Jews, those relationships have often been poisonous and lethal, so much so that absent Christianity the Holocaust would not have happened. Christianity alone did not cause the Holocaust, but it was a necessary condition for it. We Christians should always be mindful of that grim reality; we should be more aware than we usually are regarding the implications of the Holocaust for our tradition, which brings me back to the papacy, to you especially, and to events and plans in 2009.

27 January, the anniversary of the liberation of Auschwitz-Birkenau, one of the *Shoah's* epicentres, has become an international day of Holocaust remembrance. A few days before that date in 2009, perhaps without fully realizing what was being done and surely not anticipating what would follow, you lifted the excommunication of four bishops from the ultra-conservative Society of St Pius X. Apparently, that action's purpose was to open paths for reconciliation that would heal schism, a dreaded reality in Roman Catholicism. This fraught step took place during your Church's Week of Prayer for Christian Unity. Jesuit Father Federico Lombardi, director of the Vatican press office, was only one of those who hailed the move, calling it "great news that we expect to be a source of joy for the whole Church."[1] The cunning of history, however, produced irony much more than joy for the Roman Catholic Church, the Jewish community and many others as well.

"A global firestorm ensued as soon as it became clear that one of the rehabilitated bishops, Richard Williamson, is a Holocaust denier, and that you, a German, had presided over that rehabilitation."

A global firestorm ensued as soon as it became clear that one of the rehabilitated bishops, Richard Williamson, is a Holocaust denier, and that you, a German, had presided over that rehabilitation. By the time of this writing in mid-February 2009, so much outrage has been expressed about him, so many critical articles written about the Vatican's miscalculation and misstep, that one wonders what could be left to say in those veins. As stock is being taken, within the Vatican and without, as to how and why such action occurred, the probe needs to go beyond Williamson's specific case. The status of the problematic Society of St Pius X requires stern appraisal, for the Society has an ongoing record of hostility toward Jews and Judaism and the Vatican II reforms of Roman Catholicism as well.[2] Unless the Society reforms itself to such an extent that it could scarcely be said to exist any longer in its present form, unity with such persons and perspectives is not worth the price that Roman Catholics and Christians everywhere will pay for it.

Not for the first time in your reign, but with a special intensity brought on by the Williamson debacle, damage control has been necessary, particularly with regard to Christian-Jewish relations. Some of the damage control took place during your 12 February meeting at the Vatican with delegates from the Conference of Presidents of Major American Jewish Organizations. On that occasion, you insisted that, as far as the Holocaust is concerned, "It is beyond question that any denial or minimization of this terrible crime is intolerable and altogether unacceptable." You also reaffirmed that "the Church is profoundly and irrevocably committed to reject all anti-Semitism, and to continue to build good and lasting relations between our two communities."[3]

Working to control damage is anything but an optimal position for you, the Roman Catholic Church and Christianity generally to occupy as post-Holocaust Christian-Jewish relations develop. You should identify and take proactive steps that will confirm what ought to be the case: namely, that the pope is the primary Christian leader, or at least second to none, when it comes to improving Christian-Jewish relations. Therefore, wanting this open letter to be positive and constructive, I suggest good steps that you could take to move beyond damage control, especially as your trip to Israel approaches. Not all of these proposals originate with me. Others have urged some of them before. Unbeknownst to me, you may have deliberated about them and, in at least some cases, acted upon them, too. If so, more power to you. Meanwhile, for the sake of brevity, I put my recommendations in bullet points, urging them as follows:

- **Take a bold step: Issue a papal encyclical on The Church, Jews, Judaism and the Holocaust.** Written properly, which is to say forcefully and unapologetically, such an encyclical could deal, among many things, with nagging problems that compromise the clarity and credibility of previous Roman Catholic pronouncements on these subjects. The Church's *We Remember: A Reflection on the Shoah* broke some new ground when it appeared in 1998. More than ten years on, however, its language is increasingly problematic, evasive and historically inaccurate. The document, for example, lamented unspecified "errors and failures" of unnamed "sons and daughters of the Church," but this language was vague then and is even more so in 2009. Arguably the Church itself – the Church as such – failed during the Holocaust. To avoid saying so is to resort to theological mystification that obscures historical reality. Furthermore, *We Remember* takes a problematic position with respect to the wartime pope, Pius XII, crediting him far more than he deserves for resistance against Nazism and rescue of Jews during the Holocaust. Still further, *We Remember* maintains an overly sharp distinction between racial antisemitism and anti-Judaism, which puts Christianity in a better light than we Christians should allow. Racial antisemitism was a necessary and decisive condition for the Holocaust, but such antisemitism would have been neither intelligible nor persuasive absent the centuries of Christian hostility toward Jews – not just Judaism – that paved the way for Nazism's antisemitic ideology and the genocidal policies that eventually flowed from it. The encyclical you should issue, which would have special importance and impact because of your German heritage, ought to reflect the best historical scholarship, take an unapologetic stance about the Church's responsibility for the Holocaust and its less than Christ-like response to that catastrophe, and then reiterate and advance a contrite and healing Christian stance toward the Jewish people. An encyclical of this kind would not please the Society of St Pius X, but it would be very much welcomed by an overwhelming number of Christians and Jews everywhere.

"Your leadership is crucial in helping to find the way forward, which I believe should emphasize a two-state solution that strives to ensure security and a just peace for Israelis and Palestinians."

Questions

1. What are the most important implications of the Holocaust for the Christian tradition?

2. In 2009 and beyond, how should Christians respond to the Holocaust and its reverberations?

3. In post-Holocaust Christianity, what should be done with statements from scripture or Church teaching that regard salvation as coming uniquely, exclusively, universally, and absolutely through Jesus Christ?

- **Take a courageous step: State publicly that Pope Pius XII is unworthy of sainthood.** This step is needed because, no matter how many miracles may be attributed to Pius XII, his papacy is so fraught with Holocaust-related ambiguity that the proclamation of his sainthood will always be a stumbling block in Christian-Jewish relations. Christianity can never get beyond damage control where Pius XII is concerned. That problem pertains not only to ambiguities surrounding his wartime papacy, but also to his posture about the Holocaust and the Jewish people in the aftermath of World War II.[4] Every Jew and countless Christians, including most Roman Catholics, would breathe a huge sigh of relief if plans to canonize Pius XII were dropped and laid to rest forever. No immediate step that you could take to put the papacy beyond damage control in Christian-Jewish relations would likely be more successful than one that moves in this direction.

- **Take a step of solidarity: Confer special recognition on Roman Catholic priests and nuns who have used their scholarship and teaching to advance Christian-Jewish understanding.** In the American context, priest-scholars such as John T. Pawlikowski and Kevin P. Spicer and women such as Mary C. Boys and Carol A. Rittner are but four examples of those in Roman Catholic religious vocations who have devoted their lives to scholarship and teaching that improve Christian-Jewish relationships. They do this work as faithful historians and theologians. Their efforts require criticism of Christianity and the Roman Catholic Church, but their judgment is constructive, serving the good reputation of both while finding a warm reception within the Jewish community. Another superb example is provided by the French Catholic priest Patrick Desbois. His mission has been to help us – Christians, Jews and more – to remember the humanity of more than 1.5 million Jews who were shot to death at hundreds of extermination sites in eastern Europe during the Holocaust. They were murdered by Germans and their collaborators – baptized Christians undoubtedly and overwhelmingly among them – and then left to rot in unmarked mass graves that scar the earth in Ukraine, Belarus and Russia long after the Holocaust. By interviewing hundreds of witnesses who saw the killing and the dead, Desbois says that he seeks "to establish the truth and justice".[5] Desbois is a Catholic hero in many Jewish circles. He also deserves that status among his fellow Christians. Many ways to recognize and honour such dedicated Roman Catholic teacher-scholars – your own – are available to you as pope. Recognition and honour should be used constructively in ways that make clear to all your intention to advance and embrace the best scholarship about the history of Christianity and the Holocaust, and about the after-effects of that history as well.

These three steps, I believe, would take you, the Roman Catholic Church, and all of Christianity at least some distance beyond damage control where the Holocaust and Christian-Jewish relations are concerned. They would not do so completely, however, because the task of reconciliation between Christians and Jews will still be far from finished, remaining fraught and difficult. Although the situation is too complicated for elaboration here, the Palestinian-Israeli conflict looms large on the Christian-Jewish agenda that lies ahead. Your leadership is crucial in helping to find the way forward, which I believe should emphasize a two-state solution that strives to ensure security and a just peace for Israelis and Palestinians.[6]

I close this open letter by referring to one step more that should be taken for the sake of good Christian-Jewish relations. Unfortunately, I believe that your understanding of papal responsibilities precludes you from taking it, but one day, perhaps, a successor of yours will do so. This step would completely and forever renounce supercessionism, the position that Christianity eclipses Judaism. One of the surest ways toward such a renunciation, perhaps the most thoroughgoing way of all, involves your affirming that Judaism provides a fully valid and truthful path to God, one that does not require Christian mediation or conversion in any way whatsoever. By no means does such a position entail relativism, an outlook that both you and I abhor. It does reject the claim that ultimately Truth belongs to one tradition alone. That claim, which has often characterized Christianity, is at the core of religion's ethical failures. Christianity and every other religion should be done with it. Religious pluralism should be embraced instead. If you understood Christian-Jewish relations to require steps in that direction and acted on them, you would move a long way toward having my vote for sainthood.

Travel safely when you go to Israel this spring. May your journey be a blessing. If you take into prayful consideration at least some of the steps I have proposed, I believe that the chances for that outcome will be enhanced.

For Further Reading

Gregory Baum, ed. *The Twentieth Century: A Theological Overview.* Maryknoll: Orbis Books, 1999.

Alan L. Berger and David Patterson, with David P. Gushee, John T. Pawlikowski, and John K. Roth. *Jewish-Christian Dialogue: Drawing Honey from the Rock.* St. Paul, MN: Paragon House, 2008.

Stephen R. Haynes. *Reluctant Witnesses: Jews and the Christian Imagination.* Louisville, KY: Westminster John Knox Press, 1995.

Notes

1. Lombardi's comments are available online at: http://www.zenit.org/article-24903?I=english. Search for the article titled, "Lefebvre Group Step Hailed as Unity Week Success," which is dated 25 January 2009. This site also contains a link to the full text of the document that lifted the schismatic bishops' excommunication.
2. See, for example, the documentation provided on the Internet by the Anti-Defamation League: http://www.adl.org/main_Interfaith/Society_Saint_Pius_X.htm.
3. The quotation is from a Jewish Telegraph Agency (JTA) report, dated 12 February 2009, "Pope confirms Israel visit," which is available online at: http://jta.org/news/article-print/2009/02/12/1002962/pope-confirms.

4. On these points, two books by Michael Phayer are significant. See *The Catholic Church and the Holocaust, 1930-1965* (Bloomington: Indiana University Press, 2000) and *Pius XII, the Holocaust, and the Cold War* (Bloomington: Indiana University Press, 2008). See also Carol Rittner and John K. Roth, eds., *Pope Pius XII and the Holocaust* (New York: Continuum, 2002).
5. See Maria Danilova and Randy Herschaft, "Ukraine Slaughter Was Opening Salvo of Nazis' Final Solution," *Seattle Times*, 1 February 2009, A10. Desbois' quotation is taken from their Associated Press article. Desbois has written an important book about his experience and research in eastern Europe. See Patrick Desbois, *The Holocaust by Bullets: A Priest's Journey to Uncover the Truth behind the Murder of 1.5 Million Jews* (New York: Palgrave Macmillan, 2008). For an Internet exhibit about Desbois and his findings, see http://www.memorialdelashoah.org/upload/minisites/ukraine/en/en_index.htm. Desbois heads Yahad – In Unum ("Yahad" and "In Unum" both meaning "together" in Hebrew and Latin), an association of Catholics and Jews – founded in January 2004 – that seeks increased knowledge and cooperation between their traditions. Its website is www.yahadinunum.org/index.en.html. The importance and value of the reconciliation that Desbois fosters far exceeds the worth of the Vatican's initial, misplaced gestures of unity regarding Richard Williamson and the Society of St Pius X.
6. On these issues and themes, see Leonard Grob and John K. Roth, eds., *Anguished Hope: Holocaust Scholars Confront the Palestinian-Israeli Conflict* (Grand Rapids, MI: Eerdmans Publishing Company, 2008).

John K. Roth is the Edward J. Sexton Professor Emeritus of Philosophy and the Founding Director of the Center for the Study of the Holocaust, Genocide, and Human Rights at Claremont McKenna College USA. In addition to service on the United States Holocaust Memorial Council and on the editorial board for *Holocaust and Genocide Studies*, he has published hundreds of articles and reviews and authored, co-authored, or edited more than 40 books, including *Approaches to Auschwitz: The Holocaust and Its Legacy; "Good News" after Auschwitz? Christian Faith within a Post-Holocaust World;* and *Ethics During and After the Holocaust: In the Shadow of Birkenau.*

Marcus Braybrooke

states there is 'no future without forgiveness' and calls for a culture of peace.

At the World Day of Prayer at Assisi in 1986, which my wife Mary and I were privileged to attend on behalf of the World Congress of Faiths, Pope John Paul II, who had asked leaders of the world religions to join him in prayer for peace, said that they were called to be "the moral conscience of humanity".

Well beyond the membership of the Catholic Church, many people look to you above all to speak for that moral conscience, as indeed you do. Sadly, that voice is often not heard or ignored. I ask you as a matter of urgency to reflect on how leaders of the world religions can be seen more clearly to stand together on moral issues, and on how that voice may be heard more loudly.

"Yad Vashem is not only a place of remembrance, but also of warning."

Yad Vashem is not only a place of remembrance, but also of warning. Rabbi Hugo Gryn, a survivor of the concentration camps, said of Auschwitz, "the question was not where was God, but where was humanity?" – a question we continue to ask as subsequent acts of genocide are perpetrated.[1]

The world, I believe, needs to hear repeatedly and clearly the moral principles enshrined in all the great religious traditions. An important attempt to enunciate these principles, as you know, was made in the "Declaration Toward a Global Ethic" signed by many religious leaders at the 1993 Parliament of World Religions in Chicago. Based on the fundamental demand that every human being must be treated humanely, the Declaration affirms four "Irrevocable Directives":

1. Commitment to a culture of non-violence and respect for life.
2. Commitment to a culture of solidarity and a just economic order.
3. Commitment to a culture of tolerance and a life of truthfulness.
4. Commitment to a culture of equal rights and partnership between men and women.

Questions

1. To what extent do you think religions agree on ethical principles and moral teaching?

2. Do you blame God or humanity for the Holocaust?

3. What are the various faith communities where you live doing together for society? What more could they do?

4. Do you agree that the doctrine of a just war is obsolete?

5. What can you do to contribute to a culture of peace?

The need now is for religious leaders to encourage members of their faith, who have the necessary expertise, to work together on the detailed application of these principles. Much work, of course, is being done together by people of many faiths in the relief of suffering, campaigning for human rights and protecting the environment.

Again, this work is too little known, even to the faithful. Also it seems piecemeal. We need an overall vision of the steps required to create a culture of peace.

This, I suggest, requires a clear rejection of the use of violence.[2] Traditional teaching about a "just war" – or its equivalent in other faith traditions – is obsolete. Indeed at the Millennium World Peace Summit, religious leaders committed themselves "to manage and resolve non-violently the conflicts generated by religious and ethnic differences, and to condemn all violence committed in the name of religion while seeking to remove the roots of violence". The use of violence in international disputes should be condemned per se. The authority of international law and of the United Nations needs to be affirmed. As the Dalai Lama has said, a global police force is necessary "to protect against the appropriation of power by violent means".[3] I personally wish the response to 9/11 had been seen as police action against criminals rather than as a war against terror.

Nations, however, will only choose the way of non-violence if their citizens reject violence. As the Mayan spiritual leader Abraham Garcia, who was tortured in the civil war in Guatemala, said, "Peace isn't the simple silencing of the bullets. It must be an inner change toward other people, respect for the way they think and live." Peace flows from loving our neighbour as ourself – the Golden Rule taught by every religion.

The formative influence of the home – especially in early years – is of vital importance. Children, besides essential physical care and provision, need to be treated with respect and they are affected by conflict between their parents. Sometimes there is violence in the home, and all too often violence on television or in computer games.

Peace requires justice – not least economic justice. There is real fear that the Millennium Development Goals will not be met. A danger of the current economic crisis is that richer nations, in seeking to preserve their standard of living, will be even less willing to help poorer nations. Religious leaders will, I hope, continue to plead for those who are hungry or refugees.

A Culture of Peace extends beyond human relationships to our care for animal life and the natural world. Religious leaders need to help people to see that reducing our carbon footprint is not enough. We need a new reverence for nature and respect for God's creation.

Perhaps the greatest contribution to a culture of peace that religions can make is helping people learn how to forgive and how to heal past injuries. The creation of the European Community after two world wars or the emergence of a new South Africa are signs of hope. Healing the past demands honesty in admitting the evil that has been perpetrated and genuine repentance. Asking forgiveness and granting it both require courage. Yet, in the words of Archbishop Desmond Tutu, "there is no future without forgiveness." The new relationship between Jews and Christians has required contrition and a commitment to change on the part of Christians, and has been met by generosity of spirit by many Jews. Yad Vashem is a reminder of terrible human evil, but the fact that Jews and Christians and members of other faiths gather there to remember those who were killed offers us hope that together we can create a culture of peace, so that the earthly Jerusalem becomes one day the new Jerusalem of which prophets and seers have spoken.

I hope, your Holiness, that as you mourn those who were murdered, you will be also inspired to call upon the leaders of the world religions to renew their efforts to create a culture of peace and to ensure that together you speak for the conscience of humankind.

I join you in praying for the peace of Jerusalem and for peace on earth and goodwill among all people.

Notes

1. Hugo Gryn, *Chasing Shadows* (Viking, 2000), p. 251.
2. "Commitment to Global Peace," A Statement of the Millennium World Peace Summit of Religious and Spiritual Leaders, held at the UN in New York in August 2000.
3. HH The Dalai Lama, *Ethics for the New Millennium* (Riverhead Books, New York, 1999), p. 207 and p. 212.

For Further Reading

Marcus Braybrooke. *A Heart for the World, the Interfaith Alternative*. Winchester, O-books, John Hunt, 2005.

Paul Knitter. *One Earth, Many Religions, Multifaith Dialogue and Global Responsibility*. New York, Orbis 1995.

Hans Küng, ed. *Yes to a Global Ethic*. London, SCM Press, 1996.

Dalai Lama. *Ancient Wisdom, Modern World, Ethics for a New Millennium*. London, Little, Brown and Co, 1999.

Jonathan Sacks. *To Heal A Fractured World, The Ethics of Responsibility*. London, Continuum, 2005.

Marcus Braybrooke a retired Anglican priest, is President of the World Congress of Faiths, Co-Founder of the Three Faiths Forum, a Peace Councillor and former Director of the Council of Christians and Jews.

Peta Goldburg

calls for education on Judaism and catechesis of the Shoah in all Catholic schools and higher learning institutions.

"To teach religious education in Catholic schools effectively, we must address the content and meaning of Nostra Aetate, *as well as the subsequent documents such as the* Guidelines *and the* Notes."

The teachings of *Nostra Aetate*, the *Declaration on the Relation of the Church to Non-Christian Religions (1964)* and the subsequent *Guidelines and Suggestions for Implementing the Conciliar Declaration Nostra Aetate* (1974) and *Notes on the Correct Way to Present the Jews and Judaism in Preaching and Catechesis in the Roman Catholic Church (1985)* should be implemented by all teachers of religious education. Unfortunately, this is not the case as many teachers in both secondary and tertiary institutions, far from implementing these documents, are not even familiar with their content.

At an official level, the Catholic Church's changing attitudes to the Jews were formally shaped with the declaration *Nostra Aetate* (1965), which not only highlighted Christianity's Jewish roots but also the rich spiritual heritage shared by both Jews and Christians. While *Nostra Aetate* acknowledged the Church's gratitude to Judaism for her beginnings, it also stated that the Church cannot "forget that she draws sustenance from the root of that good olive tree".[1]

Ten years after the promulgation of *Nostra Aetate*, the *Guidelines* (Vatican Commission for Religious Relations with the Jews, 1974), were released. The intent of the *Guidelines* was to provide ideas for how to start a dialogue with Judaism at the local level. Its four sections dealt with the nature of dialogue, Christian liturgy, education and social action. The Preamble to the *Guidelines* stated that *Nostra Aetate* emanated as a response to the persecution and massacre of Jews during the Second World War.

The *Guidelines* offer a positive definition of dialogue which is far from the proselytising motivations of previous centuries and calls for a "great openness of spirit and diffidence with respect to one's own prejudices". The section on Liturgy begins to address one of the major problems of contemporary Christian theology, the liturgical selection of readings from scripture. Firstly, the *Guidelines* state that there is much in the Hebrew Scriptures that "retains its own perpetual value [which] has not been cancelled by the later interpretation of the New Testament". Catholics are cautioned not to juxtapose the Hebrew Scriptures with the Christian Scriptures so as to make the Hebrew Scriptures appear a religion of legalism and punishment, and then present the Christian Scriptures as documents which emphasise love of God and one's neighbour. Preachers are advised to emphasise the continuity of faith with that of the earlier covenant and to take care that homilies based on readings do not distort their meaning and do not portray Jewish people in an unfavourable way. Similarly, *Prayers of the Faithful* and commentaries should reflect this positive view.

The section on Teaching and Education stated that "a great deal of work [needs] to be done" and called on Catholics to learn about the essential traits of how Jews define themselves in light of their own religious experience. The *Guidelines* also strongly encouraged Catholic education structures, such as universities and colleges, to establish Chairs in Jewish studies. Only a few Catholic institutions have heeded the advice to appoint professors of Jewish studies or established collaboration with Jewish scholars. While the *Guidelines* acknowledge that there has been some excellent research by scholars, little of this research has impacted on seminaries and institutes of teacher education and on the everyday life of the Church. The trickle-down effect with regard to changing material on Judaism in "catechisms and religious textbooks" has been minimal. Many writers of such texts appear scarcely aware of *Nostra Aetate* and the subsequent documents. Education could play a role in fostering collaborative projects for justice and peace by Jews and Christians, as suggested by Section IV of the *Guidelines*, as this has had little uptake to date.

The *Guidelines* were not intended to be the 'end' but they were nevertheless meant to 'initiate' a process of honest and fruitful dialogue which acknowledged the strong and significant relationship between Judaism and Christianity. Unfortunately, the process has had narrow application.

The *Notes* (Vatican Commission for Religious Relations with the Jews, 1985) developed the themes of *Nostra Aetate* and the *Guidelines* much further in that they raised the question of education about the *Shoah*, the need for Christians to understand Jewish attitudes towards the land of Israel, and the significance of the State of Israel to Jews.

In the *Notes*, the Vatican Commission mandates the development of a catechesis of the *Shoah*. In this spirit, Pope John Paul II, in his address to the Jewish community of Warsaw in 1987, said that the Church's mission was to listen, to affirm and to unite its voice to that of the Jews. The importance of education to address the danger of antisemitism and to stress the unique bond between the Church and Judaism is highlighted:

> The question is not merely to uproot from among the faithful the remains of anti-Semitism still to be found here and there, but

Questions

1. How might a catechesis of the *Shoah* inform, form and transform people's understanding of Jews and Judaism?

2. How has Christianity's attitude to Judaism changed over time? How has Judaism responded to these changes?

3. How would you characterize Jewish-Christian relations today?

4. Given *Nostra Aetate*, the *Notes* and the *Guidelines*, what personal response can you make? What community response can we make?

much rather to arouse in them through education work, an exact knowledge of the holy and unique 'bond' which joins us as Church to the Jews and to Judaism.[2]

Not long after that, in *The Church and Racism* (1988), Pope John Paul II urged that there be further education to overcome and eradicate antisemitism, but much still remains to be done as new forms of antisemitism emerge.

To teach religious education in Catholic schools effectively, we must address the content and meaning of *Nostra Aetate*, as well as the subsequent documents such as the *Guidelines* and the *Notes*. Religious education in one's faith tradition not only provides the foundation for self-understanding as a member of that tradition, but it also shapes attitudes, either negative or positive, about the religious other. How teachers interpret the sacred narratives of Judaism and Christianity may result in negative portrayal of Jews. Therefore, a sound knowledge of Judaism is necessary if we are truly to understand Christianity.

It is now more than 40 years since the declaration of *Nostra Aetate* and it will soon be 25 years since the *Notes on the Correct Way to Present the Jews and Judaism in Preaching and Catechesis in the Roman Catholic Church* were published. If the next generation of Catholics is to be taught about Jews, Judaism and the *Shoah* and to work together for peace, as Cardinal Cassidy has suggested, then it is time for the Church to draw people's attention again to the significant relationship between Jews and Christians and to demand more forcefully that the calls for significant changes regarding Jews and Judaism be responded to by Catholic educational institutions.

Only a sound educational base will provide the ground for the sharing of beliefs and values. Given the history of Jewish-Christian relations and the journey travelled thus far, it is imperative that:

- all Institutes of Catholic Higher Education establish a position of Professor of Jewish Studies;
- compulsory study in the area of Judaism be mandated for all preachers and teachers;
- a catechesis of the *Shoah* be promoted in all Catholic schools and tertiary settings;
- Vatican-sponsored seminars on Jewish-Christian understanding be hosted internationally.

Notes

1. *Nostra Aetate*, #4.
2. *Notes*, section 1, #8.

For Further Reading

Cardinal E. I. Cassidy. *Ecumenism and Interreligious Dialogue*. New York: Paulist Press, 2005.

P. M. Goldburg & M. Ryan. "Jews and Judaism in Christian religious education, catechesis and liturgy." In M. Ryan, ed. *Jewish-Christian Relations: A textbook for Australian students*. Melbourne: David Lovell Publishing, 2004.

D. F. Sandmel, R. M. Catalano & C. M. Leighton. *Irreconcilable Differences? A learning resource for Jews and Christians*. Boulder: Westview Press, 2001.

Peta Goldburg, RSM, a Sister of Mercy from Australia, is Professor of Religious Education at Australian Catholic University. Her research interests include religion and the creative arts and innovative pedagogical practices for teaching world religions. Dr Goldburg's forthcoming publication is *Investigating Religion: Study of Religion for Queensland Schools*.

Patrick Henry

discusses extending interfaith dialogue and making peace the road to peace.

"... there will never be peace until there is peace among religions."

In our 21st-century world with its nuclear proliferation and long-raging generational conflicts, there will never be peace until there is peace among religions. For so long, organized religion has been such an enormous impediment to peace that it is difficult to imagine a peaceful future without a major worldwide religious contribution. No single religion will be able to make a significant impact on world peace in our century. Only a unified interfaith peace movement, including Christianity, Judaism, Buddhism, Islam and Hinduism will be able to do so. The writings of three interfaith peace activists of the 1960s, Thomas Merton, Abraham Joshua Heschel and Thich Nhat Hanh, give us the keys for the creation of an interfaith network of peacemaking for our time.

The absolutely essential foundation for interfaith peace is interfaith dialogue. There can be no understanding, no trust, no forgiveness, no reconciliation, no communion without communication. "The first real step toward peace," writes Merton, is "the recognition that the true solution to our problems is <u>not</u> accessible to any one isolated party or nation... all must arrive at it by working together."[1] In this respect, the most hopeful sign on the horizon is a very recent one: a proposal for dialogue and solidarity in the form of an 11 October 2007, 29-page letter addressed to Christian leaders in the world, entitled "A Common Word Between Us and You" and signed by 138 Muslim scholars and clerics from across the globe.[2] This is an invitation to work together for peace based on the belief that both Christianity and Islam "share the basic principles of worshiping one God and loving thy neighbor". Issued to mark the end of Ramadan, the letter quotes the Qur'an, the Christian Scriptures and the Torah. It represents a definite effort to demonstrate that Islam is a religion of peace and that moderate Muslims are willing to speak out against violence. The fact that the signatories represent all branches of Islam indicates that this is also an attempt to speak for Islam itself, which lacks one authoritative voice. "Without peace and justice between these two communities," the authors argue, communities that constitute 55% of the world's population, "there can be no meaningful peace in the world."

On 18 November 2007, roughly 300 Christian theologians and clerics signed their enthusiastic response to the Muslim initiative. Entitled "Loving God and Neighbor Together: A Christian Response to 'A Common Word Between Us and You,'" the document reaffirmed the common Christian-Muslim ground found in the two commandments of love.[3] In December 2007, you also responded favourably to the Islamic invitation to a Christian-Muslim dialogue. On 25 February 2008, the same Muslim clerics and scholars addressed the Jewish community in "A Call to Peace, Dialogue and Understanding Between Muslims and Jews."[4] Clearly an attempt to establish mutual respect and improve Jewish-Muslim relations, this call to peace, dialogue and understanding emphasized the commonalities between the two religions with their same father, Abraham, and called for an end to stereotypes and prejudices that dehumanize both Muslims and Jews. The wholeheartedly favourable Jewish response to the Muslim proposal, "Seek Peace and Pursue It," was issued on 3 March 2008 by the International Jewish Committee for Interreligious Consultations.[5]

"The absolutely essential foundation for interfaith peace is interfaith dialogue."

We must not underestimate the importance of a call for dialogue from the Muslim community. Just 40 years ago, the Second Vatican Council set out to redefine its relationship with Jewish people and that relationship has now been completely redefined. This spirit of renewal took place in the wake of the Holocaust. We have witnessed a series of formal apologies offered by various Christian Churches from different countries and one from the Vatican as well. These apologies express not only contrition for what happened in the past but deep commitment to the construction of a new Christianity totally devoid of anti-Judaism and to a future of Judeo-Christian reconciliation.[6] Just as remarkable is the fact that in the year 2000, more than 170 Jewish scholars representing all branches of Judaism issued a statement called *Dabru Emet* (Speak the Truth), which calls on Jewish people to relinquish their fears of Christianity and to acknowledge Church efforts since the Holocaust to amend Christian teaching about Judaism. Without negating the history of Christian anti-Judaism, the document explicitly states that "Nazism was not a Christian phenomenon... not an inevitable outcome of Christianity."[7]

Judeo-Christian reconciliation in the 20th century, which accomplished what must have been judged impossible only 20 years earlier, should be the model used to bring together all the major religions in the present century. Therefore, the Islamic invitation to dialogue and peace must be vigorously pursued, developed and expanded by all parties individually (Jewish-Muslim dialogue; Christian-Muslim dialogue) and collectively. This dialogue cannot simply remain at the level of clerics and scholars. It must also move into the communities of all relevant nations, where interfaith groups must be established in mosques, temples, churches and synagogues, for teaching, discussion and joint good works in peace and justice activities. In this regard, it is important to remember that by the mid-1960s, revolutionary teaching arrangements had been set up whereby Christian theologians and clergy taught in Jewish institutions and Jewish theologians and rabbis taught in Catholic and Protestant seminaries. These progressive strategies allowed members of each religion to teach their religion to those of another faith. This instilled true knowledge and trust and helped eradicate any remaining roots of prejudice from each religious culture. Similar innovations will be necessary today to ensure the accurate teaching of each faith and to establish mutual respect, trust and goodwill among people of all faiths.

"Religion is a means, not an end in itself."

The 1960s interfaith peace activists not only insisted on the importance of dialogue but of various principles without which true dialogue can never take place. From the Buddhist and Gandhian perspective, for example, as Nhat Hanh has explained, only when we have peace within ourselves is dialogue possible. It is inner peace that allows us to open up to others.[8] In order to bring together people of faith, people of faith must open themselves up to others at the level of faith. They must recognize that faith, love and understanding transcend dogma and unite all believers in deep, spiritual ways. The practice of detachment from one's doctrines enables us to receive the viewpoints of others and to hear them in a new and profound manner that opens original paths of mutual discovery. The fundamental principle of ecumenism, writes Rabbi Heschel, is that "God is greater than religion [and] faith is deeper than dogma."[9] We do not have to give up our ideas, only our attachment to them, so that an excessive attachment to dogma does not prevent us from receiving truths from outside our particular faith group, thereby undermining authentic interfaith communication.

Religion is a means, not an end in itself. As the title of Nhat Hahn and Daniel Berrigan's co-authored book makes clear, *The Raft Is Not the Shore*. We must not make a God of our religion, which is only a means of taking us to God. "To equate religion and God," Heschel reminds us, "is idolatry."[10] When we recognize that we are all united by our faith in God, we are able to perceive joyfully the holiness and validity of other religions. Rather than wanting to claim that our religion offers the only way to salvation, we begin to appreciate the richness of other faiths and our spiritual connections to them. We should understand the Roman Catholic Church's *Nostra Aetate* (1965) in this light, for it represents a virtual revolution in Christian thinking regarding the Jews. Among other things, it rejected the idea that the Jews were responsible for the death of Christ; it denounced all forms of antisemitism as

Questions

1. What are you doing today to spread the message of peace that is inherent to your religion?

2. Are you doing everything possible to counteract prejudice against people of other faiths within your community?

3. How can you interact meaningfully at a religious level with those of different faiths within your community?

affronts to the Gospels; it gave up all claims of supercessionism and recognized the Hebrew Bible as the living covenant between Yahweh and the Jewish People. What Catholic didn't feel a surge of hope and joy, what Jew didn't offer a great sigh of relief when, in April 1986, the great Pope John Paul II, the first pope to set foot in a synagogue, spoke in the Roman synagogue and addressed Rabbi Toaff as "my older brother?"

No one took on the interfaith challenge more directly, forcefully and creatively than Rabbi Heschel. Two fundamental ideas lie at the heart of his ecumenism: "No religion is an island" and "Holiness is not the monopoly of any particular religion or tradition."[11] Working together with Christians, teaching at Union Theological Seminary with Protestant and Catholic students in his classes, created new possibilities for insights and learning. Heschel celebrated this atmosphere of increasing mutual esteem between Christians and Jews and, with a remarkable generosity and originality, reached out and embraced Christianity. Strikingly, in his March 1966 "Interview at Notre Dame," he remarked: "A Jew, in his own way, should acknowledge the role of Christianity in God's plan for the redemption of all men... I recognize in Christianity the presence of holiness. I see it. I sense it. I feel it. You are not an embarrassment to us and we shouldn't be an embarrassment to you."[12] With the same interfaith fervour, 18 months earlier, Thomas Merton told Heschel that one of his "latent ambitions" was "to be a true Jew under my Catholic skin".[13] Finally, Nhat Hanh spoke often about the holiness of other religions and emphasized our ability to grow spiritually from our encounters with them: "We humans can be nourished by the best values of many traditions."[14]

"We humans can be nourished by the best values of many traditions."

Recognizing the holiness of other religions and our ability to be spiritually nourished and transformed by them means ending all attempts to convert others to our religion. There will never be peace among religions until people of all religions are treated with respect and reverence by people of all religions. To that end, we must be on the side of dialogue, understanding and communion and opposed to exclusivist concepts of salvation, denigration of other religions and attempts to convert others. Despite his embrace of Christianity, Rabbi Heschel spoke out forcefully when asked about the conversion of the Jews: "I'd rather go to Auschwitz than give up my religion," he asserted.[15] Heschel affirmed repeatedly that "religious pluralism is the will of God"[16] and objected to other religions being relegated to an inferior status: "Are the Jews and Mohammedans unable to pray or address themselves to God?"[17] he asks. Elsewhere, he answers his own question by citing Pope John XXIII's *Pacem in Terris*: "Every human being has the right to honor God according to the dictates of an upright conscience."[18] Nhat Hanh also opposes conversions and stresses that what we need is a rooted identity without separation from those in other traditions. We all have the capacity to become Buddhas in our own tradition. There is no need to convert to Buddhism. When asked, in a

1999 interview, if Merton became a Buddhist, Nhat Hanh replied: "He did not have to become a Buddhist, because he had Buddha-nature within himself. A good Christian always manifests the Buddha-nature, and a good Buddhist always manifests the love and compassion of Jesus."[19] Since our roots are important, a conversion could actually be dangerous. It is always safer to remain where we are rooted and to show reverence for all other religious traditions.

The writings of our Christian, Jewish and Buddhist peace activists all have the same message: we will have peace on earth when peace becomes the road to peace. Religions will be at peace with one another when the sanctity of the great religious traditions is mutually recognized and respected. This can only happen through a dialogue of equals which will lead to reconciliation, renewal, communion and a profound recognition that "Christianity, Islam [Judaism, Hinduism and Buddhism] are part of God's design for the redemption of all men," and that "God is either the father of all men or of no man."[20]

Notes

1. Thomas Merton, *New Seeds of Contemplation* (New York: New Directions Publishing Corporation, 1972), pp. 116-117.
2. "A Common Word Between Us and You" can be found at www.Acommonword.com.
3. "Loving God and Neighbor Together: A Christian Response to 'A Common Word Between Us and You,'" *New York Times*, 18 November 2007, "Week in Review," p. 4.
4. "A Call to Peace, Dialogue and Understanding Between Muslims and Jews" can found at www.mujca.com/muslimsandjews.htm.
5. "Seek Peace and Pursue It" can be found at www.wfn.org/2008/03/msg00012.html.
6. On Christian apologies to the Jews, see Patrick Henry, "The Art of Christian Apology: Comparing the French Catholic Church's Apology to the Jews and the Vatican's 'We Remember,'" *Shofar* 26 (Spring 2008): 87-104.
7. *Dabru Emet* appeared in its entirety in the *New York Times*, 10 September 2000, 23.
8. Thich Nhat Hanh, *Living Buddha, Living Christ* (New York: Riverhead Books, 1995), p. 10.
9. Abraham Joshua Heschel, "What Ecumenism Is," *Moral Grandeur and Spiritual Audacity* (New York: Farrar, Straus, Giroux, 1996), p. 287.
10. Abraham Joshua Heschel, "No Religion Is an Island," *Moral Grandeur and Spiritual Audacity*, p. 243.
11. Ibid., pp. 237; 247.
12. Abraham Joshua Heschel, "Interview at Notre Dame," *Moral Grandeur and Spiritual Audacity*, p. 387.
13. Thomas Merton, *The Hidden Ground of Love. Letters*, ed. William H. Shannon (New York: Farrar, Straus, Giroux, 1985), p. 434.
14. Thich Nhat Hanh, *Living Buddha, Living Christ*, p. 2. See too Thich Naht Hanh, Daniel Berrigan, *The Raft Is Not The Shore. Conversations Toward A Buddhist-Christian Awareness* (Maryknoll, NY: Orbis Books, 1975, 2001), p. 31.
15. Abraham Joshua Heschel, "Carl Stern's Interview with Dr Heschel," *Moral Grandeur and Spiritual Audacity*, p. 405. Reinhold Niebuhr and Paul Tillich agreed with Heschel in rejecting the idea of converting the Jews. See Edward Kaplan, *Spiritual Radical. Abraham Joshua Heschel in America 1940-1972* (New Haven: Yale University Press, 2007), pp. 283; 181.
16. Abraham Joshua Heschel, "No Religion Is an Island," *Moral Grandeur and Spiritual Audacity*, pp. 244; 254; 272, for example.

For Further Reading

Abraham Joshua Heschel. *Moral Grandeur and Spiritual Audacity*, edited by Susannah Heschel. New York: Farrar, Straus, Giroux, 1996.

Thomas Merton. *Faith and Violence. Christian Teaching and Christian Practice.* Notre Dame, IN: Notre Dame University Press, 1968.

Thomas Merton. *New Seeds of Contemplation.* New York: New Directions Publishing Corporation, 1972.

Thich Nhat Hanh. *Living Buddha, Living Christ.* New York: Riverhead Books, 1995.

Thich Nhat Hanh, Daniel Berrigan. *The Raft Is Not the Shore. Conversations Toward a Buddhist-Christian Awareness.* Maryknoll, NY: Orbis Books, 1975, 2001.

17. Abraham Joshua Heschel, "Interview at Notre Dame," *Moral Grandeur and Spiritual Audacity*, p. 381.
18. Abraham Joshua Heschel, "What Ecumenism Is," *Moral Grandeur and Spiritual Audacity*, p. 288.
19. Pierre Marchand, "Cultivating the Flower of Nonviolence. An Interview with Thich Nhat Hanh," *Fellowship of Reconciliation*, Jan.-Feb. 1999, p. 5.
20. Abraham Joshua Heschel, "No Religion Is an Island," *Moral Grandeur and Spiritual Audacity*, p. 249; Abraham Joshua Heschel, "Carl Stern's Interview with Dr. Heschel," *Moral Grandeur and Spiritual Audacity*, p. 398.

Patrick Henry is Cushing Eells Emeritus Professor of Philosophy and Literature at Whitman College in Walla Walla, WA (USA). His most recent book is *'We Only Know Men': The Rescue of Jews in France during the Holocaust* (Catholic University of America Press, 2007). Dr Henry is a speaker for the Jewish Foundation for the Righteous (www.jfr.org) and for the Washington Commission for the Humanities.

Carol Rittner

argues for removal of poisonous prayer, clarity on Holocaust denial and that Pope Benedict go as a penitent pilgrim to Israel and the Holy Land.

To be honest, you confuse me! As a Roman Catholic Christian, indeed, as a member of the Religious Sisters of Mercy, I have to ask, "Why in the world did you put us through the Williamson affair? Why in the world did you lift the excommunication of four traditionalist bishops who continue to reject the spirit and teachings of Vatican II and who choose to put themselves outside the Roman Catholic Church rather than accept the teachings of an ecumenical council?" As a Roman Catholic scholar involved in teaching about the Holocaust and other genocides, as well as in Jewish-Catholic dialogue, I need to know why you would plea "pastoral support" as an "act of peace" for these schismatics and their confrères in the Priestly Fraternity of St Pius X? This group, founded by the late French Archbishop Marcel Lefebvre, once identified the enemies of the Catholic faith as "Jews, Communists and Freemasons". What were you doing when you did this? Were you testing us? Trying our patience? Seeing if we were "awake and watchful"?

"I know that you are trying to find a way to repair the breach you caused in the trust we Roman Catholic faithful put in your guidance as Christ's Vicar on earth... you also must try to find a way to undo the scandal you caused within and beyond the confines of the worldwide Roman Catholic community."

We Roman Catholics know you were aware of what other priests and religious around the world were teaching in the name of Roman Catholicism. When you were Prefect of the Congregation for the Doctrine of the Faith, you had a hand in the 1997 excommunication of the Sri Lankan priest Tissa Balasuriya. To return to good standing in the Church, Father Balasuriya had to profess Pope Paul VI's "Credo of the People of God" and make other statements, including one in which he accepted "the Magisterium of the Roman Pontiff and of the College of Bishops in union with him."[1] How could you say you were unaware of Richard Williamson's rantings about the Jews and Judaism, that you were unaware of his Holocaust denial, unaware

Questions

1. What is the Priestly Society of St Pius X? What do they believe? What is their official relationship to Pope Benedict XVI and the Roman Catholic Church?

2. What does the Roman Catholic Church teach about Jews and Judaism, as evidenced in the Vatican II documents, *Nostra Aetate* ("In Our Time") and subsequent documents since the end of Vatican Council II (1962-1965)?

3. What is meant by "Holocaust denial"? What does the March 1998 document, *We Remember: A Reflection on the Shoah*, have to say about the Holocaust and why Roman Catholic Christians need to study and remember it?

of the Priestly Fraternity of St Pius X's antisemitic and anti-Jewish views, or their intransigence on everything else – from religious freedom and the education of women to the nature of the Church?

Of course, I cannot judge your motives in trying to bring these men and, indeed, the entire Priestly Fraternity of St Pius X back into communion with the Roman Catholic Church. Those motives are hidden in your heart and are known only by God, but I can judge your very public acts and statements, minimizing the importance of what you have done in lifting their excommunication. While it is difficult to judge why a person acts in a certain way, we can – and must – judge what a person does. Human beings, for better or worse, are responsible for the deeds they do, and this includes all of us, you as Head of the Roman Catholic Church, me as an ordinary Roman Catholic Christian, and Richard Williamson and his brother priests in the Fraternity of St Pius X. This responsibility for the consequences of our actions is grounded in the Jewish and Christian belief in the freedom and dignity of the human person. To deny this responsibility is to diminish the significance of all human actions.[2]

My judgment is that your actions were unacceptable and insensitive. I know that you are trying to find a way to repair the breach you caused in the trust we Roman Catholic faithful put in your guidance as Christ's Vicar on earth, trying to find a way to mend the rips and tears you caused in the fabric of the relationships we Roman Catholics have woven with our Jewish brothers and sisters since Vatican II and *Nostra Aetate* (1965). But you also must try to find a way to undo the scandal you caused within and beyond the confines of the worldwide Roman Catholic community.

I know that you and your advisors – all those priests, bishops, archbishops and cardinals who cluster around you – are trying to find ways to make amends, but your efforts must be seen as genuine, not simply as damage control, or as politically correct. You must demonstrate a sincere and long-term commitment to promoting and encouraging good interfaith relations, in word and deed, if your efforts are to help repair the unfortunate breach you unintentionally caused. I know you are not without your brotherly advisors, but allow me to offer a few sisterly suggestions as well.

First, continue to respond positively and forthrightly to your fellow German, Chancellor Angela Merkel, who stated in no uncertain terms that you must make "unmistakably clear that... denial [of the Holocaust] is unacceptable." Chancellor Merkel does not usually take a position on internal matters of the Catholic Church. She is, after all, a Protestant, the daughter of an East German minister, not to mention the Head of a sovereign country. Taking a position on a matter such as the Williamson affair has far-reaching implications. Nevertheless, she did take a position because as she said, "[W]e stand before a fundamental question... it is of great significance if the Vatican makes a decision that could diffuse the impression that a denial of the Holocaust is possible."[3] ***She*** made her position clear – "[T]here can be no [Holocaust] denial and... there must be positive relations with Judaism"[4] – now ***you*** must (continue to) make crystal clear your own position as a German, as a Roman Catholic Christian, as the Head of a sovereign state (the Vatican), and as the Head of the largest Christian denomination in the world.

Denial of the Holocaust is not insignificant or unimportant. Why? Because "the Holocaust remains a seminal event for people of faith. Particularly because of the record of Christian indifference and complicity" during the Holocaust. To waffle on this issue "raises disturbing questions about the process by which religious prejudice and discrimination gain legitimacy and power."[5] And today, more than ever, when there is a fatal intersection of religion, hatred, ideology and violence in our world, you must raise your voice repeatedly and say that Holocaust denial is not consistent with the view that "God is Love,"[6] nor is it consistent with the truth.[7] You can do this by taking every appropriate opportunity to draw attention to the March 1998 document, *We Remember: A Reflection on the Shoah*,[8] issued and promulgated by the Vatican Commission for Religious Relations with the Jews, with the approval and encouragement of your esteemed predecessor, Pope John Paul II.

Another suggestion: Do something about that February 2008 Good Friday prayer for Jews, reformulated and reinstituted by the Vatican for the Tridentine liturgy. It retains the same heading as the suppressed 1962 prayer, "Prayer for the Conversion of the Jews." That prayer conveys an attitude toward Jews and Judaism that has been disavowed since Vatican Council II:

> We pray for the Jews. That our God and Lord enlighten their hearts – so that they recognize Jesus Christ, the Saviour of all mankind. Let us pray. Kneel down. Arise. Eternal God Almighty, you want all people to be saved and to arrive at the knowledge of the Truth, graciously grant that by the entry of the abundance of all people into your Church, Israel will be saved. Through Christ our Lord.[9]

Language is important. It conveys concepts and communicates attitudes. The language of prayer is particularly important, for how we pray reveals what is in our hearts. The language contained in the 1962/2008 "Prayer for the Conversion of the Jews" is poisonous. Used repeatedly, it can dull our sensitivities toward the Jewish people, who, as Pope John Paul II said, are "our dearly beloved brothers... our elder brothers" in the faith. This prayer is inconsistent with the message of *Nostra Aetate* and with the theological understandings that have been developing in the context of official and scholarly Catholic-Jewish dialogue efforts since the Second Vatican Council (1962-1965). The "Prayer for the Conversion of the Jews" is religiously dangerous because it can be manipulated to produce poisonous falsehoods

For Further Reading

Mary C. Boys and Sara S. Lee. *Christians & Jews in Dialogue: Learning in the Presence of the Other*. Woodstock, Vermont: Skylight Paths Publishing, 2006.

Howard Clark Kee and Irvin J. Borowsky, eds. *Removing Anti-Judaism from the Pulpit*. New York: The Continuum Publishing Company, 1996.

John W. O'Malley. *What Happened at Vatican II?* Cambridge, MA: Harvard University Press, 2008.

Mordecai Paldiel. *Churches and the Holocaust: Unholy Teaching, Good Samaritans and Reconciliation*. Jersey City, NJ: Ktav Publishing House, Inc., 2006.

that in the hands of bigots could become major weapons to foster prejudice and distrust of the Jewish people. It was just such attitudes that brought havoc, suffering and death for millions of Jews over the centuries, culminating in the Holocaust, the genocide of the Jews during World War II.

My third suggestion is, go to the Holy Land as a penitent pilgrim. Your predecessor of blessed memory, Pope John Paul II, after begging forgiveness for centuries of derision, slander and persecution of the Jewish people[10] that contributed in no small way to the Nazi "Final Solution", went to Israel as a penitent pilgrim. Go to Israel with an open heart and an open mind. Go as a man of faith. Go to Israel to learn from ***all*** the people you meet – Israelis and Palestinians, Jews, Christians and Muslims, another people of faith you offended a few years ago. When you speak, as undoubtedly you will have to, begin by acknowledging that you don't know everything. Tell your hosts and interlocutors that you are there to learn, not to teach, that you are there to listen, not to pontificate. Above all, go as a fellow traveller on this fragile earth of ours, seeking to heal and repair our world, seeking to foster dialogue between and among people of good will, Jews, Christians and Muslims.

Everyone will be hoping against hope that you genuinely will try to understand their positions and problems, their hopes and fears, their dreams and desires for peace, and that you – and thus the Roman Catholic Church – will accept them for who they are, not for who you or others in the Catholic Church may want them to be. And if you can find the courage, apologize to our Jewish and Muslim brothers and sisters for the inadvertent offence you may have caused them these past years. Such words also will go a long way toward repairing the breach you caused as a result of both your Regensburg speech and the Williamson affair. And such words may even help to restore trust among all people of good will, and especially among the Catholic faithful, in your leadership in the world and in the Church that so many of us love and cherish.

Carol Rittner, RSM, an American Roman Catholic and a Sister of Mercy, is Distinguished Professor of Holocaust and Genocide Studies at The Richard Stockton College of New Jersey. She is the author, editor or co-editor of numerous essays and books, including *The Holocaust & the Christian World*. She has been involved in the dialogue between Christians and Jews for more than 30 years. Dr. Rittner is the co-editor of *No Going Back: Letters to Pope Benedict XVI on the Holocaust, Christian-Jewish Relations & Israel* (2009).

Notes

1. Hilmar Pabel, "Vatican counsel," *The Tablet*, 21 February 2009: 10.
2. Eva Fleischner, Mary Jo Leddy and Carol Rittner, "Why on earth would Pope parley with Waldheim?" *National Catholic Reporter*, 3 July 1987, 7.
3. Quoted in *The Sydney Morning Herald* [Australia], 5 February 2009.
4. Interview with Chancellor Merkel on German television, Tuesday, 3 February 2009.
5. Victoria Barnett, "Beyond Williamson: The Larger Implications of Holocaust Denial," *On Faith*, 10 February 2009.
6. "God is Love" (*Deus Caritas Est*) is the title of Pope Benedict XVI's first encyclical letter, issued in December 2005.
7. Pope Benedict XVI has made "truth" one of the central themes of his pontificate. See further, Michael Sean Winters, "Truth or Consequences for Pope Benedict." *In All Things*, Group Blog, 3 February 2009.

8. Commission for Religious Relations with the Jews, *We Remember: A Reflection on the Shoah*, Section I, par. 3. http://www.vatican.va/roman_curia/pontifical_councils/chrstuni/documents/rc_pc_chrstuni_doc_16031998_shoah_en.html (Last accessed: 9 February 2009).
9. See further, "Reformulated Tridentine Rite Prayer for Jews," http://www.bc.edu/research/cjl/meta-elements/texts/cjrelations/news/Prayer_for_Jews.htm (Last accessed: 15 February 2009).
10. "Service Requesting Pardon," (12 March 2000) in *Origins* 29, 40 (23 March 2000) 648ff. This request for forgiveness was so unprecedented that it required a lengthy justification from the Catholic Church's International Theological Commission. See the Commission's "Memory and Reconciliation: The Church and Faults of the Church," *Origins* 29, 39 (16 March 2000) 627-644.

Stephen D. Smith

calls for clear and strong leadership at this crucial time in history.

"Speak positively about Judaism; speak decisively about Holocaust denial; speak clearly about universal moral values; speak encouragingly on Jewish-Christian relations, indeed about interfaith relations generally."

I was just reminded that you are actually 'returning' to Jerusalem. As the successor of Peter, disciple of Jesus, the founder of the fledgling Church of hundreds of millions that you now lead, you are coming home. Peter, the ordinary man, the rock on whom the Church of Christ is deemed to be built; Peter, the faithful, the loyal servant; Peter who knew Jesus of Nazareth like no other person; Peter who was there to watch water turned into wine; Peter, whom the Gospels tell helped feed 5,000; Peter the believer, who watched Jesus walk on water; Peter who heard the teaching, saw the compassion of arguably the best known Jewish lay preacher of all time; Peter who understood him; Peter who followed; Peter the leader of people. It was Peter who was the only one who had the strength to revenge the arrest of his master. It was Peter who alone followed Jesus to Pontius Pilate's residence; only Peter waited in vigil in silence and fear to hear the sentence. He was a man of considerable character and resource. It is little wonder that he went on to found the Church. His is a formidable example to follow.

Yet Peter was tested – and found wanting. Faithful Peter, strong Peter, clear Peter; it was time to show his character in a moment that mattered. When asked if he was one of the disciples of Jesus, he is said to have denied his loyalty not once, but three times. It was crushing, although not, we are told, for Jesus who predicted it, but for Peter himself. He had journeyed so far with his master. He was in the right place at the right time. But human frailty overcame his spiritual strength.

We have all done it.

I am named after Stephen, another founder of the Church, who was stoned to death for his determination to preach and teach. I have never had to face the threat of death; I have often wondered if I would have the strength to live up to my namesake's courage.

Now we are at a time and place in history which requires the courage to speak out. Antisemitism is growing in visibility and potency; Holocaust denial is a sinister ghost of Nazism; Islamic activism poses a serious and violent threat to stability and security; Israel, and with it the Jews, are demonised as aggressors and troublemakers; the global economic downturn demands answers and seeks scapegoats; the rise in religious and political fundamentalism narrows minds; there is hatred and uncertainty; there is a large divide between the major faith communities, one we can ill afford.

Now the Jews are on trial. They have endured centuries of antisemitism. Accused of what? Unfairly, unjustly, history has judged them again and again. Like Jesus, who had no answer to spurious charges, there is no answer to the irrational and hateful accusations.

Now is the time for clear and outspoken leadership.

As a leader and head of the largest single religious entity in the world, congregants and loyal servants within the communion need to hear your voice clearly and unambiguously. Speak positively about Judaism; speak decisively about Holocaust denial; speak clearly about universal moral values; speak encouragingly on Jewish-Christian relations, indeed about interfaith relations generally. Let them know that your principles are clear and leave them in no doubt that they can, and should, overcome their misgivings about the Jews – and Muslims too. You have upheld *Nostra Aetate* and reinforced the principles of *Dabru Emet*. But now it is time for a more vocal and visible statement which reaches everyone within the communion. The clergy need informing, training, encouraging and supporting. If they deliver, so do you. Change praxis at the grass roots.

As a world leader, your reach extends well beyond the Roman Catholic communion. Not all will want to admit it, but you also give leadership to Protestants, to Jews and Muslims. Your influence stretches beyond religious communities to political leaders, and statesmen and women too. It affects charities and humanitarian support, as well as penetrating right into the heart of local communities. You are not a religious figure for those outside the communion; you are a public figure. If you lead your Church with clarity and openness, then greater openness will follow between many people beyond the Church. You could be one of the few world leaders whom people listen to and trust. Such trust is not easily won, and indeed never will be won if it is not truly in the interests of humanity as a whole. People of all creeds and none want to hear your voice clear and strong, unambiguously promoting our shared human values.

There are some things you may want to keep in mind as you lead on these issues:

Antisemitism creates well-grounded fear. Fear is the enemy of hope. Without hope, we cannot move forward. To restore hope, we must be resolute in our stand against antisemitism.

Questions

1. Is the Pope a religious leader or a world leader?

2. On what subjects would you expect the Pope to speak?

3. What role could education play in better informing members of the Catholic Church?

4. Is it necessary for Christians to know about Judaism and the Holocaust?

5. Has the Pope given clear leadership on the Middle East?

Deity does not subscribe to religion. Religion subscribes to deity. Remind people that God is not a Christian, a Muslim or a Jew.

Religious persuasion is never reason enough to exclude or harm another human being. Remind people that the true worship of God always engenders respect for the 'other'.

Holocaust denial is an affront to the Church, not only to the Jews. It offends truth; it apologises for evil; it sides with the enemies of Christian values.

Genocide is a real possibility against Jews living in the State of Israel. The would-be perpetrators are not united enough, nor do they have the political capital or tactical means to execute their intent. But there are rapidly growing numbers of Islamic activists, and sympathisers, who share the goal of eradicating the Jewish population of Israel. It constitutes a real long-term threat.

Leadership is needed in times of crisis. You are a leader. Jews need your reassurance; Muslims need your friendship; Christians need your direction.

There are some things you should consider doing:

Train your clergy to understand more about Judaism, and also about the Holocaust. It will inform them and empower them.

Provide educational material for youth and adult catechesis so that those learning the faith understand the spiritual links to Judaism and learn about the Holocaust and its meaning to Christians.

Speak clearly about the failure of the Catholic Church to confront its own antisemitism and its ignorance about Islam.

Encourage Catholics to be on the frontline of combating antisemitism.

Explain that anti-Zionism is a form of antisemitism. Remind them that the State of Israel is a democratically governed nation state that will be judged by international law and history, and not by public opinion.

Build a positive and public relationship between the Vatican and the State of Israel.

Be outspoken on matters of conscience and bring together other religious and political leaders towards solidarity in the Middle East.

Peter was a leader. He was human too. No one expects you to be more than human. But among us, you have a voice which is unequalled in its reach, its scope and its persuasion. I ask you, as successor of Peter, the Jew, on your return to Jerusalem, do not turn away from the high calling you have. Use your unique voice, with clarity and with courage.

Never respect the office alone, but rather respect all those who look to you in that office.

Give us all the leadership we need, when leadership is needed most.

For Further Reading

John Allen. *All the Pope's Men: The Inside Story of How the Vatican Really Thinks.* New York: Doubleday, 2004.

Marcus Braybrooke. *Christian-Jewish Dialogue, The Next Steps.* SCM Press, London, 2000.

Edward Kessler & Neil Wenborn, eds. *A Dictionary of Jewish-Christian Relations.* Cambridge University Press, 2005.

Stephen D. Smith is a Christian theologian. He is the founder of the UK Holocaust Centre; co-founder of Aegis, the crimes against humanity prevention organisation; Chair of the UK National Holocaust Memorial Day and Project Director of the Kigali Memorial Centre, Rwanda. Dr Smith is the co-editor of *No Going Back: Letters to Pope Benedict XVI on the Holocaust, Christian-Jewish Relations & Israel.*

Concluding Comments

Your Holiness,

There is no going back.

Sixty-five years ago, the imperative to create a new relationship between Christians and Jews was painfully clear. The pall of human smoke was still settling on a landscape of destroyed Jewish communities. Christianity did not cause the Holocaust, but it was the uncomfortable bed mate of too many of those who did. Complicity in the genocide of the Jews is an indictment too far. It is unconscionable that Christianity should ever be in such a situation again.

Fifty years ago, Pope John XXIII announced that he was convening an ecumenical council.

Forty-four years ago, the Roman Catholic Church took a bold step at Vatican Council II and issued *Nostra Aetate*, giving a way forward and providing the long-awaited hope that trust could be established between Catholics and Jews and within the Christian-Jewish relationship.

Nearly ten years ago, Pope John Paul II, the best friend the Jews ever had as Head of the Roman Catholic Church, went to Israel and the Holy Land. He did so as a penitent pilgrim and as the leader of the Church.

Today we live in challenging times again. There is a renewed need for clear leadership and direction, particularly when it comes to interfaith relations.

These collected letters have overwhelmingly and appropriately paid respect to your high office as you make your 'way' to the Middle East. Jews, Muslims and Christians of many denominations have invested their trust in your good will and intentions regarding your visit. Nevertheless, these letters reveal that there are also high levels of concern and some feelings of uncertainty about the future of Jewish-Christian relations. There are stern words in these letters, some bordering on reprimand, and of course many words of encouragement.

Common themes have emerged, including the need to focus on the spiritual and theological validity of Judaism; the necessity of promoting and extending the spirit and tone of *Nostra Aetate*, its subsequent guidelines and other documents issued by the Vatican on

Jewish-Christian relations; the requirement to recognise the power of the past, but not to be dominated by it; the importance of finding, respecting and listening to one another; the challenge to work actively across religious and community boundaries; the desire to replace ambiguity with clarity, particularly in terms of Jewish-Christian relations; the demand to deal firmly with Holocaust denial; the hunger for inspiration and hope; the importance of not being afraid of change; and the need to provide leadership in times of crisis.

Practical steps that have been suggested include, among others, developing education about Judaism and the *Shoah* at all levels of religious education and training, including seminary education; encouraging grass roots participation in Jewish-Christian dialogue; bridging divides; revising areas of liturgy and theology that unintentionally demean others; publishing a new encyclical on the Jews, Judaism, the Holocaust and Jewish-Christian relations.

Still, we do have some questions:

- Is the Vatican trying to finesse the Williamson affair and the more sinister issue of Holocaust denial within the Catholic Church? Is it, in fact, exercising 'damage control' rather than genuinely embracing a position?
- Is there a difference between your theology as an individual and your theology as Pope? If so, please explain the difference – we want to know what *you* think.
- Do you fully acknowledge the validity of Judaism, or do we detect latent supercessionism? Can you be clear with us all on this?
- Is your recognition of the State of Israel and engagement that of real partnership, or do we hear grudging diplomacy? How will you express partnership in concrete terms?
- Have you clearly denounced antisemitism inside and outside the Church? Are you really a defender of the Jewish people against this most noxious influence? Are the Vatican and the Roman Catholic Church generally?
- Do you acknowledge the legitimacy of Islam as one of the Abrahamic faiths? Are you engaging Jews and Muslims equally and at a deeper level than ever before?
- Are you committed to education about Judaism and the *Shoah* at the grass roots level? If so, how are you, how is the Vatican investing in our shared future?
- Are you doing all that you can to ensure that Roman Catholic liturgy promotes the well-being and harmony of Jews and Christians and does not undermine the legitimacy of Judaism?
- Are you helping Catholics to understand that for peace to prevail in the Middle East the rights and security of Israel *and* the Palestinians must be protected equally?

We think,

- You are held in high esteem, but more work must be done on the issue of Jewish-Christian relations, inside and outside the Roman Catholic communion.
- The official Catholic Church has become more ambiguous about Jewish-Christian relations under your pontificate, which is a step in the wrong direction.
- There will be no scope for positive collaboration on peace in the Middle East if you do not support the rights of Israelis *and* Palestinians.
- Non-Catholics are not interested in the finer details of theology, doctrine or liturgy. They want to hear clear moral guidance on the 'big issues' of the day.
- Christian-Jewish relations are the cornerstone of interfaith work, without which there will be no progress on peace-building between and among religious communities more generally. We are not convinced that you have given this matter the priority it deserves.

Jewish-Christian relations is well on its way since Vatican II. There is no going back. But, Your Holiness, we need you to lead us forward.

Carol Rittner
Stephen D. Smith
May 2009

Index